THE LIBERAL
WAR ON
TRANSPARENCY

Confessions of a
Freedom of Information "Criminal"

Christopher C. Horner

THRESHOLD EDITIONS
New York London Toronto Sydney New Delhi

Threshold Editions
A Division of Simon & Schuster, Inc.
1230 Avenue of the Americas
New York, NY 10020

First Threshold Editions hardcover edition October 2012

THRESHOLD EDITIONS and colophon are trademarks of Simon & Schuster, Inc.

For information about special discounts for bulk purchases, please contact Simon & Schuster Special Sales at 1-866-506-1949 or business@simonandschuster.com.

The Simon & Schuster Speakers Bureau can bring authors to your live event. For more information or to book an event, contact the Simon & Schuster Speakers Bureau at 1-866-248-3049 or visit our website at www.simonspeakers.com.

Designed by Renata Di Biase

Manufactured in the United States of America

10 9 8 7 6 5 4 3 2 1

Library of Congress Cataloging-in-Publication Data

Horner, Christopher C.
  The liberal war on transparency : confessions of a Freedom of Information Act "criminal" / Christopher C. Horner.
      p.   cm.
  1. Freedom of information—United States. 2. Freedom of information—Political aspects—United States. 3. United States. Freedom of Information Act. I. Title.
KF5753.H67   2012
342.7308'53—dc23
                                                                    2012019381

ISBN 978-1-4516-9488-8
ISBN 978-1-4516-9490-1 (ebook)

Contents

THE LIBERAL WAR ON TRANSPARENCY

1.

When Freedom of Information Requests Are "Criminal," Only Criminals Will Request Information

Liberals love transparency. Except when they don't. Which is often, as transparency increasingly inconveniences them. In fact, it is more accurate to say that liberals used to love transparency. Now that transparency threatens their franchise, they've had enough of it.

Freedom of information was the liberals' idea. Today, firmly in control of the institutions that they demanded be open to inspection—government and publicly funded academia—the bloom is off that rose. Openness has outlived its purpose. It needs "reform." Transparency should still be available, but for the right kind of people. To be on the safe side, it must also acquire new meaning: Publicly funded institutions need privacy, so politically select classes subsisting on your labors should be outright exempted, protected from your scrutiny. It is private citizens and companies who need to be examined more closely, should they involve themselves in the public debate. That is, if they pick the wrong side.

Until the courts or even compliant lawmakers formally turn transparency on its head, the laws are being flaunted and subverted as political needs dictate. Release information if it helps a liberal cause, even when classified and its release places operatives or allies in danger; when exposed in scandals involving taxpayer money, shriek "harassment!" "fishing expedition!" and of course "witch hunt," and stonewall efforts to scrutinize public records elaborating on the evidence of abuse. Welcome to the new normal of liberal open government.

This Orwellian inversion of the idea of "transparency" is toward avoiding public awareness and informed debate. Apparently those are no longer likely to be of much help to the liberal cause.

Transparency in American politics, as originally conceived by liberals, was rightly deemed vital to our system of governance. This is because of the threat that sunshine poses to those who might misuse public office or money in the darkness of secrecy. Transparency allows the taxpayer to pull back the curtain on operations of government.

Now that transparency threatens liberals' use of government and other taxpayer-financed institutions, it is a problem to rein in; we've started asking questions and obtaining embarrassing answers, meaning the wrong kind of people are using transparency laws to the wrong ends. Other voices have also entered the political debate. Thanks to transparency and a more engaged public the liberal agenda is being impeded, and passage of laws they disfavor is made more likely. So the threat liberals now see is not misuse of public institutions, including publicly funded universities, a key ally in designing and expanding liberal government. Instead, the threat is exposure of how these institutions are being used, and the ability to spread the word of these abuses far and wide.

This is a cynical revolution, whereby private parties, more than a lack of public institutional accountability, must be protected against. To keep the marketplace of ideas free from competition, public debate must be kept unpolluted by undesirable content and unwanted voices. And so liberals demand that private citizens or businesses reveal all, if they dare support or otherwise engage in political activities standing in the liberals' way. The left works to obtain private parties' information with the same zeal and attitude with which they work to keep what belongs to the public secret. This means constructing flimsy arguments that the public is rightly private—hiding and even destroying records—and that the private is rightly public, employing deception, even theft and fabricating records in the name of a greater good. Day is night and black white, and their claim of righteousness justifies all when they are questioned about this perversion of principle.

But this also represents abandonment of a grand liberal achievement: institutionalizing the doctrine that public access to information about public service is "vital to the functioning of a democratic society, needed to check against corruption and to hold the governors accountable to the governed."[1] That is as articulated by a majority of the U.S. Supreme Court more than thirty years ago, although for many years before that liberals championed allowing the public to see what their government was up to. (The first freedom of information law was adopted by liberal heartthrob Sweden in 1766. Hinting at coming hypocrisies, it also tacked on illiberal speech code provisions.)

Transparency was a dream of American political progressives since they first graced the world with their presence. Progressive Hall of Famer Louis Brandeis wrote, "Sunlight is said to be the best of disinfectants; electric light the most efficient policeman."[2] Suitably, he offered this wisdom in the context of "Other People's Money," the title of his work containing the axiom.

The man who appointed Brandeis to the Court, Woodrow Wilson, waxed on about the ideal well before his elevation to the presidency. In 1884 Wilson wrote, in his typically deathless prose, that "[l]ight is the only thing that can sweeten our political atmosphere—light thrown upon every detail of administration in the departments; light diffused through every passage of policy; light blazed full upon every feature of legislation; light that can penetrate every recess or corner in which any intrigue might hide; light that will open to view the innermost chambers of government," and on and on for one hundred twenty words before rediscovering the dreaded punctuation mark, the period.[3]

All quite earnest, as liberals are known to be. And the sermon tells us that progressives would be appalled if, say, an out-of-control EPA administrator, who also ordered records being sought by the public destroyed, demanded creation of a secret, "secondary" email account despite insisting she never really used her computer anyway (when asked about having her hard drive be wiped clean, oddly, and in violation of a court order). About this secret account, an agency document I obtained in 2012 states, "Few EPA staff members, usually only high-level senior staff, even know that these accounts exist. Therefore, responsibility for identifying, printing and submitting records for filing in accordance with EPA records schedules falls to the Administrator." This document openly acknowledges that not even the office that created the account for the administrator knows whether she—or the current administrator, running similarly amok if not more so—has turned over emails from them that are responsive to freedom of information requests.

Surely that sort of thing would be an enormous affront to liberal principles? As you'll read, the answer is that it depends on whom we're speaking about, and what end or which master the secrecy or transparency is intended to serve. That is what dictates the righteousness or outrageousness of an act.

This is not a complete surprise, particularly given the admissions by liberal activists and interest groups of such situational principles. For example, they would protest the Obama administration more if only it weren't the Obama administration.[4] So, for liberals, disclosure is no longer necessarily a good idea, if it threatens the liberal enterprise (government, academia); it is, however, worthy indeed when useful to find any cudgel against private parties opposing said liberal enterprises.

The perversion of the law is now institutionalized. President Obama has installed political appointees into the machinery designed to provide the public with information it is owed. Through them the administration stonewalls requests for information from perceived enemies while providing immediate turnaround to friends; strategically abuses the law by attending to languishing requests once the release becomes politically beneficial to them; and even promiscuously leaks classified information from the highest political levels in efforts to bolster Obama's electoral standing while conducting the most aggressive prosecution campaign against whistleblowers and leakers in the country's history (and that's according to fellow liberals).

Then there is the matter of their dirty laundry, and the often extreme ploys to impose Obama's agenda, including through the bureaucracy.

About this, I have found scandalous cronyism and internal admissions of damaging truths that are denied publicly. Their efforts to avoid scrutiny range from awkward use of code names for high-profile political appointees to using "cutouts," or intermediaries, to frustrate information requests. I have also uncovered widespread use by activist employees of the federal government—both career and political appointees—of private means to conduct official business: unofficial computers, off-site servers, and private email accounts that, like those secret email addresses created to keep correspondence from being seen, all were presumably free from prying taxpayer eyes and record-retention systems. It will require a fierce battle in court to obtain access to records always under the exclusive control of the employee choosing to conduct business away from official channels, and these are most likely being regularly purged.

Transparency in government can be as entertaining as it is illuminating, if sadly so. My first indication of this came when I used the Freedom of Information Act (FOIA) to elicit an admission by the Clinton-Gore administration that no, they never considered using emergency authority to impose a certain regulation despite hysterically claiming it would immediately save tens of thousands of American lives . . . each year! As I delicately reminded them, this is the same emergency authority invoked for seemingly lesser crises, like sparing a handful of sea turtles.[5] *So . . .*

By their own terms, then, with forty-plus Americans dropping dead each and every day and the time it would take to hash things out in boring old Federal Register notice-and-comment proceedings, this cruel decision to treat the unprecedented public health crisis like just another rule-making sentenced as many as thirty thousand citizens to premature, avoidable death.

But, as they plainly agreed, *not really*. What was really going on was that this was a particularly expensive and controversial regulation—at the time, expected to be "perhaps most costly regulations the EPA has ever promulgated"[6] and about which internal documents revealed grave administration concerns not acknowledged to the public.[7] Their "no records" response to me proved the claims to be alarmist rhetoric of the worst variety, nothing more than cynical politics, trying to scare the public into sympathy for the costly scheme while framing opposition as heartless. (The ruse so outrageously exposed bureaucratic abuses, it led to a law requiring that certain claims by the government at least meet a minimum threshold for quality, the Information Quality Act.)

FOIA proved useful to my policy work as years, issues, and political administrations came and went. After some wrangling, one particularly productive FOIA request to the Obama Treasury Department in 2009 unearthed internal documents laying out the true plan for the "cap-and-trade" scheme, to raise up to $400 billion per year, an enormous, job-killing cost denied by the plan's supporters. An open-minded writer with CBSNews.com reviewed the material, analyzed it on his own, grilled me about my take, and wrote a pair of devastating columns. These caused terrific liberal outrage and surely helped lead to that scheme's death in the Democrat-controlled Senate, and an electoral body count among those who voted for it in the House of Representatives.[8]

Then there are the smaller fry, if still often highly instructive. In 2012 I obtained an email sent to the Department of Energy political appointee in charge of renewable energy from her close pal the managing director of Solyndra's outside political consulting firm. Just a note to let her know he was "at [the] poolside bar at Caesars having a drink" with her "Senior Advisor" (a twenty-something poli sci grad, which might explain a lot about these "green jobs" disasters except, as further information requests revealed, it was more cronyism than lack of experience or understanding driving the boondoggles). Right about then, back in Washington, President Obama's political team was leaning on colleagues in government to get a campaign bundler's company—Solyndra—a historically wasteful loan guarantee, soon to be predictably squandered.[9]

Raise a glass in return to toast this insight into how our dollars get spent, if a year late and a half-billion dollars short. Other emails showed the same DOE political appointee in charge of "green energy," assistant secretary Cathy Zoi, bantering as close confidants do with yet a different partner in Solyndra's political firm, Mike Feldman. One thread discussed dinner at her house that weekend, if he could make it, which promised to be a blast as "a couple of other fun political animals will be there."[10] Other Zoi emails showed her enlisting the same firm, apparently pro bono (although that would seem to be a legal no-no),[11] to help pull together materials she wanted to consider when developing DOE's campaign, pushing the same agenda but from the inside.

But, no, that whole Solyndra and "green stimulus" boondoggle and the cronies who made out at the taxpayer's expense,[12] that money was "invested" on the merits.

These emails discussing drinks and dinner parties were originally withheld in full by the administration, with no legal basis and precisely the sort of defensive crouch that President Obama so loudly insisted would not occur on his watch, crowing upon his inauguration that "[t]he Government should not keep information confidential merely because public officials might be embarrassed by disclosure, because errors and failures might be revealed, or because of speculative or abstract fears. Nondisclosure should never be based on an effort to protect the personal interests of Government officials at the expense of those they are supposed to serve."[13]

In truth, despite all of the promises and boasts, this presidential directive merely reflects long-standing policy on information dissemination and access, and is routinely ignored.

With the current administration, risibly self-congratulating as the most transparent in history, we now know to ask sooner than we did with Solyndra, even if by the time that scandal broke I had already used information requests to expose the basic but thorough corruption of Obama's "green energy" operation. For example, another of my FOIA requests to the Department of Energy led to a treasure trove of emails exposing what *Investor's Business Daily* called "The Big Wind Cover-Up." This also uncovered the collaborative effort to smear the Spanish "green jobs" economics professor and his team's work documenting the true disaster of liberal plans to reorganize America's economy as "the clean energy economy." FOIA allowed me to chase down the genesis of this panic-driven attempt at discrediting people viewed as political opponents; this instance confirmed aggressive violations of Barack Obama's promises of transparency and to banish lobbyists from insider roles in the policy process.

But documents pried out of the administration also let slip revealing details of how this defense of a "renewables" industry that Solyndra later made famous was coordinated with the windmill lobby and left-wing pressure groups. These included George Soros's project, the Center for American Progress (CAP), using the industrial wind lobby as the go-between in anticipation of DOE claiming, for example, to Congress that it "had no direct contact with" CAP or another pressure group to which the windmill lobbyists served as DOE's "cutout" contact. *Investor's Business Daily* described these records as being as substantively explosive as the previously described "Climategate" leak in 2009 of emails and computer code, because it showed senior Obama political appointees doing the bidding for industries that were propped up in the name of an anti-energy ideology and crony capitalism, joined with the assault on abundant domestic energy sources that work and are therefore also disfavored for ideological reasons.

So, the FOI Act, properly implemented, provides a useful tool. It enabled me to obtain emails from a career activist federal employee working with outside liberal ideologues to lobby and pressure the George W. Bush administration to come around more to their way of thinking. The law allowed me to out an activist running a third-party website supporting Obama policies from a taxpayer-funded office, on taxpayer time and without having obtained ethics clearance to do so. Then there were the other, career employees dedicated to advancing Obama's ideological agenda, neutered by FOIA revelations from being useful future witnesses before Congress or courts as supposed unbiased authorities, or who simply found themselves spending more time with their families and pursuing other interests, after exposure of what they were all up to on the taxpayer's time.

Of course, FOI laws are equal opportunity vehicles, notwithstanding the faddish claim that certain bad people like me shouldn't be allowed to use them anymore. Texas's FOI law enabled me to affirm that there was a reason presidential candidate Newt Gingrich was less than convincing when telling an Iowa voter about a chapter in his upcoming book to be written by a global warming alarmist, "That's not going to be in the book. We didn't know that they were doing that and we told them to kill it." In fact, an email that appeared to be the final correspondence between Newt's coauthor and the public-university academic and activist before that revelation and denial confirmed plans for her chapter's inclusion.[14]

These are reasons why transparency laws are tools that liberals believe have outlived their usefulness and demand "reform" of, now that they can only cause unwanted problems for the institutions subject to these requirements.[15] You will read how FOI laws are subverted in the meantime, as they take matters into their own hands. There are tactics you should expect to confront in order to navigate your government to find out what we deserve to know. (Activists in career government positions and academia also regularly use these same moves.)

This book relates my own experience and the experience of others with this campaign to deny access to information about the activities of government, to bar access for those people viewed as a threat to what one character repeatedly called "the cause," just one of many causes liberals use government and academia to advance. I relate these experiences to expose how liberals are trying to stop us from seeing what else they are up to, and how to take them on.

Chapters one through ten detail these tactics and how they are being more aggressively abused in the age of Obama. It assumes a basic understanding of freedom of information laws as transparency statutes guaranteeing the taxpayer the right to inspect public records reflecting how the government conducts its business, with limited exceptions and a presumption of honest implementation by employees charged with providing this information.

I then return to the statute's governing principles and its nuts and bolts, providing background information and a road map for you to hold your government and the activists within it accountable as they test or even ignore the limits of the many vague, sweeping grants of power provided by Congress. This offers the basic framework for dealing with the hurdles placed in your path, and lets you in on the tricks of their trade.

Liberals have come to despise the requirement of transparency and you must now press the truth upon them that, if they want taxpayer money, there are indeed strings that come with it, principal among them being transparency and thereby (presumably) accountability. If not, the solution is to find another job, or live off other money. It is not to undermine the public's right to open government and transparent use of our tax dollars.

What you read should disappoint you about your government and occasionally infuriate you. My hope is that it motivates and energizes you to enter the fray and take effective action yourself to pull threads, find and then follow trails of bread crumbs, work around or plow through obstacles, and become someone your government begins to treat with respect.

Transparency is a condition of living off the taxpayer as well as a necessary condition for liberty. If liberals succeed in undermining it, they will be unencumbered in using the money and authority afforded them by our laws, as grants from us. And we will wake up one day to realize we are far less free.

Use this tool, and your freedom of obtaining information, or risk losing it. As you will read, taking this right away from you is a liberal priority.

2.

A Life of FOI "Crime"

Over the course of three presidential administrations I have used freedom of information laws scores, if not hundreds, of times to seek information from federal offices and the states. Some requests were simple and some resembled litigation discovery; some have been handled promptly while some agencies have forced me to sue them.

I began using these laws after, and in great part inspired by, an eye-opening stint in 1997, after I left my law firm to become director of federal government relations for a little energy company out of Houston. I was gone from the company within weeks, but it found itself in the news a few years later and its very name, Enron, became a cultural metaphor in 2001. The reasons behind this were not unrelated to the reasons why my fling with them was as brief as it was, management not appreciating indelicate objections to their new, great big idea to design, but not so much "earn," a fortune thanks to favors from friends in political office.

That big idea was the "global warming" industry—known in other quarters, as explained momentarily, as "the cause"—cooked up and deliberately constructed to reward Enron and other founding fathers, such as BP, for having purchased uneconomic properties like windmills and solar panels on the cheap (being, after all, uneconomic). Obama pal Jeffrey Immelt's GE Wind, for example, was previously Enron Wind. Enron's large solar venture became BP's after the . . . unpleasantness down in Houston, though BP soon enough moved "beyond solar" after the failure of Obama's cap-and-trade legislation. The plan was for these companies to underwrite the desires and campaigns of politicians and pressure groups sharing a pro-statist agenda of central control and managed scarcity. You might know it from its current popularity as "cronyism."

This agenda was truncated as "cap-and-trade" until the liberals' aforementioned debacle with that in 2010, which cost many lawmakers their jobs for having voted to wipe out the jobs of so many others in the name of environmentally meaningless but economically depressing dogma. It was restyled as "the clean energy economy," a poll-tested rebranding[1] that provides insight into President Obama's repeatedly stated vow to "finally make clean energy the profitable kind of energy in America." So I began poking around the federal government on behalf of various pro-market, pro-environment groups (those recognizing that wealthier is healthier, and cleaner).

I discuss this later in the context of Obama's own series of Enrons demanding scrutiny, including Solyndra, which actually stood on the shoulders of such earlier rent-seeking giants. The whole enterprise always reminded me of an old Far Side cartoon in which two spiders admire a web they've spun at the bottom of a playground slide, one telling the other, "If we pull this off, we'll eat like kings." Specifically, after enacting their scheme Enron and the others would frolic in a gusher of revenues from artificial markets and wealth transfers, all at the expense of the unsuspecting taxpayer and electricity ratepayer. And the overall economy.

This sort of scheming stunned me at the time, though I came to learn just how widespread these Baptist-and-Bootlegger coalitions—and the practice of helping whip up crises and, by chance, solutions promising "rents"—were in Washington and state capitals. Also, certain internal Enron documents were later passed to me elaborating on Enron's close relationship with the Clinton-Gore administration to jointly promote the agenda—which included an Oval Office meeting with the president and vice president on August 4, 1997, at which Enron CEO Ken Lay advised them (successfully) to ignore the unanimous Senate instruction under the Constitution's "advice and consent" clause, and agree to the Kyoto Protocol anyway.[2]

The media never bothered or even seemed to care to get basic facts remotely correct about an issue over which they were nonetheless excitedly activist. They loved the political "narrative," chose a side immediately, and repeated the dogma. For example, Bill Clinton acted further on Enron's wishes, even signing the Kyoto treaty in November 1998, which did not stop the press from agitatedly, absurdly excoriating George W. Bush for refusing to do so in 2001 (which he couldn't), a supposed favor for his energy cronies at Enron (who practically invented the blasted thing). That's how badly out of touch the media were, with no interest in actually reporting the news as opposed to repeating a political line or otherwise engaging in political activism.

This left a void, which I sought to help fill. My first freedom of information requests began by probing further into the agenda and the relationships. I inquired after records discussing the scientific, economic, and political angles, moving to a range of issues and seeking the deliberations in agencies throughout government about the relationships, the costs, and the agendas of those in government.

All of this led to my sitting in 2010 in a local courtroom where an admission by one of the lawyers set in motion a chain of events, including appalling revelations about the behavior of public servants, more courtrooms, silly fulminations about "abuse" of FOIA laws, and an Obama agency head calling my requests for public information "criminal." It seems that in that particular case, as with many others, there is information that you paid for, that you are entitled to, held by institutions working to cost you much, much more, that liberals simply do not want you to see.

It was muggy, a typical August afternoon in central Virginia as the sparse crowd filtered into the historic courthouse that is home to the Albemarle County Circuit Court. We came to observe a hearing, the first public installment in the very local contribution to an international scandal that was playing out in this company town, where the University of Virginia is the company.

Charlottesville, Virginia, is much like university towns all over America—politically "progressive" and prone to taking its progressivism dreadfully seriously. It differs possibly by degree with "Dear Old UVa" (as it is known in the school's alma mater, "The Good Ole Song"), and its attendants, who are possessed of a singularly elevated self-importance. After all, as its lawyers and supporters would note at odd intervals, Thomas Jefferson founded the school.[3] Therefore, went the implication, however absurd the university's words or deeds, Mr. Jefferson would have wanted it this way. As to the matter at hand, if the school didn't find certain allegations and an awful lot of incriminating evidence worth investigating on its own, well, that should be good enough. (Wait until you read why they opted against this.)

It wasn't good enough for everyone. The day's event was oral argument in a case styled as *The Rectors and Visitors of the University of Virginia v. Cuccinelli*. The university filed this action, on its "home court," to quash a civil investigative demand—essentially, a pre-investigation subpoena—by the commonwealth's attorney general, Ken Cuccinelli.

Cuccinelli sought certain records he believed to be in the possession of the university, known as one of the nation's finest academic institutions and one that takes particular pride in its honor code for students, underpinned by principles of trust and self-policing coupled with strict demands of integrity. This pride often seemed misplaced as the university extended the depths to which it would burrow to keep secret a cache of taxpayer-funded documents that would shed light on "the worst scientific scandal of our generation,"[4] centered in great part at UVa. Clearly, the administration and faculty did not choose to hold themselves to the same expectations. This public university would fight at all costs to keep further evidence of scandal that had occurred on their watch from the public.

That scandal came from the 2009 "Climategate" release by an anonymous leaker of one thousand emails, some computer code, and annotations to that code all subject to at least one and often several freedom of information laws, requests for which were being stonewalled.[5] They showed a deliberate and organized effort, at the highest levels of taxpayer-funded academia and research institutions on at least two continents, to promote a supposed scientific basis for what one of the saga's protagonists (Michael Mann, teaching at UVa from 1999 until 2005, and then Penn State) called "the cause" in these emails.[6] The methods: pressuring journals to avoid publishing "not helpful" research papers; organizing campaigns against perceived enemies, thereby violating the freedom of those who dared challenge the cause to publish ideas or findings without fear of retribution ("academic freedom"); and subverting statutes designed to provide taxpayers access to taxpayer-funded records.

This "cause" was the imposition of an agenda of spending, prohibition, and regulation embraced and feverishly demanded by a broad coalition of "global governance" enthusiasts, businesses, and academic and scientific institutions. By way of ever more politically directed riches, and elevation in the economic and societal hierarchy of certain academics and industries, the cause's promoters would fulfill a long wish list of the international political left and the crony capitalists aiding the agenda's political component. Although this particular manifestation of "the cause" was pitched as a means of remedying "global warming" or (alternately) the "climate crisis," its demands revealed it to be nothing more than the latest rhetorical disguise to market an otherwise unappealing utopian agenda of control, wealth transfers, and artificial scarcity sold as liberty, equality, and plenty.

Sure, the odd "useful idiot" from elsewhere on the political spectrum embraced "the cause": unable to resist the lure of handing out its goodies to favored, politically helpful constituencies, encouraged by the career boost that can come from showing just how caring and sophisticated he is (or cowed by the threat of the noise machine if he didn't go along).

Cuccinelli gives a different impression, one of being the kind who is instead drawn to the sound of such conflicts. Given that taxpayer funds underwrote the scandalous behavior revealed by the leaked materials, he invoked an antifraud statute to see the rest of the related documents that might be sitting on UVa computers.

Although the Virginia Fraud Against Taxpayers Act had passed unanimously in both chambers of the commonwealth's legislature just a few years before, suddenly the establishment found the law an outrage and began clucking about necessary exemptions for certain kinds of people, which had not previously occurred to them and clearly had not struck the legislature as worthwhile. But then, as was soon obvious, laws protecting the taxpayer from abuses were meant to be applied to *other* people. And so the university called on the courts to protect it from the tyranny of taxpayer scrutiny.

Cannons outside the courthouse symbolically stood guard to this forum for obtaining justice, while inside three parties all claimed to represent the public. The retired judge called in to hear the case was no stranger to the university, whose law school now served as his employer and for years employed his wife in the very department whose actions were at the core of the case. He prominently looked down in black robe upon counsel for the attorney general and the flagship state university. All very solemn.

Then, not long into the proceeding, I was startled to hear an acknowledgment casually placed into the record. Apparently, the University of Virginia did in fact possess a cache of email traffic between the former UVa faculty member and central player in the scientific scandal, Mann, providing further context and discussion of that which had been leaked. This was undoubtedly great news all around, as Mann et al. had implausibly insisted that the leaked documents were "out of context," even though they were released with entire email threads attached, without editing or otherwise amended. Here, at last, was the missing context.

However, this breakthrough gave rise to another, somewhat sticky aspect of the matter: the University of Virginia had told a completely different story to members of the public seeking the information under a different law, the state's Freedom of Information Act. It was after a law enforcement officer asked the same question that they provided this different answer. I was to learn that this was not an isolated example of that progression of denying the existence of records to nosy members of the public, only to later inform authorities of one sort or another that, upon further consideration, the public institution indeed did have those records after all.

I turned in surprise to a gentleman seated next to me, a professorial scientist, former U.S. Public Health Service surgeon, electrical engineer, and all-around thorn in the side of the statists in Virginia named Dr. Charles Battig. We both flashed expressions to the effect of *How about that?* A copy of the trial transcript, promptly obtained, affirmed that UVa had indeed acknowledged to the attorney general that it possessed the records it had claimed to have destroyed. Finally we could put to rest all of the terrible doubt that the supposedly out-of-context but nonetheless deeply troubling emails had raised in the minds of the public and their policymakers!

With a colleague of mine, a lawyer and PhD environmental scientist named David Schnare, and a lawmaker to whom the university had told its no-longer-operative story, through the American Tradition Institute (ATI) I then submitted what was up to that moment viewed everywhere as an unremarkable thing—a Freedom of Information Act request. We reiterated the lawmaker's call for the university to release these same records the attorney general had requested, which effort already had been successful by revealing the university did in fact possess them after locating a computer server holding the controversial material, according to their revised position. They had missed this during the diligent search performed for mere citizens.

The university revised an earlier position to state that only *certain* academics' records were destroyed upon their departure from the school (even if it turned out these actually still existed). This tweak emerged after a group very different from ours sought the records of a less politically correct academic who by chance had left the same department, former state climatologist Patrick Michaels, chased out of the position for his scientific views. The school had no problem with this.

However, when it came to the very-PC Mann, who had also left the same department and was a star activist in a fashionable "cause," the university made clear it would fight at all costs to withhold his records. UVa treated us with the same disdainful practices they used

with the attorney general,[7] indicating they had no interest in producing these particular records that apparently had to be kept more secret
than, say, records of other former faculty, or other faculty elsewhere at
Virginia public universities, which requests had received very different
responses.[8]

UVa had decided to stonewall these two requests for Mann's records,
in my case taking every possible delay allowed for in the statute, implausibly misreading the request—causing further delay and so as to
justify their demand for a spectacular fee of tens of thousands of dollars
to hunt for records on a computer we specifically identified and they
had acknowledged having already located. *Why, we would have to search
an entire, decentralized campus record-keeping system!* Unless they simply
looked where we directed them. After we surprised them by agreeing to
pay their subsequent, reduced search fee of mere thousands of dollars,
they found other ploys to keep the publicly owned records secret. It was
clear then, and is ever more clear now, that at no time during these hi-
jinks did the University of Virginia ever intend to produce the requested
records.

So, after several months, we decided enough was enough was
enough. We filed suit.

That is when the furor really began. And it came from far beyond the
Albemarle County line. It revealed that our elites believe that transparency laws were drafted by them, for them, and that the wrong people
using these laws constitutes "harassment," is "abusive," and must be
stopped.

Everything is politicized to those for whom everything is about government, which is to say power—the authority to control, the desire to
dictate to others.

Peggy Noonan and George Will made this point in columns published on the same day, mourning the passing of two different champions of liberty. Will noted, "[S]ince the 1960s, liberalism has been
concerned with who thinks what, who acts when, who lives where and

who feels how."[9] Noonan wrote of the left, "Because they seek to harness government and the law in pursuit of what they see as just and desirable ends, everything becomes a political fight."[10]

So today we battle a state "acknowledging no limit to its scope and responding to clamorous factions that proliferate because of its hyper-activity," that is "no longer constrained by either the old constitutional understanding of its limits or by the old stigma against deficit spend-ing."[11] Our weapons in this battle are few, but the greatest of them is an informed electorate. As citizen journalists fill the void left by the establishment press's migration firmly into the left's political sphere, now more than ever we require the guarantee of transparent government of-fered by federal and state freedom of information acts.

But transparency poses a political threat to those in power so they politicize it. The liberals now control the institutions they previously demanded be open to public scrutiny, using the institutions to impose their values and their isms, their peculiar faiths, on us all. The bureau-cracy had long resisted transparency, but now, under President Barack Obama, appointees and career activists working in government at all levels fear and loathe FOIA for very good reason. The same reason you need to join the fight and begin poking around. The bureaucratic, politi-cal, and academic left have embarked on a systematic push to diminish our ability to peer behind the curtain and see their work to "fundamen-tally transform America."

Their leader and his administration expended great effort proclaim-ing theirs was "the most transparent administration in history." Mean-while, they ran so hard and so fast in the opposite direction that even some left-wing watchdog groups complained that Obama's team made the hated, supposedly secretive Bush administration look good on this account.

Like left-wing academics, the Obama administration has deliber-ately politicized the FOIA process just as it has everything else, ignoring politically unnerving requests outright, erecting obstacles by imposing fee barriers, and delaying production of records regarding their many scandals until the spin can be prepared and sold through friendly media outlets. They employ tricks to ensure that your request will turn up nothing and, if it does, that the records are withheld. Friends get what they need and "enemies," as President Obama famously labeled some universe that apparently consists of those who oppose his agenda, are stymied.

Yet the contempt for transparency of their machinations extends even further.

On a November afternoon in 2011, President Obama's administrator of the Environmental Protection Agency (EPA), Lisa Jackson, made a startling assertion at the University of California's Berkeley Law school:

> One of the things that drives me nuts are . . . you know . . . we have scientists being sued, we have climate scientists who are being persecuted, prosecuted, through persecuted [*sic*] by prosecution, by doing, for doing their job. I think that's, I think that's criminal.[12]

Jackson's overwrought rhetoric about persecuting scientists was obviously directed in whole or in part at our FOIA request for those records from the University of Virginia, in the news at the time due to other outbursts by media and academic elites.

Though typical of the bilious outrage about my and others' requests for public information—and by no means restricted to their environmental agenda but extending to their various mis- and malfeasances— this was the first instance exposing such fury from a high government official. Jackson sought to instigate lawyers and apprentices, for some purpose, by declaring the pursuit of public records "criminal."

Her mutterings were also somewhat incoherent: the only "climate scientist being sued" was one who had been singled out for his condemnation of Jackson's activist allies, saying one particularly notorious character "should be in the State Pen, not Penn State." Retired and without a visible support structure to help with his defense, Dr. Tim Ball appears to have been targeted by champions of "the cause" as someone more likely to be broken and made an example of for those thinking about fighting back. The plaintiff in that case was the very same former UVa professor Michael Mann. Ball nonetheless is admirably fighting back, at great personal cost.

Although this particular "cause" Jackson erratically chimed in to support is just one leading vehicle for a larger agenda, liberals view challenge of any sort to their agenda more as a threat than part of a healthy process. The *New York Times'* Thomas Friedman complains that we know too much now about what our political class is up to, now that "the Internet, the blogosphere and C-SPAN's coverage of the workings of the House and Senate have made every lawmaker more transparent,"[13] such that, darnit, they aren't able to do as much as they'd like. Particularly galling to Friedman and company is that part about transparency "making back-room deals by lawmakers less possible." This was echoed in similar quarters,[14] forgetting that Obama ran against backroom deals he still finagled anyway[15]—only Friedman, it seems, forgot the promise to broadcast negotiations on the same C-SPAN he now finds so corrosive—but which Obama also now desperately needs more of in order to become that most transparent president ever or something.

When Friedman finds that institutions of our democracy are getting in the way of his team's big plans, he pines for an enlightened totalitarianism, just for a short while, to allow liberals to make the right things happen[16]—if it need be longer, why, you'll be among the first to know. The celebrated columnist is merely saying what his kind are thinking.

They're doing more than thinking it now that some of us have put their pet projects and the "cause" at risk. As with any inconvenience to their utopian engineering it must be struck back at with vengeance. Their behavior and words also betray their fear.

They are hiding things, things that we paid for, and for which we are intended to pay more dearly if they succeed. They best articulate what they're up to among themselves and in their own words. When these words are committed to writing using resources we provided, we are owed them. We increasingly have to fight much harder to obtain them.

Scrutiny is anathema to this movement, to the entire project of using taxpayer-funded enterprises to create ever more costly and intrusive ones.

But it was they who created laws ensuring that government comes with the "strings" of openness and scrutiny. Now that government is their institution, it's no fair peeking. Liberals sneer at the prospect of those who do not share their motives accessing the same rights they regularly exercise.[17]

And they assail those who try. Think through this worldview proudly broadcast by Jackson. Consider the implications of this mind-set, in the hands of those placed in positions of authority. When Freedom of Information Act requests are criminal, only criminals will make them. Is this over-egging the rhetorical pudding? Not if you take them at their word, and by their deeds.

They really do view a demand by the wrong kind of taxpayer for information he paid for, revealing and explaining transformative policy agendas, to be the same as or worse than a crime. Jackson did not misspeak.

As you will read, to our political, media, and academic elites, any means necessary are acceptable for their movement, but you are not supposed to ask for information about them.

If you do, they don't want you to know how to do so effectively, limiting their avenues for escape. They have developed tradecraft to frustrate your presumptuous, illegitimate desire for information about what they're up to. If you catch on to them, they ever more flagrantly violate the laws in order to avoid producing.

They hope you never consider the ways to avoid or counter their tactics, which were honed over time and designed to frustrate your desire to learn what your government is up to.

I hope you do.

You have a right to transparency. Use it or lose it.

3.

Transparency for Me, but Not for Thee

The ACLU does it. Big Labor does it. Environmentalist pressure groups do it. The *New York Times* and *Washington Post* love doing it, most of all. Indeed, the Society of Professional Journalists embraces it as "the cornerstone of openness."[1]

Each of them argue that doing it is fundamental to their rights as Americans, and essential to liberty. The United States Supreme Court agrees.

And yet, I'm not supposed to do it. Nor are people like me. If you're reading this, you probably shouldn't be doing it, either. And the more I have done it during this "most transparent administration in history," the more cynically and furiously the establishment fought back to keep "it" for themselves.

This forbidden activity? Asking for records to which we all are entitled by law and that reveal "what your government is up to," to "shed light on an agency's performance of its statutory duties."[2]

Those are the words of the Supreme Court assessing a law enacted to impose sunshine on an ever-expanding government, a statute intended to ensure the rule of law, with just and equal treatment for individuals by the collection of institutions captured by the ruling class as vehicles to serve their own ends. This statute, the federal Freedom of Information Act, or FOIA, was adopted in 1965 in order to overcome an earlier such law defanged by institutional resistance to transparency. That was Section 3 of the 1946 Administrative Procedure Act (APA), which the Court, in

23

its first case reviewing FOIA's reach, noted "was generally recognized as falling far short of its disclosure goals and came to be looked upon more as a withholding statute than a disclosure statute."[3] State FOI laws soon abounded, further codifying the guarantee that taxpayers may request and receive government records in a timely and thorough manner.

FOIA was followed in 1976 at the federal level by the Sunshine Act, also replicated throughout the states. In 1978 Congress adopted the Presidential Records Act (PRA), requiring among other things that a president and vice president properly create and maintain records, and allowing for public access to presidential records through FOIA beginning some years after the end of the particular administration, all on the grounds that ownership of these records does not rest with the officeholder, but with the public.[4] You may recall how "President Barack Obama negotiated a compromise at the start of his term allowing him to use a private BlackBerry for personal and official business—provided that some messages would go to the National Archives at the end of his term."[5] The dispute was the result of Obama resisting PRA's requirements.

The broader federal government must similarly retain and preserve the record of its ministrations, under the Federal Records Act.[6]

Liberals reveled in transparency. But now it is causing them a great big headache.

Controlling the institutions subject to these requirements, the critical levers of power to reorganize society to their liking, they no longer get the joke. Lately, as with the left's views on other aspects or institutions of democracy, transparency has become inconvenient. The stupid masses don't want what the left's selling, and they are resisting. Some are even asking questions.

Generally frustrated at the hurdles that democracy and open society throw in their path to Utopia, liberals are increasingly angered by our making use of this law to scrutinize them and their noisy constituencies, well fed at the trough of taxpayer dough but no longer willing to accept this condition of bellying up to it.

Now they mewl about freedom of information being misused, that it has apparently outlived its usefulness; by their deeds they escalate old-school steps to block access to information while innovating newer ones. They are pulling out all stops to ensure that the madness—as they see certain people exercising privileges apparently reserved for preferred classes—cannot continue.

Sure, their continued use of FOI laws to obtain information the taxpayer paid for makes them "watchdogs," pursuers of "good government," accountability, and the public's "right to know." In fact, they even do precisely what they claim to abhor (when I do it), "harassing researchers" with requests for information of academics identical to my own. Our use of the law constitutes "targeting" and "attacking" selfless public servants; we are said to be not only engaging in "harassment" but also "abusing" the law.

The Society of Professional Journalists' Freedom of Information Committee to this day touts on its website a 1996 homage to the FOI law, which many of their ilk view as principally a journalist's tool to assist in their role as public watchdog. "FOIA: It's always there: Debated, disliked, sometimes scorned, it remains the cornerstone of openness."[7] In it, former SPJ president Paul McMasters trumpets that, "[c]omplaints aside, the FOIA has compelled federal agencies to yield millions of documents relating to government operations and performance. Every week, a news organization, scholar or public-interest group somewhere reports information of significance to public health or safety or good governance—based on material gleaned from FOIA requests."[8]

The Associated Press somewhat more narrowly "encourage[s] all news organizations to fight for freedom of information."[9] And fight like hell, they do, when it involves, say, Sarah Palin's email. Which apparently was "of significance to public health or safety or good governance." When we seek information on the activities of a few taxpayer-supported sacred cows, well, that's different.

This emerging idea that the unwashed should leave the role of public watchdog to the press, as they know what's good for us, is of a piece with Dan Rather's famous comment captured for posterity, "I understand keeping secrets from the viewer, I don't understand keeping secrets from me."[10]

But FOI laws are not merely tools for some people to go after certain other people, the wrong kind of other people, as seems to be the fashionable view. These laws acknowledge the necessity of publicly scrutinizing the machinations of the state's rapid expansion—in size, cost, and scope, which is profoundly greater today than at the time of FOIA's enactment. Government continues to move further away from the governed, with power concentrating in Washington at a pace rarely approached before in our history. Rightly or wrongly, government is at the same time increasingly viewed as unresponsive, and even out of control.

This perception is a dangerous one, as there is great moral hazard in the public losing confidence in the laws, the lawmakers, and those who are charged with executing these authorities. Widespread use and evenhanded application of FOIA to enable citizen watchdogs and citizen journalism are therefore as important as ever, if not more so.

Coincidentally, liberals now demand that it's time to stop the transparency train—they want to get off.

"Change": The Liberals Lose Their Love for Transparency

Liberals' concerns about transparency, abandoning their history as originators of transparency laws, are truly newfound. Academics, bureaucrats, and ideologues watched in silence in recent years as a group with which they plainly sympathize, Greenpeace, not only was outed for its information-gathering practices of stealing the trash of those with whom it disagrees—such as me, and a White House aide during the George W. Bush administration named Philip Cooney—but also as it serially requested records of academic scientists and researchers, including their emails, under state and federal FOI laws. Not one peep of discomfort issued. No threat to research was alluded to, nor was there any keening of how this signaled the death of science, or the republic. No cries of violating some sacrosanct if elusive right to "academic freedom" residing somewhere in the emanations and penumbrae of our Constitution's First Amendment.

Then they suddenly hit the roof when I submitted a request just like Greenpeace's—it's not like I stooped to cart off the academics' garbage, although Greenpeace showed some real cheek by suing others for allegedly taking theirs[11] (liberals like their hypocrisy ostentatious). In fact, my requests for information that have drawn the most fire from this noise machine, the ones prompting cries for unequal rights of access to public information and charges of harassment and threatening our national fabric, were those that simply replicated requests made by the left—who then froth at the unfairness of it all. They really don't like us working their corner, so righteously occupied.

Soon after my audacious replication of the left's move, two other groups initiated similar pursuits of activist state-employee academics. These were filed in Michigan and, of course, Wisconsin, ground zero of the left's effort to protect the governing class from the tyranny of the governed. Both sought records shedding light on how activist faculty used their taxpayer-funded positions for political, nonacademic purposes (not that taxpayers need a reason under these laws to request records: we do not).

By their howling, these recipients of the FOIA requests and their enablers equated the looming end of their world—comfortable taxpayer-funded perches to advance ideological agendas and more wealth transfer, free from any reasonable measure of scrutiny, accountability, or responsibility—with the end of the world.

They unleashed an orchestrated if painfully insincere symphony of outrage. Faculties rose up, cowing administrations into raising and spending hundreds of thousands of dollars to fight the very transparency to which the faculty agreed as a condition of their cushy public jobs, apparently only so long as it didn't inconvenience them. Media friends were engaged to assist with the outcry. It was time to change the rules of the game, retroactively, which also meant retroactively changing the terms of their employment and the larger compact with the taxpayer.

A sudden urgency dawned on them—the laws must be changed! In the near term this required the courts to helpfully interpret them, to afford liberals transparency for me, but not for thee. However, the laws as written beg to differ, making it difficult, though of course not impossible, to end the matter there. Legislatures have concluded that we have a right to see what our government is up to. No matter who you are, whether a felon, global warming skeptic, or even, gasp, a Tea Partier. Freedom of information laws are one of the average citizen's best tools as government and its sprawling institutions, including publicly funded academia, assert and exaggerate various threats, which, they assure us, require more government (and more academia).

And so the bureaucracy and the ideologues have developed routines to frustrate these pursuits by certain of us, until such time as they are able to negate FOI laws' utility. Subsequent chapters illustrate how these are employed, and how to avoid or counter them. But we see them employed to treat similarly situated requesters differently, for no apparent reason other than the requesters' views. Or, as enablers of this outrage admit in their more candid moments, because one's "objective" is different than theirs.[12]

My particular request using the Virginia Freedom of Information Act so angered the chattering, statist class that the *Washington Post* dedicated its Memorial Day 2010 editorial—"Harassing climate-change researchers"—to it.[13] More specifically, to me. Acknowledging that of course they like and indeed avail themselves of transparency laws as much as the next guy, this leading mouthpiece of the political left cited its distaste for the title of one of my books as evidence that my use of such provisions, to expose their pet projects and scandals, was abusive.

This is the same *Washington Post,* incidentally, that hailed President Obama[14] and his administration's promiscuously phony posturing about ringing in an age of oh-so-transparent government[15] only to have precious little to say about exposure of his administration as having trampled all over its own promises, so rapturously received.

Reaffirming the selective view of transparency further, the same *Post* claiming that request for public information is "harassment" soon demanded complete disclosure of any and all privately held information they could mine to damage those it doesn't like. Like Mitt Romney, about whom they parroted a campaign theme then being rolled out by Team Obama[16] by penning a sneering editorial titled "Mr. Romney's Secret Life: The public has a right to know what is on his tax returns and who is raising money for him" (online version: "Mitt Romney's secrets"[17]). It opened on the rather self-unaware note, "Mitt Romney's contemptuous attitude toward the importance of public disclosure is increasingly troubling. Whether it involves the details of his personal finances or the identity of his big fundraisers, the presumptive Republican is setting a new, low bar for transparency—one that does not augur well for how the Romney White House would conduct itself if he were elected."[18]

No, this does not mean the *Post* is now suddenly interested in Barack Obama's, say, academic records. Their principles about transparency, as good modern liberals, are grounded in identity and ideology. They'd made the decision to embrace Obama, based not on any details demanded of him, a legislative record, or other accomplishments, so presumably it was based on what he chose to tell us in his memoirs. As scrutiny of these—finally, in 2012—proved, attention to his writings and his own "compelling personal narrative"[19] had been outsourced to Oprah's book club or set aside for reading sometime tomorrow. But it's different because, as we've learned, transparency is for other people.

The paper's tantrum about my UVa request failed to articulate an argument, grounded in the law, for treating one class of records or people differently from the rest of those expressly covered by the act's terms. It also failed to acknowledge a critical point: Virginia's public universities routinely provide such records of academics, even the specific class of records we sought. Instead, the *Post*'s point was simply that the wrong people using FOI acts reveals a loophole that must be closed.

We know this because history actually began before my request that so unnerved them, a point obscured when the splendorous outrage purveyed by Big Academia, EPA's Jackson, the *Post*, and left-wing pressure groups was directed only at one in a long, unprotested series of similar FOI requests. Consider:

- Two 2009 requests of the very same University of Virginia for records and emails of academic scientists, one of whom was ultimately forced out as state climatologist by a nonscientist politician who did not share this scientist's views—on science.

- A request of the University of Delaware for the records and emails of an academic scientist, also subsequently ushered out as state climatologist for the same reason.

- Requests of the University of Alabama–Huntsville for the records and emails of two academic scientists.

- Requests of Harvard-Smithsonian for the records and emails of two academic scientists. In turning over requested emails, Harvard-Smithsonian acknowledged that, while not actually covered by FOIA, it wanted to comply with the spirit of the act.

Smelling salts, anyone? Yet there was no outcry in all those right quarters now grasping for heretofore undiscovered constitutional rights and scrambling the activist machine to ensure that FOIA laws are not evenly applied. Of course, the subjects of each of the above requests held politically incorrect views and the people using the law were left-wing activists. All good. Even though, on its face, this is an effort to protect select individuals, a select cause, and a nearly unprecedented revenue stream. But as Victor Davis Hanson has written of these times, "Identity in this ill society is everything—something to be put on and taken off as one sees advantage."[20]

Closer to home, a *USA Today* reporter was promptly provided emails of a researcher at Virginia's George Mason University, and even prepublication correspondence with a journal editor, with no delays, ruses, or financial hurdles. Naturally, the academic had published work critical of the statistical methods and use of "pal review" by the *Post*'s beloved global warmists (particularly UVa's Mann and his colleagues) to get the right kind of papers published and keep the wrong kind out. So he was fair game.

You may detect a pattern here as to what are acceptable uses of FOIA, and which represent grave threats to science, the academy, and the republic. From Greenpeace to academics and labor unions to the *Washington Post,* our thought leaders see the state as the proper dispenser of rights and privileges, and themselves as the proper executors of the state. If you have the wrong objectives, they prefer that you be out of luck and on your way. Worse, we see demands that the state be trusted and records we paid for placed off-limits, but individuals' private information revealed. As circumstances dictate.

This turns on its head the old liberal ideal that the FOIA laws are tools to protect the taxpayers. According to the laws' terms they are to be construed liberally in favor of disclosure, their exemptions interpreted narrowly and applied without regard for political sacred cows. They are not to be reinvented as certain, correct constituencies find the moment requires. Selective bias and self-preservation are not legitimate grounds for policymaking. To bow to that is abuse of the FOIA.

Objecting to this is how I became a FOIA "criminal."

Turning Transparency on Its Head, by Whatever Means Necessary

The UVa case study is illustrative of the true nature of our supposed champions of liberty and freedom of inquiry, and of their view of how taxpayer-financed academic institutions are to be used (politically) and treated (not like the rest of the taxpayer-dependent world). This is true throughout the federal government, state governments, even local governments, and most certainly state-funded universities. They unevenly treat citizens when it comes to allowing access to public information, borne of ideological prejudice or a desire to keep secret that which is meant by the laws to be public.

This campaign to snuff out the average citizen's ability to look into the operations of the state can be traced back to the United Kingdom, as a reaction to embarrassing revelations in emails covered by, but unlawfully withheld under, their FOI law. That law, while fairly new, is the one European Union version that was suddenly being used and so became the focus of a campaign by government and academia to shut it down. It was introduced in 2000 "as part of an attempt to create what Tony Blair called 'a new relationship between government and people.' The process of releasing previously private [*sic*] Civil Service information was intended to have signalled that the public are 'legitimate stakeholders in the running of the country.'"[21] This would soon lead to a revolt.

By the time of his 2010 memoir, Blair already sang a starkly different tune, writing of the tongue-lashing he claims to have given himself for enacting an FOI law: "You idiot. You naive, foolish, irresponsible nincompoop. There is really no description of stupidity, no matter how vivid, that is adequate. I quake at the imbecility of it."[22] Transparency for the public servant, he discovered, can be a difficult journey.

Blair is not alone in his horror. BBC News reported that a request for information to a taxpayer-supported university on a sensitive issue—politically sensitive, that is (yes, global warming)—managed to draw the attention of law enforcement.[23] A Mr. Adrian Kerton also attested to this to investigators for the British Parliament's Justice Committee as part of its postlegislative review of their FOI Act, published in February 2012. Kerton's written evidence stated, in pertinent part:

> I was surprised to be contacted later by the Norfolk constabulary, asking for personal details of me, my family and our computing equipment, purely on the grounds that I had made an FOI request.[24]

Kerton told investigators that the police acknowledged in writing to his member of Parliament that Kerton "was not and is not currently a suspect in [an] investigation."[25] Yet he was visited and was not the only FOIA requester to draw such attention, leading to his suggestion that this "exercise was designed to intimidate myself and others into not making legitimate FOI requests."[26] (On a completely unrelated note, a North Carolina IT consultant who asked for "contact information" for the EPA official caught boasting of his enforcement philosophy—to "crucify" random oil and gas companies to keep the industry respectful of the agency's authority—received a similar visit, from a local police officer and two EPA agents claiming to have no business cards.[27] He was asking for it, not because his email was threatening: apparently on its face it merely asked EPA external affairs for "Mr. Armendariz's contact information so we can say hello?", not Armendariz's home address or indicating a desire to physically find him. But he was inherently suspicious, being a known Tea Party activist. I FOIA'd the same bureaucrat's emails referencing iterations of "making examples" and "crucify," but as of this writing still face a stone wall.)

Surely the volunteer army recruited by media sources to paw through Governor Palin's emails, some of which were plainly not related to official duties and are therefore the sort that are typically excluded from production under FOIA, received similar treatment in 2011?[28] I missed that. A few years before, California's attorney general used the courts to demand the release of any correspondence that might exist between the then-private company General Motors and certain identified private parties, including me and a few others. His stated reason was that we were uniquely effective advocates on a policy issue on which he and we disagreed. At least in my case there was no such correspondence, but we were people whose views he didn't like and so he used the courts to go fishing through private parties' records. Again, like me, you may have missed the hue and cry.

The double standards and move to turn our system on its head became exaggerated beyond coherence in 2012. A "Three-Year Plan" emerged from the left-wing activist group Media Matters, sketching out a campaign to furiously compel transparency across the land. Well, from private institutions anyway.[29] The ones whose objectives don't (yet) satisfy the coalition behind this, "such labor unions as the state and local government workers (AFSCME) and groups like the Center for Political Accountability, whose work is funded by George Soros's Open Society Institute."[30]

Liberals, the original champions of such disinfection, now obviously believe in "disclosure" not as a safeguard of public funds and against the misuse of government, but for purposes of intimidating private parties.

So, psychological projection of their own thoughts onto others may explain in great part their selective enthusiasm for and newfound opposition to transparency. They did, after all, leap in unison to call FOI requests—of precisely the variety they had routinely issued— "harassment" once the favor was returned and such requests sought records of left-wing activists. Although this likely speaks volumes about their own intentions in issuing similar FOIA requests, the fact of the matter is that such requests were a condition of the liberal activists' employment. (The same cannot be said of private parties.) But holding employees to this condition was legitimate only when the academics at issue were disfavored by liberals.

Meanwhile, individual donors to Mitt Romney's campaign deserve to be publicly named and shamed by the president and his team, with an accuracy inversely proportional to the slippery verbiage, for "betting against America" and having a "less-than-reputable" record. "The message from the man who controls the Justice Department (which can indict you), the SEC (which can fine you), and the IRS (which can audit you), is clear: You made a mistake donating that money."[31] It has become clear about several such statutes that, in the eyes of the political left, "the real point of these disclosure laws is not to inform voters but to get donor names in order to intimidate them from participating in politics."[32]

The aim of their demands that select politicians turn over everything that is private, and that private corporations "disclose" support for think tanks or policy groups that liberals abhor, is "to stigmatize and shut down funding sources for any business group that seeks to influence policy debates," providing the basis for planned "ad hominem attack . . . right out of Saul Alinsky's playbook."[33] This is part of their modern formula.

Transparency was a liberal cause, but intended for less ignoble purposes. Now, as part of their modern formula, demanding disclosure has become the background music for the political left as they tee up their Nixonian machine. Transparency as contemplated by the law applies to public institutions, which liberals now extend to people who choose to engage in public debate while determining the original application— open government—poses a threat.

So in short, the argument that has emerged is that transparency is useful for intimidation purposes and therefore private parties must surrender information to liberals, to whom use of transparency laws applying to public institutions are also reserved; nonliberals who insist on using these laws are also to be intimidated out of using such laws, lest liberals on the public dime feel intimidated, themselves, by virtue of letting the public know how public money is spent.

Like most bullying, this derives from a deep-seated insecurity. In this case it involves the sense that substantive debate that might not serve the liberal agenda should be avoided where (and however) possible. In my 2008 book *Red Hot Lies: How Global Warming Alarmists Use Threats, Fraud and Deception to Keep You Misinformed*, I detailed the widespread, unprofessional, often sleazy and in some cases organized effort to intimidate scientists from publishing or even expressing views not helpful to "the cause," tactics elaborated upon by the 2009 and 2011 leaks of the same crowd's taxpayer-funded emails. All of this perfectly captured the liberal fear of transparency: in the liberal's mind the public can't handle the truth, for the reason that they'd consider it instead of just letting themselves be led.

Also in 2012, suddenly all manner of like-minded thought leaders in the fields of science, media, activism, and elective politics—many of whom had wrung their hands over certain people employing such legal means as FOIA and other laws to obtain public records from public, taxpayer-funded institutions—completely lost it. They openly condoned criminal activity to obtain private records from a private organization[34] and forge another that they then falsely touted as a leaked original.

Once again the identity or objectives of the parties involved was the distinction cited to rationalize this. A more medieval twist was that the thief was pursuing something he believed in passionately, so no biggie.[35] Whatever the fervor, somehow this made the miscreant a "whistle-blower,"[36] because after all he was just responding to beastly people whom these apologists disagree with, and so, come to think of it, he was a "democratic hero" for forcing a taste of "transparency" on these private actors standing in the way of progress.[37]

There was some muttering, generally inchoate, about how if you draw attention to public records subject to the legal process of FOI laws, well, you're asking for all of your private records to be made public by whatever means, however illegal.[38] That served as the backdrop for our betters at the *Washington Post* and *Los Angeles Times* to declare that this fraud was simply taking a page from the playbook and employing the tactics of those awful, other people. No such similar plays or tactics of these critics were offered, as there were none.[39]

One incident victimized a private party, whose private records were obtained (and a fake document forged)[40] by unlawful means. It was hailed as heroic. After all, people use FOI laws to get records, too. The Oxford University student newspaper quoted another journalist defending the thief, saying he "acted in a way that served the 'greater good.'"[41]

The supposed parallel and justification was an apparent leak[42] of publicly funded records subject to FOI laws but which had long been improperly withheld. The thief's cheerleaders condemned that. That leak exposed violations of ethical and moral obligations, as well as serial, continuing scientific misconduct and conspiracy to unlawfully thwart FOI requests in the name of a "cause," the same cause that made it okay to steal private records. Meanwhile, no malfeasance was revealed in the stolen, private records.[43] Just the grievous offense of private actors opposing the "cause"; therefore such actors were asking for it. As to the thief—recently named chairman of a new task force on "scientific ethics and integrity" at the august American Geophysical Union—he sent the documents he had stolen and a phony one that a forensic analysis concluded he "more likely than not" also faked[44] to colleagues with an email saying he was providing them "[i]n the interest of transparency."[45] Of course.

And yet despite such obvious distinctions and disparities, and the odious celebration of thievery of private materials while condemning revelation in public documents of unethical behavior, parity was feverishly proclaimed among these apples and road apples. This was done not by random Occupy types but by those at the upper levels of elite institutions, who then declared the illegal activity justified and the legal activity the worse of the two.

Theirs is worse than noble-cause corruption. Not only are criminal acts in pursuit of their "cause" acceptable—legally opposing the noble cause is somehow, or else should be, criminal.

Identity Politics Infects Transparency Practice

Liberals obsess about identity. Identity alone resolves so much for them. The phrase "identity politics" was coined to capture their political oxygen. In keeping with this and extending it, the Obama administration, beginning with the man at the top, famously seeks to divide Americans by class and advocates ideas like "We're going to punish our enemies and we're gonna reward our friends who stand with us on issues that are important to us."[46] Columnist Charles Krauthammer calls the approach "Slice and dice, group against group," and Obama our Divider in Chief.[47]

We now know the administration's use of the power of the presidency to disparately treat citizens, and identify them by what group they identify as being members of, extends to our rights to access public information. This is information that the taxpayer paid for and is by statute entitled to so that they can, as the Supreme Court famously wrote, know what their government is up to.[48]

From that court's first ruling on the law it has been settled that the Freedom of Information Act may be invoked by any member of the public—with no showing of need or motive—to compel disclosure of confidential government documents.[49] Whether a document is properly released depends as a matter of law solely upon the nature of the requested document and its relationship to the act's purposes. It does not turn on any particular objective of a party requesting the information, or that party's identity.[50]

As detailed in the next chapter, the concerted, deliberate obstruction of inconvenient taxpayer requests for openness escalated in the earliest days of the Obama administration. New presidential administrations regularly take office still to some degree in campaign mode, not yet transitioned to governance. But over time matters got worse, not better, with a demonstrated systemic practice of providing or denying access to information on the basis of a requester's identity and presumed motives. This is precisely the approach expressly admitted to and demanded by the emerging bloc of antitransparency liberals in academia and elsewhere.

This is to say that the ad hoc legitimacy of transparency is determined by the specific cause the content of the records serves, not the broader cause of open government. Consider the 2010 and 2011 WikiLeaks episodes in which stolen official records pertaining to the Iraq War and Guantanamo Bay detention facility—few if any of which records were the kind required to be released under any transparency law—drew huzzahs from liberals as just the kind of openness required for healthy government.

One liberal writer who styles himself "Mr. Transparency," David Brin (he wrote *The Postman,* which unforgivably led to a Kevin Costner movie, and *The Transparent Society: Will Technology Force Us to Choose Between Privacy and Freedom?*), wrote, "This is clearly the sort of transparency that—while it may short-term inconvenience some western governments—could help the secular trend toward an open world that (in turn) fosters and strengthens enlightenment nations and people. In other words, embrace this! The answer to most modern problems may boil down, time and again, to a more aware citizenry."[51]

True. And we have laws for that. But liberals' joy over WikiLeaks was narrowly targeted, their celebration obviously deriving from the fact that the leaks generally, if often indirectly, related to left-wing bêtes noires the Iraq War and George W. Bush. It was this discrediting and embarrassment that they cheered, for transparency to them is a beloved talking point and theory to selectively embrace. But in practice they view it as a threat and something to be carefully, politically managed.

On the other hand, the *New York Times'* beat writer for environmental and related political issues, Andrew Revkin, refused to publish the first release of Climategate emails in 2009, given that they represented "private" conversations and were therefore off-limits.[52] No, they didn't, but nonetheless that's not actually a standard the paper adheres to any more than the rest of the left when they want to promote information obtained by whatever means necessary. WikiLeaks is simply a flamboy-ant example.[53]

Further, Revkin was among several at the *Times* who rushed to (gull-ibly and uncritically) report on the above-cited stolen and even faked nonpublic records as a "leak," one that placed a group not of the *Times'* liking in a bad light, without verifying that the documents were even real.[54] Revkin was apparently even the first to claim "confirmation" of the faked document's validity (in a classic transparency move made famous by some Russian leftists, the version of the *Politico* article quot-ing Revkin has been disappeared).[55] This standard of not writing about something unless it is properly in the public domain—as they seek to define what is proper—only applies when the *Times* and liberals gener-ally want to avoid discussion of information they view as unhelpful. Writing about leaked records which, for legal sticklers, aren't "public re-cords" but in fact sealed under court order, is cool if they reflect badly on liberals' political opponents.[56] (In fact, in one of those rare coincidences, sealed court records involving not one but two political opponents of Barack Obama made their way public at convenient moments; the victo-rious Obama proceeded to install political operatives in agencies helping stonewall access to actual "public" records.)[57]

When they feel like it liberals can be very, very much in favor of "transparency," defined as the moment requires. But asking for an ID to see if who is voting is who they say they are—talk about basic "transpar-ency" requirements for those who seek to participate politically—why, that's an invasion of privacy of the highest order clearly meant to dis-courage minorities from exercising this right so fundamental that we can't dare do anything to protect its integrity. But public records subject to FOI laws are "private" when liberals don't want them viewed; gov-ernment documents not subject to FOI laws are public if they help a "cause" or two; sealed records, stolen records, and faked records actually or supposedly belonging to a private interest, those are public as well when circumstances require. These principles are very circumstantial.

When emails are obtained from Goldman Sachs, a big liberal supporter but more importantly a useful political object to tie to

Republicans for pretty much any reason that the moment requires, what matters is the substance, not their provenance![58] We're very lucky to have liberals around to assure us that this is consistent and not the raging, self-serving hypocrisy it appears.

As a general matter, liberals' particularly aggressive if selective fight to keep information from the public does show we're on to something. They politicize because there is a "there" there. Exposure of what they're saying among themselves about what they sell to the public threatens to queer the deal.

This is not, however, merely a function of the current occupants of the White House trying to "fundamentally transform America." Also, academics whose ranks had always been subject to FOI laws, who had no problem when the odd dissenter or conservative was the focus of requests under these laws, are shocked, shocked that it would also apply to them and theirs. They are all going to great lengths to escape transparency.

Another example of this involved a publicly funded academic institution stonewalling a known troublemaker, while coming clean to a lawyer who decided to conduct an experiment pressure-testing the stone wall by identically replicating the request. Both parties were initially rejected at the weeding-out stage, by the institution playing dumb and muddying the request. The university unilaterally interpreted the requests as being for records the parties did not ask for even though the requesters had deliberately employed the university's own jargon in identifying the documents sought. So the school was an equal-opportunity stonewaller at this stage. After that, the responses differed starkly.

The lawyer, Richard Brearley, countered the rebuff and requested clarification of this puzzling denial. The school clarified promptly and in seemingly forthright fashion. He checked with the other, notorious requester, whom the university in fact continued to obstruct with a tendentious and legally specious response.[59]

Brearley sought to explain how two identical requests could result in two such different responses when the reasonable expectation is for identical requests to receive identical treatment. He concluded that the institution's approach was one of not believing it should comply with certain requests, given its "assessment of the assumed motive of request-ers of information—an entirely invalid consideration" under the law.

> [I]f, as may be the case here, there is obfuscation operating within public authorities in response to requests that they don't like, then where does that leave us? The Regulations provide numerous excep-tions upon which requests can be refused. . . . What the Regulations do not do is allow a public authority to obfuscate on requests from people they do not like. . . .
>
> What can be the justification for public authorities apparently treating identical requests differently based on who the requester of information is and what motives the public authority, rightly or wrongly, attributes to the requester? The Regulations are blind to motive for a reason. It is not the public authority's concerns about disclosure that matter—at all. It is the right of access to information granted to the public at large that matters. . . . [60]

Not to them it isn't. Elites are squirming under scrutiny, and they seek to carve themselves out from under the prying eyes of those whose labors pay to support them. Consider the following statements made to the British House of Commons, released in that previously cited February 2012 compilation of written evidence of how their FOI law is working out.

FOI 92, Written evidence from the Society of Editors

> It has been suggested that the lack of a "motive clause" should be re-dressed and that in future, people making requests should be forced to explain why they want the information. [61]

To its credit, this particular media outlet weighed in to disapprove such a move, but a push to gut the law like that is startling. Reluctant bu-reaucrats and taxpayer-dependent academics actually want permission to refuse production on a claim that the information would only be put to an unfortunate use that good people really shouldn't want. On the other side of the ledger, the campus gang offered gems such as these:

> Whilst the Freedom of Information Act may have been intended to operate in the public interest by subjecting public bodies to increasing transparency and accountability, it has, in our experience, been too frequently used by some whose motives are far removed from the general public interest.[62]

And:

> [Certain] requests are not looking for confirmation of information held and disclosure of it for the public benefit, but rather are requests aimed to "fish" for information for motives entirely personal to the requestor and which are arguably not for the public's benefit.[63]

The police chiefs' association, also not thrilled with the burden of scrutiny, weighed in in support of the academics' complaint, asking that the information commissioner "provide clear guidance to authorities, and more importantly the public, that when considering Section 14 an analysis will be made of the individual and their motives."[64]

Taxpayer servants subject to transparency just aren't that into it. The condition is especially acute among the liberal establishment that now leads the charge to undermine the public right of access to public records. And they are actively seeking permission for improper practices that many of them, on both sides of the pond, are already employing anyway.

Further illustrating the panic, the political left in the United Kingdom has tried something our First Amendment would (presumably) never allow: a fitness test conducted by a political committee to determine whether an individual is the sort they believe should be permitted to disseminate information (specifically, run a media company).[65] It was aimed at a notorious if overmythologized conservative Rupert Murdoch, backer of such right-wingers as Tony Blair. The free-speech left want to control the flow of information, period.

The panic is already spreading across the continent. As the euro teetered in mid-2012, a rare media request under a mostly dormant FOI law that went into effect in 2006 led the German government to release hundreds of pages of documents on the inclusion of less stable economies in the euro zone.[66] What could possibly go wrong, right? This exposed that the common currency's design, and even formal defenses by the German government against a serious legal challenge to its creation, were premised on dismissing clear warnings, in favor of political dogma, on a falsehood that may prove to be one of the most expensive ever told a public by their government.

The previously secret papers show that "German officials gave numerous warnings that Italy was not ready to join the euro but were ignored because Helmut Kohl, the German chancellor, believed the single currency was Europe's destiny."[67] This secret abandonment of previously agreed standards in turn led to Greece's acceptance into the Euro. The rest of the story continues to play out before us.

Such a notorious introduction of the public to a transparency law that few Germans even knew existed can only lead to more widespread use, which in turn will prompt an expectation of transparency. Which, once institutionalized, is not easily undone. Hence the push to reverse these laws now.

It is for enabling such troubling exposures that European (and now American liberal) elites want to strangle this notion of freedom of information laws.

4.

Rhetoric and Reality:
Obama's War on Transparency

olitico wrote of President Obama, "A minute after he took office, the White House website declared his administration would become 'the most open and transparent in history.' By the end of his first full day on the job, Obama had issued high-profile orders pledging 'a new era' and 'an unprecedented level of openness' across the massive federal government."[1]

Later, Obama said, "This has been the most transparent government, most transparent administration that we have seen in a very, very long time, perhaps in the modern era. . . . We very much believe in transparency and accountability."[2]

"We have put in place the toughest ethics laws and toughest transparency rules of any administration in history. In history. By the way. This is the first administration since the founding of the country where all of you can find out who visits the White House. First time in history. And that's just one example of how we're trying to constantly open up the process."[3]

Ignore the fact that while President Obama was patting himself on the back, his lawyers were busy fighting off parties seeking these logs in court, and then appealed their loss, "which would appear to be in tension with Obama's repeated pledges to operate the most transparent administration in history."[4]

As George Will wrote around the same time with the Obama

administration in mind, "As government expands, its lawfulness contracts."[5] Things were indeed much changed when it came to transparency and open government issues. Just not as Team Obama said they would be.

Instead, soon after all the breast-beating about just how openly wonderful he would be, for all practical purposes Obama's promises were old news, something we should all "move on" from. Further, Obama's performance has every indication of being deliberate and systematic. A lawyer, Katherine Meyer, who had handled FOIA cases since 1978, reluctantly admitted to being "stunned—I'm really stunned. . . . It's kind of shocking to me to say this, this administration is the worst on FOIA issues. The worst. There's no question about it."[6] Political researcher and columnist Michael Barone writes, "Obama talks a good game on transparency and openness, but he's ready to flout the law . . . and to break his high-minded campaign promises."[7]

The overriding problem with this is not the hypocrisy and the lie of yet again loudly boasting to be one thing while striving so aggressively to be another. It is that the law says what it says. Ignoring and abusing this runs against our legal construct. But, sadly, laws are a lesser concern to many liberals than their movement and its requirements. It is acceptable to twist and even ignore the laws as the political moment requires so long as they are the ones doing it.

This is a strong statement, but as I have noted elsewhere Barack Obama openly decries our system once it stops working his way, and insists he will find ways to work around it for that very reason.[8] Some of President Obama's moves have been plainly unlawful, and others too gray on that count to be responsibly pushed by someone sworn to uphold the Constitution.

He uses laws for purposes never intended for them, in order to push through an agenda that the elected representatives rejected (the Federal Communications Commission's activism and EPA's "global warming" agenda, for example); he subverts the rule of law to the benefit of cronies, from Solyndra to Chrysler (and gets away with it, while also playing the thug);[9] he ignores the Constitution and precedent (making "recess appointments" when Congress is in session, the very same "pro forma" session in which they rammed through ObamaCare on a partisan vote); and he decides not to enforce laws he is sworn to uphold (New Black Panther case, Defense of Marriage Act, immigration laws).

True, existing laws can feasibly be used as legitimate means to achieve those ends that the failed efforts to revise, supplant, or supplement the law aimed to obtain. But these other times, when existing legal frameworks are simply vehicles that will do in a pinch thanks to the extreme deference that courts grant regulatory agencies, challengers have an extraordinary burden of proof in seeking to have rules overturned by the courts.

And when justices advanced legitimate questions about the constitutionality of one of these follies, Obama orchestrated a campaign of public intimidation, calling in advance any effort to exercise their traditional function of determining a law's consistency with the Constitution "judicial activism."

Arguably lawless, this approach also manifests itself in systemic, often systematic flouting and flagrant abuse of our transparency statutes.

The rule of law is a basic premise of a free and prosperous society, demanding that laws be evenly applied to all, regardless of a citizen's economic profile, political correctness, or standing in society. This is our Declaration of Independence's affirmation that we are all created equal in the eyes of the law. There are no footnotes "Unless you don't like them," "Except when I disagree with them," or even, as it sometimes now seems, "When another's use of the laws threatens my own standing, or my agenda."

The thuggishness and cronyism may be all Chicago but it is an import from Europe, increasingly home to the developed world's greatest "democracy deficit" (where, incidentally, Eurocrats are also seeking to gut the proposal for releasing official European Union documents to the public).[10] It is wholly at odds with American values and the letter of the law. And it demands scrutiny. We underwrite their "cause." And they say it's awfully mean for those of us who foot the bill to exercise our rights, laid down in the law and equitable principles, to see what these people we are paying are up to.

Strike a Pose, There's Nothing to It

Not one but two Obama administration memoranda were immediately issued after the president's inauguration proclaiming his transparent wonderfulness. The memo referenced by *Politico* addressed the Freedom of Information Act,[11] and another, "Transparency and Open Government."[12] These words "pleased good government groups and . . . journalists."[13] That was according to a journalist.

This is something Democrat presidents do, part of the sneering and poking at the man they replaced, a largely symbolic chord in the ritual anthem preening about their moral and other superiority. President Clinton issued a memo in his first year also mandating a new attitude toward the FOIA to make a clean break with the Reagan-Bush years. "The act is a vital part of the participatory system of government. I am committed to enhancing its effectiveness in my administration."[14] This was paired with Attorney General Janet Reno reversing a 1981 Department of Justice policy, saying that the department no longer would defend an agency's denial of a FOIA request merely because there was a "substantial legal basis" for doing so.[15] The Clinton administration proceeded to be secretive (even if also infamously pursuing something of an enemies list compiling information on private citizens, just as Obama's campaign is promoting against Romney donors).[16]

Obama followed this script to the letter, with an attorney general pronouncement and his own boast similarly representing a misdirection play, hinting at the coming secrecy. In the Clintons' case the latter was driven by a Nixonian paranoia originating with the First Lady, to wit, that the institutions that for years had covered for her and her husband were actually out to get them. Obama, having joked to the press that "[m]ost of you covered me. . . . All of you voted for me,"[17] suffered no such delusions.

Regardless, Attorney General Eric Holder added a seemingly legal imprimatur in a third memorandum published on March 19, 2009.[18] This follow-up guidance to Obama's memoranda deserves particular scrutiny given its contrast with Holder's operation later being declared the worst FOIA offender in the worst administration for FOIA compliance.

Wrote Holder's DOJ, "On his first full day in office, January 21, 2009, President Obama issued a memorandum to the heads of all departments and agencies on the Freedom of Information Act (FOIA). The President directed that FOIA 'should be administered with a clear presumption: In the face of doubt, openness prevails.'"[19] Holder instructed chief FOIA officers to support career staff by ensuring they have the tools necessary to respond promptly and efficiently to FOIA requests.

March 19 is apparently "Opposite Day" in some circles because the investigation by the chairman of the House Committee on Oversight and Government Reform, Darrell Issa (R-CA), discovered that political staff actually impeded execution of the law, taking control of FOIA operations and seizing up the machine to stop embarrassing information from coming out. This investigative report contained excerpts from interview transcripts affirming this. And later revelations showed these were not isolated instances. Yet it was precisely that imposition of political interference that Holder stated would not occur.

Holder similarly instructed that, when a record has information that is properly withheld, the agency should look to redacting portions, not the entire record. This instruction is simply consistent with long-standing law, so on its face it had a whiff of the pose about it.

"The Attorney General also 'strongly encourage[s] agencies to make discretionary disclosures of information.'"[20] This refers to the fact, also discussed later, that many exemptions to FOIA simply authorize an agency to withhold information, but do not compel it. "Consistent with such discretion provided in the Act, the President also instructed agencies that information should not be withheld merely because 'public officials might be embarrassed by disclosure, because errors and failures might be revealed, or because of speculative or abstract fears.'"[21] This proved to be no more than hand-waving, as they still regularly do this.

"The President's FOIA Memoranda directly links transparency with accountability which, in turn, is a requirement of a democracy. . . . For every request, for every record reviewed, agencies should be asking 'Can this be released?' rather that [*sic*] asking 'How can this be withheld?'"[22] Holder airily held forth that the presumption of openness established by the president meant that "an agency should not withhold information simply because it may do so legally."[23] I say airily because my firsthand experience with dozens of FOIA requests submitted to this administration unambiguously affirms that when they do not want politically sensitive information to come out, they employ this practice as if they were born to it.

Holder piled on with more, gratuitously emphasizing that the FOIA "reflects our nation's fundamental commitment to open government," with the new guidelines "meant to underscore that commitment and to ensure that it is realized in practice."[24] Similarly, "The President also directed agencies to act in a 'spirit of cooperation' with requesters." As Holder stressed: "Unnecessary bureaucratic hurdles have no place in the 'new era of open Government' that the President has proclaimed."[25]

The Most Transparent Administration in History?

The Obama administration's praise of itself doesn't credibly reconcile with what has been exposed, largely by private citizens diligently keeping tabs on what their government is up to.

Despite all of the self-congratulation, the administration went to great lengths to dodge disclosure, violating the spirit and the letter of laws they vowed to adhere to with historic purity. "The most transparent administration in history" showed its openness by systematically arranging to meet with lobbyists off campus to avoid creating a history of their business-hour relationships as the law clearly intends, and by closing "transparency" briefings even to the press.

Then there were the cries for help. Gunwalker and Fast and Furious come immediately to mind, with the administration sealing up tight and risking a highly damaging legal fight. The Troubled Asset Relief Program (TARP) "resolutely refused repeated requests from . . . members of the House Oversight and Government Reform Committee for TARP documents, particularly those concerning decisions affecting auto industry pensions during the General Motors and Chrysler bailouts."[26] The Obama White House forced congressional subpoenas for records about their politicizing of the BP oil spill to promote an ideological offshore deepwater drilling moratorium (the "permitorium"),[27] but even stonewalled themselves on this. When a federal inspector general looked into the editing of expert conclusions and recommendations in the Obama administration's report on the spill, erroneously suggesting these outside experts supported the administration's drilling moratorium—less politely known as manipulating peer reviewed recommendations—he "was denied access to a White House official and full email records" needed to conduct the investigation.[28]

They promiscuously granted waivers for Obama's political allies like the labor unions (but not for conscientiously objecting religious hospitals and schools).[29] "I'd like to work my way around Congress."[30] They met with Democrat governors to "discuss ways of bypassing Congress."[31] Carol Browner and her order, "Put nothing in writing, ever."

Then there was the issue of Obama's 2008 campaign chief of staff (and 2012 campaign manager) Jim Messina—called by left-wingers "the Obama administration's designated 'fixer'" who "jet-sets around the country, huddling with big donors," and "Obama's Enforcer" known for "hardball tactics"[32]—found to have used his personal email account to do public business. Specifically, while serving as White House deputy chief of staff he used his private email account to work with the drug lobby crafting their deal on ObamaCare. Surely by accident. Each time. (Oddly this came right on the heels of a Democrat congressional investigation of Karl Rove using a Republican National Committee email account.)

The *Nation* wrote in 2011 that Messina is "a savvy, experienced operative who played a key role in the passage of Obama's legislative agenda"; it precisely wrote, "The inside strategy pursued by Messina, relying on industry lobbyists and senior legislators to advance the bill, was directly counter to the promise of the 2008 Obama campaign, which talked endlessly about mobilizing grassroots support to bring fundamental change to Washington . . . he spearheaded the administration's deals with doctors, hospitals and drug companies . . . . When they were negotiating special deals with industry, Messina and [a leading Senate staffer] were also pushing major healthcare companies and trade associations to pour millions of dollars into TV ads defending the bill."

Upon release of the ObamaCare email traffic pried out of the drug lobby, the *Wall Street Journal* subtly headlined its editorial, "Emails Reveal How the White House Bought Big Pharma."[33] What they did not note, or possibly did not know (the addresses are blacked out),[34] is that Messina had used his AOL account to do his business with the drug lobby that the White House otherwise publicly demonized, stepping outside of his official account for which the law requires that records be kept, and which was provided for precisely that reason. (In addition to such legal considerations, I suggest that this is several steps removed from broadcasting all negotiations on C-SPAN, among other campaign promises broken by such tactics.)[35] He also coordinated the administration's tag team with left-wing groups called the Common Purpose Project.[36] So, maybe his continued memory lapses that he was no longer a campaign operative but doing public business, subject to laws like the Presidential Records Act, wasn't so accidental.

Plenty of signals hinted at a need for heightened scrutiny. The National Labor Relations Board and Boeing. ACORN. Dodd-Frank. Van Jones and other unconfirmable czars and czarinas. Then "recess" appointments to avoid Senate confirmation, even though the Senate was in session. Backdoor, "other ways to skin that cat" of cap-and-trade.[37] Obama's vow to "bankrupt" politically disfavored industries, and the rest of his administration's war on domestic energy. Keystone XL, which reminded us of the cronyism that begs for citizen journalists to do the job of the slumbering "real" kind. Andy Stern. General Electric. Light-Squared. Stimulus. Fisker Automotive, Beacon Power, BrightSource Energy, Ener1, Amonix. Serious Materials. Solyndra.

Solyndra embodied the administration's rampant cronyism, breaking laws in the name of "finally mak[ing] clean energy the profitable kind of energy in America." That curious formulation found its way into Obama's first two addresses before Congress. He made that same pitch verbatim in his first speech to the United Nations General Assembly, of all places, to upbraid Congress for not giving him what he wants. That deliberate word choice soon gained meaning when the scandal broke, not just the handout, but the facially unlawful move to subordinate the taxpayers' enormous financial interest in the already teetering "green jobs" venture in favor of campaign "bundler" George Kaiser. It was in all the papers. If not so much on the network news, which preferred to focus, if at all, on how awful it was to ask questions about such an over-blown affair.

The experience of the lawyer claiming to be shocked and dismayed by Obama's reality, like my experience and that of others, led even some leftist groups to become appalled at the administration's clampdown on the flow of public information. In early 2012 two left-leaning, self-styled FOI watchdogs, Citizens for Responsibility and Ethics in Washington (CREW) and OpenTheGovernment.org, released an assessment of Obama's compliance with the Freedom of Information Act. They surveyed fifteen major federal agencies, comparing compliance data from fiscal 2008 and fiscal 2010, President George W. Bush's last full fiscal year in office and Obama's first.[38] They found an increase in the reliance upon exemptions, and particularly on FOIA Exemption 5 (discussed in detail later), "used often to protect internal deliberations from disclosure."[39] Two-thirds of agencies increased the frequency, on a numeric and percentage basis, with which they denied routine requests to waive related fees for those taxpayers too nosy for their own good (fee barriers being one means of obstruction).[40]

The unavoidable overall conclusion, affirming the findings of an earlier investigation by the House Committee on Oversight and Government Reform, was that the Obama administration had clamped down on the release of publicly owned information. "This data reveals the Obama administration has been less transparent than the Bush administration in allowing the public access to some of the internal workings of government."[41]

A closer look also revealed how this was a result of severely politicized implementation of the Freedom of Information Act, examples of which are discussed later. Therefore, the administration's ostentatious proclaiming of itself as a breath of fresh, transparent air seems little more than a cynical attempt to create the prism through which the public would view such real-world evidence. If they ever did. Because, other than the odd one-off story, the public weren't often exposed to these complaints.

A few media outlets at least acknowledged problems discovered by yet another group, the National Security Archive. These included no actual, detectable follow-up by the administration on their loudly proclaimed reversal of the dark days of the prior administration.[42] But this systemic assault on disclosure and transparency under Obama seemed so passé as to not warrant elevation to, say, a theme for framing media coverage of the (politically appealing, to the media) administration.

Reality and these templates have a complicated relationship. Bush was so stupid, of course, that he would never have lived down that whole "fifty-seven states" thing that we all knew signified nothing about Obama, who actually said it. Because he's really worldly and was just tired, probably from being so smart, when he said Austrians speak Austrian (possibly he was thinking about Australians). Similarly, the pattern of abusing transparency laws was indicative of nothing about Obama, so the press disregarded this even though it represented an assault on something they claim to cherish.

Once again a party's identity or presumed intentions apparently determine the righteousness of their actions, as the media rationalized paying no heed to a move to undermine transparency so plainly intentional, and not mere incompetence or hypocrisy on Obama's part. Something was going on here, yet, generally, the media treated each revelation in isolation when they deigned cover it at all, with an apparent perspective that Obama said he was going to be open and certainly means well, he's our kind of guy . . . so this must just be a bunch of yahoos who want to embarrass or distract his administration.

If there's another explanation, we deserve to hear it. But the watchdogs specifically entrusted by the Constitution with asking the necessary questions left it to citizen journalists to fight the press's battle for them, in the vain hope the press would take interest in a government waging war on transparency. But they will not, because, after all, anything not done by them isn't the product of real journalism. Now excuse them while *New York Times* reporters ask President Obama what most enchants him about the office,[43] and the *Los Angeles Times* frets about Ann Romney's hobbies while "refusing to disclose the contents of a video tape in its possession that reportedly shows Barack Obama lavishing praise on his friend Rashid Khalidi, a close associate of Palestinian terrorist Yasser Arafat."[44]

These public guardians of what warrants scrutiny have their standards, after all, and we should learn to live with them. Except that we have laws allowing us to decide otherwise.

"Just Words"

In "a testy exchange" with Fox News reporter Wendell Goler in 2011, White House spokesman Jay Carney hinted that specific deeds exist proving the administration's actual openness, even though he only pointed to what were by then two- and three-year-old words as his evidence. Though Carney insisted vaguely that "[t]his president has demonstrated a commitment to transparency and openness that is greater than any administration has shown in the past, and he's been committed to that since he ran for President and he's taken a significant number of measures to demonstrate that,"[45] even the most self-congratulatory rhetorical commitments are not deeds. The president's memorandum that marked the apex of his historic transparency closed by reminding everyone, "This memorandum does not create any right or benefit, substantive or procedural, enforceable at law or in equity by any party against the United States, its departments, agencies, or entities, its officers, employees, or agents, or any other person." That boilerplate escape hatch signaled the coming reality.

After hearing an earful from watchdog groups—several of them liberal groups aghast at just how bad the Obama culture of state secrecy is—left-leaning *Politico* acknowledged the chasm between Obama's rhetoric and the truth. Sympathies die hard, however, and, possibly after getting another earful from the White House when calling for comment, *Politico* played the pattern down to a series of isolated "stumbles." Stumbles like "aggressively fighting FOIA requests at the agency level and in court—sometimes on Obama's direct orders. They've also wielded anti-transparency arguments even bolder than those asserted by the Bush administration."[46] But of course not every watchdog group resisted housebreaking. At about the same time spokesman Carney was lecturing the cheeky Fox reporter, "representatives of four open-government groups visited the Oval Office to give Obama an award for his 'deep commitment to transparency.'"[47] Really. ("The event prompted some snickering because it was closed to the press and was omitted from Obama's public schedule.")[48]

Efforts to tamp down the snickering proved further amusing, with supporters offering hopefully naïve apologies, rationalizing this award despite the by-then-obvious secretiveness, calling the honor "aspirational." Steve Aftergood, director of the Project on Government Secrecy at the Federation of American Scientists, said, "And in that sense, one could say it resembles the award at the Nobel Peace Prize. . . . It's not because Obama brought peace to anyone but because people hoped he would be a force for good in the world, and maybe that's the way to understand this award."[49]

The *New York Times* was among the outlets unhappy with at least one aspect of Team Obama's code of *omertà*: cracking down on whistleblowers, unseemly given the administration regularly leaked classified information from political sources to suit its political needs. Even though the Obama team "promised during its transition to power that it would enhance 'whistleblower laws to protect federal workers,' [it] has been more prone than any administration in history in trying to silence and prosecute federal workers."[50] This was for grave offenses, like telling a reporter (accurately) that an internally developed software program would cost far less than an outside vendor's product for which the administration planned to spend hundreds of millions of taxpayer dollars. Ironically, the whistleblower, named Thomas Drake, also warned that the administration was going with a product that violated personal privacy rights in ways the internal software would not. He faced up to thirty-five years in prison, until the prosecution against him collapsed.[51]

The *Times* quoted Jesselyn Radack, Director for National Security and Human Rights at the Government Accountability Project, as saying, "The Obama administration has been quite hypocritical about its promises of openness, transparency and accountability." How hypocritical?

> Reporters were immediately and endlessly briefed on the "secret" operation that successfully found and killed Osama bin Laden. And the drone program in Pakistan and Afghanistan comes to light in a very organized and systematic way every time there is a successful mission.
>
> There is plenty of authorized leaking going on, but this particular boat leaks from the top. Leaks from the decks below, especially ones that might embarrass the administration, have been dealt with very differently.[52]

A week later the *New York Times* reporter who published the details on that bin Laden raid, for which he received the Pentagon's furious anger, acknowledged the story was leaked to him by the White House, which doesn't punish itself for self-serving actions, however harmful.[53] As when the White House leaked details about the bin Laden raid to filmmakers working to make Obama look good.[54] Those leaks that apparently sprung from the top were irresistible to the Obama camp desperate to make a hero out of their guy but were damaging to a different and somewhat more important "cause" than a radical environmental agenda or reelection campaign.

About the same time came an "inexplicable leak" of details about the intelligence operation snaring another "underwear bomber," right "on the heels of a series of disclosures" over the first few days of May 2012 and described by intelligence professionals as "really tragic," "despicable," and "a tawdry political thing" putting future operations at risk.[55] One intelligence veteran questioned the future of British intelligence cooperation "with their American friends, who are far more leak-prone than they. In their place, I would think two and three times before sharing with the Americans, and then only do it if I had to."[56]

Okay, so it later came out that the administration had even falsely implied credit was due them for what was in fact an MI6 operation, whose agent's life their insecurity-driven preening endangered.[57] But, hey, it allowed Obama to strike a pose for political needs.

No one said being the most transparent administration would be easy. In fact, by June 2012 the promiscuous leaking of sensitive information apparently to make Obama look tough drew bipartisan outrage in both houses of Congress and calls for a special counsel.[58]

And yet, also by 2012, the *Washington Post* would acknowledge (as a political item in Al Kamen's all-in-good-fun "In the Loop" column, not as hard news) that Holder's Justice Department won the "Rosemary Award," named in misspelled fashion for President Nixon's secretary Rose Mary Woods, famous or infamous for erasing eighteen and a half minutes of Watergate tape.

According to the *Post,* "The seventh annual award, presented by the George Washington University–based National Security Archive, honors the agency that has done the very most in the previous year to enhance government secrecy and keep the public in the dark. The agency's actions 'seem in practical rebellion against President Obama's 2009 open-government orders,' said Tom Blanton, director of the Archive."[59] The administration, "among other things, engaged in 'selective and abusive prosecutions of espionage laws against whistleblowers as ostensible "leakers" of classified information' and conducted 'more "leaks" prosecutions in the last three years than in all previous years combined.' . . ."[60] This, using a law whose "sordid history" liberals describe as including use against political opponents.[61]

DOJ is seen by liberals as the worst offender, that is among many, as it turns out that Obama is "a president whose administration has led a vigorous attack on journalism's most indispensable asset—its sources," according to Edward Wasserman, Knight Professor of Journalism Ethics at Washington & Lee University.[62] Despite the rhetoric it is "prosecuting [whistleblowers] with a zeal that's historically unprecedented."[63] Before a recent spate of prosecutions one liberal wept that "most whistleblowers say his administration and his DOJ treat whistleblowers worse than any previous president."[64] Later, even left-wing commentators at Daily Kos,[65] Salon,[66] and CommonDreams.org[67] became startled.

Administration behavior justifying these condemnations, and the lofty Rosemary Award, included drawing the ire of self-described investigative journalists for "aggressively pursuing" leaks[68] all while still publicly maintaining its objective of protecting whistleblowers, constituting an "attack on journalistic sourcing"[69] in response to which "fervor . . . the news media have largely rolled over and yawned."[70] One exception was ABC News's Jake Tapper, who told Obama spokesman Carney at a press briefing, "There just seems to be a disconnect here. You want aggressive journalism abroad; you just don't want it in the United States."[71]

Possibly the press otherwise yawned because journalists are decreasingly pressed to reveal their sources. That is because, "[a]s a national security representative told Lucy Dalglish, director of the Reporters Committee for Freedom of the Press, 'We're not going to subpoena reporters in the future. We don't need to. We know who you're talking to.'"[72]

Reason magazine's Peter Suderman quipped, "Investigative reporters are supposed to be the ones keeping an eye on the government. Instead, it turns out, it's the other way around."[73] Please pause for the obligatory "imagine if this was George W. Bush" moment. But of course, one need not leave it to the imagination. Bush waged a "war on whistleblowers."[74] President Obama matched that war,[75] and raised it, to a war on transparency. (Incidentally, this discussion also revealed that the left-wing Federation of American Scientists apparently demands the right to unlawfully leak classified information at their discretion without prospect of prosecution;[76] that's the same class who now are also supposed to receive exemption under transparency laws that require those who rely on taxpayer money for their work to allow the public to see it, even if with many exemptions to ensure appropriate privacy and intellectual property protections. This helpfully puts the demand for exemption and the hypocrisy of those who make it in cartoonishly stark relief.)

It was, after all, national security information that was the focus of those Bush administration practices seized upon rhetorically by Team Obama as the supposed scandal off of which Obama keyed his "transparency" pose. This traced back to a directive from then–attorney general John Ashcroft, issued weeks after the September 11, 2001, attacks, "put[ting] the burden on the requester of sensitive information to show why it should be disclosed."[77] Obama ordered declassification of some Bush administration records addressing leftist hobbyhorses, then dropped any tangible pretense at the whole "transparency" shtick.[78] Only the misdirecting rhetoric proclaiming their miracle of transparency lived on.

Reality proved so contrary to the pose that even the Environmental Protection Agency began invoking what is known as a "Glomar response" to requests for information. This response, by which an agency is permitted to refuse to either confirm or deny that requested records exist, was pioneered by the National Security Agency to hide information about "Project Azorian," a secret plan using Howard Hughes's ship the *Glomar Explorer* to raise a sunken Soviet submarine.[79] The request then goes before a judge for a private look at the files, for the requester who takes matters that far. It can also be used to shield exposure of informants. Now EPA is invoking it. Or at least they did upon Obama taking office, that is.[80] But no, not during that hermetically sealed Bush administration.

I challenged the administration's apparent use of Glomar with me when they were at first oddly cagey about whether certain NASA records existed—ethics records—without actually daring to invoke the exception in a case already drawing unwanted attention. These records involved the spectacularly compensated (by sympathetic, private parties) James Hansen of NASA's Goddard Institute for Space Studies. They worked hard to protect Hansen, a valuable advocate in pushing "the cause," from having his records disclosed despite their legal claims being specious. Then he made a pain of himself by drawing even more unwanted media attention by getting arrested in front of the White House and helping keep alive the conversation on Obama's opposition to the Keystone XL pipeline.

Suddenly NASA's cageyness evaporated, and I soon received a call saying the entirety of Hansen's relevant ethics records would be sent to me by messenger.

Then, as if the existing ability to simply refuse to confirm or deny the existence of a record were not enough, Attorney General Holder sought sanction for the practice of lying to requesting parties about whether records exist.[81] Addressing the administration's resistance in the courts against complying with FOIA, the *Post's* Kamen noted, "Another Justice lawyer argued at the Supreme Court last year that claims of an exemption from FOIA should be given a broad reading. Justice Antonin Scalia ventured that the high court's prior opinions 'assert, do they not, that exceptions to FOIA should be narrowly construed?' 'We do not embrace that principle,' the lawyer replied."[82] About this, David Sobel, senior counsel at the otherwise sympathetic Electronic Frontier Foundation, told a reporter, "It's just incredible for an administration that says it's committed to an unprecedented level of transparency to be telling the Supreme Court, 'Hey, we don't accept long-established Supreme Court precedent favoring disclosure.' It's just jaw-dropping."[83]

Actually, it is illustrative of this administration's rhetoric being so starkly at odds with its reality. It reflects who they are. So it is no surprise that Obamaphiles soon summoned the ghost of Orwell by claiming that, well, it really is "good government" that's important, not "open government." "Good" offers a little more leeway for the eye of the beholder. This came from the former administration appointee charged with the, er, "Open Government Initiative," Beth Noveck. Now returned to (surprise!) academia, she "noted that the White House has subtly shifted from the 'open government' theme, setting up a new Web page last year focused on 'good government.' A few months later, it rebranded the effort again, as '21st Century Government.'"[84] Twenty-first-century government that was stuck, somehow, in 1984.

Noveck, who took to the *Huffington Post* to assist with the rebranding,[85] later argued in defense of the administration's record that the public needs to get over its obsession with FOIA and instead be happy that the administration puts out data at places like NASA, to enable citizen involvement.[86] But of course, it is manipulation and exaggeration of data at places including NASA that prompted FOIA battles, with the administration fighting tooth and nail to avoid you seeing the truth about the data and accompanying doomsday proclamations—in support of guess-who's floundering policy prescriptions?—that you should be happy receiving. So it seems the whole "most transparent administration in history" thing, translated, goes something like this: Just take our numbers, get hysterical about them, and demand our agenda on the basis of them. Or shut up. Your call.

More systemically, as *Politico* wrote while also affirming its charitably inaccurate use of "stumbles" to describe the Obama cloak of secrecy, "Compliance with agencies' open-government plans has been spotty, with confusing and inaccurate metrics sometimes used to assess progress. Some federal agencies are also throwing up new hurdles, such as more fees, in the path of those seeking records. The Office of Management and Budget has stalled for more than a year the proposals of the chief FOIA ombudsman's office to improve government-wide FOIA operations."[87]

And then, of course, there was the practice of leaving inspector general positions unfilled. "The State Department (think Keystone XL pipeline), the Interior Department (think BP oil spill), the Justice Department (think Operation Fast and Furious), and the Department of Homeland Security (think airport pat-downs), all are without IGs. It has been [as of February 2012] 365 days since DHS had an IG. The Department of Justice hasn't had an IG for 395 days. And Obama has not even bothered to nominate people for either the State (1,503 days) or Interior (1,099 days) IG jobs."[88]

That is, he's even stonewalling his own executive branch, very similar to the way his team blocked an inspector general from investigating the manipulation of expert recommendations regarding a drilling moratorium after the BP spill. As the *Washington Examiner* editorialized, citing a string of embarrassing and expensive administration boondoggles:

There is no mystery in Obama's aversion to independent IGs. . . .
Back in 2008, candidate Obama extolled transparency in government. But now IGs investigating his record for the past three years
could hurt his re-election efforts.[89]

As could citizen-IGs doing the work of the real kind, or citizen journalists doing the job of "real journalism," both wielding FOIA as their
weapon. Which explains Obama administration stonewalling, politicization of the process, and use of tricks to avoid detection of records that
taxpayers seek, paid for, and deserve.

5.

Obama's Tactics: The Most Transparent Administration Ever's Tricks and Tradecraft to Escape Transparency

The *New York Times* revealed that senior Obama administration aides met with lobbyists away from the Presidential Records Act's prying eyes "hundreds of times" to discuss "front-burner issues like Wall Street regulation, health care rules, federal stimulus money, energy policy, and climate control—and their impact on the lobbyists' corporate clients."[1] Before getting excited, note that this was a one-off story, reflecting no investigative reporting but only repeating others' findings and from which big red flag the Grey Lady then walked away, with a shrug of her narrow shoulders.

Still, we later learned elsewhere that Obama's White House compounded this, instituting a practice of moving meetings to "row houses just off Lafayette Square," across from the White House and where "[t]here are no records of meetings," in order to avoid detection.[2] "It allows the Obama administration to keep these lobbyist meetings shielded from public view—and out of Secret Service logs kept on visitors to the White House and later released to the public."[3]

In addition to then–chief of staff Rahm Emanuel, "Other Obama aides—like Jim Messina, the deputy chief of staff, and Norm Eisen, the special assistant for ethics—and senior aides in the Office of Management and Budget, the energy czar's office, and elsewhere have also taken part in off-campus meetings, lobbyists said."[4]

Administration defenders claim that these off-campus meetings are held because, well, sometimes governance requires spontaneity that the White House screening does not allow for; except that emailed invitations expose that claim to be spin, as meetings were called with plenty of notice to proceed according to the rules.[5] They're hiding things. Including "a steady stream" of lobbyists ultimately found out to be working with Team Obama once the requisite records were created, despite all of the promises.[6] It was apparently better to risk being exposed as obvious hypocrites on a transparency vow Obama never meant than on the lobbyist vow he never meant.

Then there is the "list of administration failures on transparency," presenting a compelling pattern at stark odds with the self-congratulation, including:

> Obama's Housing and Urban Development Department demanded confidentiality orders from lobbyists with which it was meeting.
>
> A telecom advisor to Obama's transition team did not disclose he was pushing policy that helped his client.
>
> The State Department used flimsy reasons to reject a FOIA request over a former pipeline lobbyist now working on pipeline issues for State.
>
> The Recovery Act, or "stimulus" website, didn't meet standards for transparency, according to the Government Accountability Office.
>
> A total failure to post nonemergency legislation online for five days before signing.

When Obama sent his transparency czar to the Czech Republic, he never replaced him, giving his duties to a partisan ex-lobbyist not too enamored of transparency ("disclosure is a mostly unquestioned virtue deserving to be questioned").[7]

The revelations show a deliberate avoidance of record-keeping, disclosure, and transparency laws. "Attempts to put distance between the

White House and lobbyists are not limited to meetings."[8] For example, to arrange their sneaky coffee klatches and otherwise to correspond, lobbyists regaled the *Times,* in its one-and-done story, with how "they routinely get e-mail messages from White House staff members' personal accounts rather than from their official White House accounts, [the latter] which can become subject to public review."[9] (The *Times* appears unaware that disclosure policy in fact extends to official business on private accounts.) Even *Mother Jones* noted, with sobriety reserved for unlawful behavior by political allies, that aides "using private email accounts to schedule coffee shop meetings with lobbyists (an apparent attempt to prevent these sessions from appearing in White House visitor logs)" leaves no record memorializing meetings, which do appear to be the very records that not one but two statutes require White House officials to preserve.[10]

At least one appointee in the White House Office of Science and Technology Policy (OSTP) also was publicly outed for his practice of improperly and regularly using personal email to conduct official, policy-specific business but on an account from which he may permanently delete mail, over which only he has control, and which supervisors cannot search in response to a FOIA request or otherwise.[11] There are, after all, reasons why employees are assigned government addresses and computers, and they are expected to perform their official business using them. An administration lawyer opposite me in a FOIA dispute admitted that the practice of using private email accounts is well-known and widespread, which sentiments were echoed by a career FOIA specialist at a different department.

So we have a campaign to avoid creating records in the first place, efforts to avoid preserving records that are created, and the broad array of abuses and outright subterfuge to avoid releasing those records that somehow nonetheless manage to get created or preserved. One ally of the Obama administration, commenting on the significant worsening of what were often decried as the dark days of Bush, noted that Obama elevated the matter of FOIA compliance to senior political appointees—somehow, a good thing (just like if a Republican did that, right?). Even better, it was assigned to Bob Bauer, White House counsel and husband to Anita Dunn. Dunn was made briefly famous for her expressed admiration for Chairman Mao and the Obama administration's War on Fox News when she formally worked on the inside. Having left the administration she is now business partner of the delegated "War on Women" attack dog Hilary Rosen,[12] whose joint consulting firm also flacks for Sandra Fluke, once again of the "War on Women" initiative.

The Sunlight Foundation's John Wonderlich told *Politico,* "Their line was, 'Remember, Bob Bauer is the White House counsel. It's a big step up. These issues will really be addressed. . . . ' We never heard anything again from Bauer. . . . The transparency portfolio did get upgraded: It was upgraded to the president's senior political staff who aren't specialists in it and view it as a liability."[13] That's right. It was "addressed."

It's not for nothing that Obama found lapses among even friendly media, who occasionally quoted allies bemoaning his performance as "the worst on FOIA issues. The worst. There's just no question about it." Washington lawyer Katherine Meyer, quoted earlier about being "stunned—I'm really stunned," continued, "This administration is raising one barrier after another."[14]

Disclosure and transparency were just talking points; their reality proved a threat. So the tricks to avoid it began. How unforeseeable, really, was the result described above from involving hyperpolitical lawyers in what is supposed to be an apolitical, straight exercise in timely and evenly responding to requests for information? Therefore it is difficult to imagine that the tricks were anything but deliberate.

Committed bureaucrats can do many things to frustrate FOIA requests—like making improper assumptions or reading the request in a way other than its plain meaning, and by playing dumb in other ways, such as redefining the search parameters on their own and/or farming the request out to too few or the wrong locations to be searched. These moves limit what is captured by a search as "agency records" and ensure an improperly narrow response, keeping documents hidden.

There can be goals behind an inadequate search other than limiting what is produced. Sometimes buying time alone is enough, to allow the team to get their spin in order and twirling madly in allied quarters. Sometimes delay and otherwise being difficult is just a tactic to weed out those who will fade away before they can cause too much trouble.

A congressional investigation of the Department of Homeland Security confirmed this deliberate practice of delay,[15] and I and several others have experienced painfully obvious examples with "Fast and Furious" and the Department of Energy regarding Solyndra-related records. Consider the administration's stonewalling of Congress on that latter episode, not using FOIA but pursuant to Congress's oversight function (remember, this authority and constitutional delegation is serious enough that they have subpoena power and the power to hold someone in contempt, referring prosecution to the Department of Justice). It is a necessary pursuit, with even the Treasury Department having concluded that the administration broke the law.[16] But this ritual illustrated the tiresome predictability with which they play out their routine of delay while trying to put a gloss of cooperation on it. They'll say, why, we've released (some number, exasperatedly uttered) pages; it's just politics to say we're not cooperating. Implication: what more could a reasonable person want from us? Answer: the pages you've chosen to withhold, usually known as the good stuff.

If there are eleven pages of responsive records and they release ten, and only one page—guess which page—says that your campaign bundlers really need the bag of money, does providing the ten pages indicate compliance? When ten thousand pages are released, what is more illustrative and informative: ten thousand pages being released or the refusal to release one hundred pages? Phrased otherwise, precisely how many pages should we expect to smoke? Waving around hundreds or thousands of pages of released documents usually aims to distract from the pages being withheld.

When the administration turned over four hundred thousand pages of Solyndra records—in at least six distinct dribs and drabs, generally late on a Friday afternoon—they and their apologists pedantically prattled on about how this proved they'd been cooperative and aren't hiding anything, disproved by each subsequent release. Except of course the documents they admit to withholding, even in the face of subpoenas.[17] To that they replied that what they released is what they've on their own determined satisfies the "legitimate oversight interests" of Congress.[18]

Similarly, evidence emerged about secretive White House meetings with various industries and special interests as ObamaCare was being developed, "trading policies for public support and treating pieces of our health care system like a series of bargaining chips to be doled out in an effort to deliver a political victory,"[19] as suspicious House Republicans put matters. When they sought details about these deliberations, the White House first suggested that pulling the information together would be too "vast and expensive." To this the Republicans saucily replied that the admission, if that is what it was and not just more stonewalling, "rais[ed] questions about the sheer number of closed-door meetings between the White House and these outside groups. Eventually the White House did turn over some documents, consisting largely of press releases, publicly available information, and an incomplete copy of [Deputy White House Chief of Staff Nancy] DeParle's schedule. (It would have been cheaper to simply televise it all on C-SPAN as promised.)"[20]

But after promising transparency the White House continued asserting that it had given the House what it needed to satisfy any legitimate inquiry; now go away. So just as with the liberal mind-set that all we need to know about a liberal candidate for the highest office in the land is what he chooses to write about himself, those of us seeking information about his White House's questionable escapades apparently only need those pages the White House is willing to give us. Those pages they don't want us to see, well, demanding them is illegitimate and . . . drum roll . . . politicizing the process.[21] Which justifies making up their own rules as they go. Because people seek records about something even the administration acknowledged was unlawful, apparently, they're the ones really being political. The law and White House obligations under it play little role in this playacting.

It is this sort of logic that led to the claim that Chairman Issa's request for records from the disastrous Solyndra boondoggle, representative of Obama's "green jobs" obsession, including subordination of taxpayer interests in recovering the squandered half-billion dollars, was a witch hunt. Just as they decried my use of the very same FOIA request that liberals pioneered, to seek academics' records. And the Virginia attorney general's pursuit of taxpayer-funded records under an antifraud statute. All were "witch hunts."[22] If so, they came amid revelations looking an awful lot like a broom, a boiling kettle, and many eyes-of-newt.

So the White House joins those who believe that the wrong people seeking information is on its face illegitimate, it is up to the state to determine what the curious really need, and that blocking these requests is the noble cause in the name of which any corruption is acceptable. They and their defenders deride citizen investigations using FOIA just as they sneer at congressional oversight or law enforcement. "Fishing expedition," "witch hunt," and all other labels recast inquiries into apparent or possible illegitimate activity as themselves being the illegitimate activity, all deriving from the requesters' identity or "objectives." I know that my objective was transparency and good government. The sort that would upset certain well-laid if half-baked plans. Which makes one wonder what their objective is.

This ritual of partial releases followed by claims of full cooperation is a close cousin of the secretive appointee's ploy of withholding documents in full when they could simply redact any properly withheld information. In so clinging to entire documents they withhold the to, from, when, and subject information, as a matter of course, calling it "pre-decisional" even though keeping such basic, identifying information from the taxpayer is not a legitimate use of that exemption.

As with the "Big Wind" cover-up described next, they do this because your learning merely who is corresponding with whom about what, and when, is sometimes enough to help piece together the particular puzzle.

The law requires redaction of releasable information as opposed to withholding records in full, unless that is impossible without giving away the game about the properly withheld information; it is also specifically ordered by Obama's and Holder's memos to staff. Yet the Obama administration generally and White House specifically still as a matter of course withhold entire documents as "pre-decisional," making us fight to pry the public records loose. Forcing us to expend effort and expense, delaying their embarrassing releases, and discouraging others from pursuing the matter can in itself be a victory for them. But some of us have pushed back. The National Right to Work Foundation, for one, had experienced enough stonewalling over a request to the Department of Labor seeking information about cozy ties with unions, and so they sued. That got Labor's attention, fast. The department "apparently didn't think that there was any value to responding until it hit the courts and the media."[23]

This is similar to my experience, most notably with one FOIA request that NASA sat on, hoping I would go away. I didn't. After too long, I instead notified them of my intention to finally sue, and two years of pretending I didn't exist evaporated amid the heat from negative press coverage of their obviously hiding things.[24] Those things include an admission to a reporter for *USA Today* (who never wrote about it) that NASA does not in fact have an independent global temperature record despite all of its alarmist and self-promoting claims indicating otherwise; emails showing an even chummier and mutually beneficial relationship with the *New York Times* writer covering them; that NASA had terrible record-keeping practices, inconsistent with their precise claims within hundredths of a degree comparing contemporary and historic temperatures; that activists at NASA were running a third-party activist website on taxpayer time, using private computers to do official business, and other revelations that in turn led to more FOIA requests and more damning releases.

As I have already quoted one open-government advocate complaining, this administration in particular also has been known to impose unwarranted fee barriers, on one improper ground or another. House investigators explained an egregious case to me, again involving Obama's Labor Department, which, after detecting that one nosy taxpayer's probing stirred preliminary media interest, suddenly ground down the requester's follow-up searches with enormous fee demands. Leftist groups ended up suing Team Obama over this fee-barrier tactic, particularly exercised over the Central Intelligence Agency being uniquely inventive at creating obstacles. And in 2012, "five nonprofit groups, including the American Civil Liberties Union and the Electronic Frontier Foundation, asserted that the Department of Homeland Security was demanding thousands of dollars in 'exorbitant fees' to process FOIA requests, even though the groups regularly obtained waivers in the past."[25] These are not the actions of an administration driven by a desire to be transparent, to disclose in the absence of compelling reasons not to.

This is also the same move tried on me by UVa, implausibly reading my request for records not as written but so as to warrant a $35,000 search fee—for records they'd already searched for and had found, which discovery I expressly stated had prompted my request, which went so far as to specifically identify the computer where the records resided. And UVa first replied with that line about a woefully decentralized computer system that would have them searching all over creation, demanding we show our good faith by coughing up tens of thousands of dollars before they agree to look.

State FOI laws typically provide far fewer days to respond than the federal law (five days in Virginia, plus one extension); although the university knew that they could not sustain their reinterpretation, it was simply a delaying tactic most likely so they could internally confront their strategic decision about which way to diminish their reputation, by disingenuously stonewalling or by revealing more dirty laundry. So delay was the name of the game as they "addressed" the problem they had created for themselves, the solution to which was to take the position that the law somehow does not fully apply to them. That this was their thinking was seemingly affirmed by subsequent behavior, all consistent with what we ultimately learned: the faculty had rebelled and was insisting that the school fight, at all costs, to wear down me and others, including the Virginia attorney general.

Using FOIA, I also uncovered a deeply troubling development, which was Obama officials showing good discipline—good, not great, which was what led to exposure of the tricks—in employing tradecraft. That is, using code names, and industry groups as "cutouts," or intermediaries with groups whose communications would be likely targets of

FOIA efforts, discussed later. If your EPA is going to invoke the NSA's Glomar response to FOIA, why not go all out and employ the day-to-day habits of the espionage community?

The goal of these particular evasive maneuvers is similar to that of the Obama White House's "simple rule," as reported by the *New York Times* in another story the liberal press broke only to walk away from its implications: "Put nothing in writing."[26]

This rule is of a piece with White House staff using private email and outside meeting places for the conduct of official business. It was outed after having been communicated to automakers with no little gravity in a series of meetings called to strong-arm them into supporting an administration agenda item—back when that was still necessary, in the days before a certain, ah, change in the automakers' organizational structure left them more amenable to the Obama agenda.[27]

The problem there was the troublesome, post-Watergate Presidential Records Act, a law ensuring that records of an administration's dealings are created and maintained even for White House offices exempted from FOIA. But if a White House tries such an obvious end run around the law, unless someone squeals, who's to know? The evidence of something not being done is not typically a smoking gun, but more likely is testimonial or circumstantial. It just might be crazy enough to work. As one participant told the *Times*, "We put nothing in writing, ever. . . . That was one of the ways we made sure that everyone's ability to talk freely was protected.' She added, 'It's an astonishing thing that on something of this magnitude there were no leaks.'"

It is useful to note at this point that to the extent any such records would be subject to FOIA, the act has an exemption to exclude from production those which are necessarily withheld to encourage the "deliberative process." It is FOIA's most abused exemption. Carol Browner, of all people, knows this (see below) and is convinced that nothing less than absolute secrecy will suffice in doing the public's business.

It was inevitable that the administration's promiscuous self-promotion as the most transparent ever would lead officials to expect their activities would be the stuff of public interest, of calls for transparency, meaning the subject of FOIA requests, and thus would adopt these and other defensive tactics (however lawful or unlawful) to defeat taxpayers who take up the challenge.

It makes it logical. It doesn't make it right or legal where otherwise illegal. And some of these moves are going to require judicial review to get to the bottom of them, like the rakish use of private email accounts by White House aides and other political appointees to conduct official business. For the moment, what we do know is that Browner either set or reflected the administration's tone in that auto meeting by ordering no notes be taken (speaking of foreseeable outcomes, she did, after all, have a "czar" position created for her so as to avoid Senate confirmation hearings due to her own history of destroying records that were being sought by FOIA litigation).[28]

The practices this mind-set begged soon became a way of life, reaching its logical zenith with that Justice Department request to lie outright about the existence of records sought under FOIA.[29] Investigations and experience affirm that, when it comes to FOIA, this administration employs stonewalling and deception as routine practice.

Politicizing Transparency

Obama and company crafted an image of reversing an existing system of improperly refusing access to information, institutionalized by the preceding administration. That supposed condition was overblown at first by the combination of specific angst over the "war on terror" and more generally by Bush Derangement Syndrome; it was further hyped by candidate- and president-elect Obama for reasons of political, self-promoting optics. The boastfulness shrouded the fact that he was in fact politicizing the FOIA process for nonsensitive information the release of which posed a threat not to the nation but to his administration, his cronies, and his allies.

The Obama administration handles requests differently based upon the requester's identity, whether he's a perceived ally or friend, or if the congressional office seeking information is Republican or Democrat. In addition to slow-walking requests that make them nervous, they've been shown to ignore[30] or even just spike planned responses to requests from undesirables.

Former Department of Justice career attorney J. Christian Adams drew attention by protesting the Obama DOJ's politicization of voting rights enforcement cases with which he was involved (particularly the New Black Panther Party case of voter intimidation at Philadelphia polling places). Looking into departmental bias, he noticed that the media were very interested in Bush personnel hires at DOJ, but not so much when it came to Obama and Attorney General Eric Holder's team. It's not that there was no interest in DOJ under Obama: Adams also noticed liberal media outlets reporting on records they obtained from the new administration while he, writing after his departure from DOJ for the conservative Pajamas Media, was getting the cold shoulder.

So he dug into the matter further. Liberals seeking DOJ records got five-day, three-day, and even quite often same-day service from their pals in government, eager for stories assisting with their own agenda or trashing political opponents. A review of DOJ records led Adams to conclude, "FOIA requests from liberals or politically connected civil rights groups are often given same-day turn-around by the DOJ. But requests from conservatives or Republicans face long delays, if they are fulfilled at all."[31] "[W]ell-known conservatives, Republicans, or political opponents had to wait many months for a response, if they ever got one."[32]

The FOIA process under Obama had been immediately hijacked by political appointees. Friends got information, as their motives were surely pure; perceived opponents did not, and this meant anyone seeking embarrassing information or information relating to particular key projects. And friends came immediately, looking for evidence to continue their obsession with the previous administration, or else to otherwise give a hand to the new one.

In his book, *Injustice: Exposing the Racial Agenda of the Obama Justice Department*, Adams cites specific examples derived from reviewing DOJ's own records, documenting that certain taxpayers were treated with shoddy, outrageous service ranging from a six-month wait (Michael Rosman of the Center for Individual Rights; Jerry Seper of the *Washington Times*; Jed Babbin at *Human Events*) to no service at all. Adams found cases where DOJ simply did not even reply (the *Washington Post's* "Right Turn" nod to the idea of balance, Jennifer Rubin, who sought records precisely of the same class that a left-wing requester received immediately; Jim Boulet of English First; Jason Torchinsky, former DOJ lawyer who went to work for the Republicans).[33]

When asked about Adams's reporting, Attorney General Holder dismissed it by arguing that "it did not account for different complexities in the requests,"[34] referring to the routine under FOIA of sorting of requests into classes depending on, for example, the number of search terms or offices to which it would need to be sent. But Adams's research affirmed that "the liberals enjoyed this speedy favoritism even when they filed intricate requests."[35] He concluded, after deconstructing Holder's dissembling, "The only explanation for why FOIA requests from liberals are fulfilled much faster than those from conservatives is that the DOJ is systematically stonewalling the latter."[36] Left-wing radicals hired by Holder moved papers out the door with immediate turnaround unheard-of in FOIA implementation, and shut out requesters they deemed unfriendly.

Adams writes, "Politicized compliance with FOIA might be an administration-wide pattern. The revelation that the Obama Department of Homeland Security has politicized the FOIA process may be just the tip of the iceberg,"[37] referencing the investigation by the House of Representatives Committee on Oversight and Government Reform that documented egregious and systemic political interference at the Department of Homeland Security, detailed below. That found, for example, "unprecedented intrusion" by "political staff into the department's FOIA procedures."[38] I found the same practice, and even had it admitted to me, at other agencies.

Funneling information to help friends grind commonly shared axes is a great side effect of politicizing FOIA, but the administration's overriding objective in so egregiously straying from their promises and their continuing rhetoric by withholding, complying, or even overcomplying is to attain political advantage.

Think back to Obama's unseemly politicization of the bin Laden raid in Pakistan. The incessant effort to capitalize on the event's anniversary in 2012 reminded us of how the administration had no qualms about releasing operational details of the strike, and in shameless haste, despite the foreseeable consequences of doing so. According to a disgusted former Pentagon chief Robert Gates, an agreement among the highest decision-makers was struck on a Sunday to do no such thing, an agreement which "all fell apart on Monday—the next day."[39]

This politically expedient but reckless embrace of transparency seriously compromised capabilities and future actions and made SEAL Team 6 reluctantly famous, placing them and their families in jeopardy.[40] Military officials seethed "at the White House and CIA and Pentagon officials for releasing so much detail."[41] "There is an awareness that the threat of retaliation is increased because of the attacks—because of the action against bin Laden," Gates said.[42]

But, like the similar leaks of sensitive information which came in a flurry as the 2012 re-election campaign heated up, it momentarily made Obama look good, which was apparently the principal consideration. Meanwhile, routine information not reasonably withheld is clung to, and citizens are forced to sue their own government to obtain information owed to them simply because some political appointee found their request a threat. This is a pattern, and indeed a universal practice by this administration of politicizing the laws including those designed to provide all taxpayers equal treatment.

Equal treatment under the law is intended to apply regardless of the impact of releasing information on, say, the political prospects for a liberal agenda. In one tidy example, EPA immediately turned over to the newspaper *Politico* "pre-decisional" documents, exempt from FOIA, involving the agency's original plans to impose the failed "cap-and-trade" energy tax through the back door.[43] These indicated that the original proposal was a much more obvious assault on coal-fired power plants, going further on its face than the rule that was actually published. This was a distinction without a material difference because instead of effectively banning the construction of new coal-fired power plants, with responsibility in Obama's hands, the rule set the greens up to sue the agency to mandate that.

Here the administration did not refuse to provide these records plainly covered by, and precisely the sort they routinely withhold under, the "pre-decisional" exemption to FOIA, which is also the exemption they most egregiously abuse (according even to lefties). They pushed the documents out the door to help strike a needed pose of moderation on one of Obama's most radical agenda items. It was posturing. The administration used selective transparency to create the image of there being a step back—he could have done what they say he wants to do, but see here, he didn't!—where there was no such thing going on.

This aided the effort to spin the general public while setting the greens up to sue them to force adoption of their shared agenda in a classic sue-and-settle move. Win-win.

The sole distinction was image, crafted in tandem with the reelection effort. As the brief, selective, and politically self-serving moment required, transparency was all the rage in an ostentatious rush to position Obama as not really being as radical as his own promises to kill the industry he targeted for extinction with these and a suite of other rules.

Then, right on the heels of this episode came release of more documents under another FOIA, a request that had sat for eight months—possibly because on its face it was not a friendly request—but which now could serve a purpose, for release as a follow-up to the other pile of documents, both reassuring anxious greens that the administration really was with them. A left-wing group the Center for Progressive Reform had asked for these records, which, as the *Washington Post* heralded the release, showed the White House supposedly bringing its own EPA into check, an agency whose "officials thought the White House failed to adequately capture their work on anti-pollution rules opposed by Republicans and industry officials."[44]

There goes that moderate Obama White House again, led throughout, one should not forget, by a man who staffed this EPA with radicals[45] and said he wanted to use these same rules to "bankrupt" politically disfavored industry under a scheme that would "also raise billions of dollars."[46] The same moderate who insisted that government is there to ensure that "[w]e can't drive our SUVs and eat as much as we want and keep our homes on 72 degrees at all times."[47] That moderate who will not tolerate an out-of-control EPA running amok with expensive regulations. But of course EPA was running amok, which did leave him in a difficult election-year quandary, one he resolved by continuing with the agenda, while pursuing a campaign of seeming to be very troubled by its excesses at the hands of, well, his own people.

The *Wall Street Journal*'s editorial writers presumed that this release was the product of committed left-wingers within the bureaucracy, striking back at the White House for daring to acknowledge a list of rules costing the economy over $1 billion, each, per year.[48] (Something else about which liberals are loath to be transparent.)[49] However, these emails released were between senior Obama political appointees, and their content did not damn the White House, but laid out the administration's environmental dogma that EPA has an entire media department and campaign arm working overtime to spread in the public domain.

In this case they managed to get widespread national repetition of the lines by issuing them not as a press release, pleading they be the hook for some story, but by dropping them into the public domain at their chosen moment and as an internal dispute, thereby irresistible to even the friendly media. As the same editorial writers noted just days later, in another context yet again involving a ploy to fire up Obama's base, as a general proposition regarding this administration's actions "you don't have to be a cynic to wonder about Team Obama's political re-election calculations."[50]

And certainly this spasm of transparency had more than a slight odor of being part of a managed narrative. Given how a detailed House investigation had demonstrated the practice of Obama political appointees seizing control of FOIA operations to manage what goes out, when and how, the scenario of EPA ambushing the politicos over at the White House seems less likely than this being yet more strategic use of

FOIA. This conclusion seemed to gain further currency with the revelation, just weeks later, that an otherwise sleepy agency that had turned whistleblower and exposed the fact that EPA's same agenda threatened blackouts and the basic reliability of our electrical system found itself the subject of "a highly unusual audit" by the administration. Suddenly, by speaking up the North American Electric Reliability Corporation (NERC) "may have exceeded [its authorized] functions" and was warned that its continuing activity might have to be "revisited."[51]

Never mind that NERC had, as its mission as a guarantor of "reliability," been providing its opinion on just this for decades. The agenda was not to be upset, and to keep things under control, including to manage what sort of "transparency" would be allowed, the Obama gang were corrupting the laws, for both political stagecraft and to get heavy with those who caused problems.

Similarly reflective of political interference with the law, one career FOIA officer informed me in 2012 of a massive reduction in backlogged FOIA requests. When I asked if the common denominator of the 10 percent of well-overdue responses that remained to be fulfilled was that they were "politically sensitive," this aide responded in the affirmative. The same person stated that most delays experienced by parties seeking information from that disastrous hive of Solyndra-style cronyism begging public scrutiny, the Department of Energy, are because the responses "get hung up in the GC [general counsel, a political appointee] review." Follow-up questioning revealed that the department's general counsel, early in the Obama administration, altered the system to run all FOIA responses (from career employees) through his (political) office. "They wanted to see everything that was going out," this aide told me. Previously, responses would go through a FOIA specialist and then, if particular legal consideration was required (for example, privacy issues), then through the office of general counsel.

Apparently they want to see everything that's coming in, too. There are biweekly meetings between FOIA officers and the general counsel or his office, giving the latter a heads-up for what they will need to get ahead of, politically. Or, if the politicization that House Oversight

Committee chairman Darrell Issa uncovered at the Department of
Homeland Security (DHS, see discussion below) is as widespread as the
evidence suggests, what other work the political operatives will confront
in the way of having their labors probed, and possibly exposed.

Naturally, the individual cases of politicization, of the sort I and
others have experienced and Chairman Issa and Christian Adams uncovered, can hide in the statistical background noise when "the federal
government receives some 600,000 formal Freedom of Information
requests a year."[52] An administration will target requests it finds particularly threatening, due to the requested information, the identity of
the requesting party, or otherwise. They don't simply stop producing
requested information. Still, the defense that the overall numbers aren't
any different than under Bush[53] is disproved by investigation[54]—the
relevant numbers, such as denial of fee waivers and invoking the more
easily abused exemptions, are demonstrably much worse than under
Bush—and only dodges the question of the specific cases, each of which
shows a fear of letting the public know what their government is up to.

Case Study in Obama's Politicization of FOIA: DHS

The Committee on Oversight and Government Reform is the House of
Representatives' principal watchdog body. As already indicated, prolif-
erating anecdotal evidence indicated to Chairman Issa that the realities
of transparency were getting to the Obama administration and its fellow
travelers. After committee staff uncovered political interference with the
FOIA operation at the Department of Homeland Security, they conducted an eight-month investigation of that bureaucracy's practices.

The staff report to the chairman noted that, in this promised "new
era of openness and transparency[,] Executive branch agencies under
an Obama administration were to assume a presumption of disclosure
when responding to citizen requests for records that did not impinge on
the federal government's responsibility to keep America safe or violate
certain narrowly-defined executive privileges."[55] The truth, however, was
that in practice "the FOIA response process is less transparent and more

politicized than when President Obama took office."[56] This echoed the conclusions, cited previously, of Citizens for Responsibility and Ethics in Washington (CREW) and OpenTheGovernment.org.[57]

Committee staff specifically inquired into allegations and early findings "that political staff under DHS Secretary Janet Napolitano have corrupted the agency's FOIA compliance procedures, exerted political pressure on FOIA compliance officers, and undermined the federal government's accountability to the American people."[58]

It turned out that, within months of the inauguration, the politicos at DHS "introduced a directive requiring a wide range of information to be vetted by political appointees for 'awareness purposes,' no matter who requested it."[59] This begged trouble, which soon followed. Despite basic FOIA principles such as that "the identity of a requester and the purpose of the request can have no bearing on the agency's response . . . political staff at DHS probed FOIA Officers for such information."[60] The career employees handling requests "were ordered to provide Secretary Janet Napolitano's political staff with information about the people who asked for records, such as where they lived, whether they were private citizens or reporters, and about the organizations where they worked. If a member of Congress sought such documents, employees were told to specify Democrat or Republican."[61]

The investigation found something that most of us who have FOIA'd this administration learned firsthand, which is that DHS "abused the 'deliberative process' exception" specifically identified in the Holder and Obama proclamations as an area where they would brook no such nonsense.

Original versions of documents that were heavily redacted before being released to the Associated Press show the Office of General Counsel relied on exception (b)(5)—normally meant to protect pre-decisional records—to prevent the release of embarrassing records.[62]

Other damning conclusions included:

- "The Committee investigation has uncovered evidence that career FOIA professionals at DHS have been compromised in their statutory compliance by the unprecedented intrusion of Secretary Napolitano's political staff into the department's FOIA procedures."[63]

- "DHS political staff ceased using official email to approve FOIA responses. Instead, political staff contacted FOIA compliance officers via telephone to end a paper trail that could prove scandalous."[64]

- "FOIA professionals were burdened by an intrusive political staff."[65]

- "The Front Office reviewed and approved responses. By the end of September 2009, copies of all significant FOIA requests were required to be forwarded to the Secretary's political staff for review. The career staff in the FOIA Office was not permitted to release responses to these requests without approval from political staff."[66]

- "The Front Office stopped using e-mail. Political appointees stopped using e-mail to clear response packages in the second quarter of 2010. Instead, they contacted the career staff in the FOIA Office by telephone. . . ."[67]

- Although a software "system simplified the approval process for significant requests [and] the FOIA Office no longer need[ed] an affirmative statement of approval from the Secretary's political staff, the Front Office retained the ability to halt the release of a FOIA response."[68]

- "Political appointees conduct their own searches. Documents and witness testimony show political appointees run weak and incomplete searches for their own documents. They were allowed to choose their own search terms despite lacking a basic understanding of the statute."[69]

This was again systemic, involving a concerted effort to avoid creating FOIA-eligible records in the first place and hobbling searches and otherwise blocking access to those that did exist. And it exhibited the hallmark of the left's approach to FOIA, targeting requests for slow-walking or outright derailing requests depending upon the kind of information sought or who sought it.

Repeated experience proves that the administration's self-congratulation, which got far more media attention than the reality of cheating and scheming, was at best empty and more likely a deception preceding an organized, deliberate campaign to broadly block access to public records as they engaged in their sweeping transformations. The truth is that the Obama administration shamelessly claims the mantle of transparency while working aggressively to rip it to shreds.

6.

You Never Know What You'll Find:
Obama's "Big Wind" Cover-up

Former secretary of defense Donald Rumsfeld was mocked in all the right quarters for saying something equally appropriate to his occasion as it is to using FOIA to learn what your government is up to. "[T]here are known knowns; there are things we know we know. We also know there are known unknowns; that is to say we know there are some things we do not know. But there are also unknown unknowns—there are things we do not know we don't know."[1]

A FOIA request often proves to be the first in a series, yielding bread crumbs that, properly followed, lead to a bigger prize that was more carefully hidden; unknown unkowns that, once revealed, beg further inquiry.

My experience with FOIA has produced some intriguing revelations about things I didn't know we didn't know. For example, the FOIA request and then successful litigation for the ethics records of Dr. James Hansen of NASA—the Millionaire Bureaucrat—came about by chance. When reviewing records produced under a FOIA inquiry into his protégé's busy schedule blogging as an activist while at his day job at NASA, promoting his and Hansen's shared cause of global warming alarm, I learned by NASA's own admission that Hansen's underling was not filing the required ethics forms, NASA's Application for Outside Employment or Other Activity. It begged the question that if his boss Hansen did not view this as a priority for the subordinate, possibly Hansen with his notoriously lucrative outside life also had eschewed compliance with the minutiae of ethics requirements that come with his fat $180,000 annual paycheck from the taxpayer.

We were proved right, discovering correspondence from NASA's ethics officer chiding Hansen, the media darling, supposed victim of "muzzling," sage for partisan axe-grinding on Capitol Hill, and all-around voice of integrity, for noncompliance. Other shortcomings found in these records included failing to report enormous sums received in the form of travel all over the world for him and his wife, as well as questionably benefiting privately from his public employment. (On a less happy note, though offering a lesson for aspiring FOIA activists: this FOIA went cradle to grave, including litigation, settlement, and payment of our fees, while a single motion on the case that spawned it languished with no action for a year and a half, and counting, before the U.S. District Court for the District of Columbia.)

Remember, most staff worth FOIA'ing are acutely aware that what they are up to makes them of interest, and so they employ tactics to defeat such curiosity from bearing fruit. We have seen Obama administration appointees use private email to avoid creating records, and politically intervene in the FOIA process to block production of records for requests they find threatening. I learned from a 2008 document produced to me in 2012 that sometime "in the 1990's" EPA "assigned its Administrators two e-mail accounts," the second of which carried an address designed by the Administrator, remained unpublished and essentially was a secret about which even the office that assigned the email knew no details such as whether it was ever used, or searched as required for FOIA requests for emails.[2]

It is noteworthy when and how this occurred, during the Clinton-Gore administration and according to this EPA document, at the instigation of then-administrator Carol Browner (later Obama's energy and environment "czar"). On her way out the door Browner had ordered her computer records wiped clean and emails erased in violation of a federal court order, and computer backup tapes also were then erased. In defending her instructions to have this done, Browner claimed ignorance of the court's order (EPA later admitted the agency was aware; she was the administrator and the order applied to her, so draw your own conclusions); she said she was actually concerned with making sure her computer was properly formatted for the incoming George W. Bush administration and besides, she didn't usually use her computer.[3]

But this computer-avoiding administrator happened to order creation of a secret email account that even now EPA does not know whether she used. Because, well, she destroyed all of her records. Which probably didn't exist anyway.

I learned of this move after probing for documents referenced in a Government Accountability Office (GAO) report about FOIA's failures. I pursued its cited authorities, and one document that was identified revealed EPA writing to the National Archives of this "dual-account structure," in the context of learning that emails were improperly destroyed with no record maintained. "Few EPA staff members, usually only high-level senior staff, even know that these accounts exist," and—disturbingly given that it was Browner who initiated this practice—"Therefore, responsibility for identifying, printing, and submitting records for filing in accordance with EPA records schedules falls to the Administrator." EPA acknowledged to the National Archives that records of activity on these "secondary" accounts were for the most part nonexistent. Browner's, for example.

Other tactics emerged to fill the gap between these two steps of not creating records and blocking production of records that are created given the modern reality that email cannot be avoided entirely. They play a game of hide-and-seek, adapting along the way to nosy taxpayers' moves, actual and anticipated.

These are amply illustrated in a case study I stumbled upon in pursuing some political hatchet-jobbery out of the Department of Energy's windmill and sun-catcher shop, Energy Efficiency and Renewable Energy (EERE), led by an assistant secretary who, as luck would have it, was the former CEO of Al Gore's pressure group the Alliance for Climate Protection.

I uncovered a breathtaking function being played for the windmill lobby by that office, as well as for and with the active participation of left-wing activist groups like Center for American Progress and Union of Concerned Scientists (actually just a pressure group with a lofty name but accepting anyone as union members, even dogs).[4] This came from a previously sleepy operation called the National Renewable Energy Laboratory (NREL) in Boulder, Colorado. NREL happened to fall under EERE, run at the time by Gore's pal Cathy Zoi. The story reveals quite a lot about the Obama administration, and its dealings both with transparency and with industry cronies.

The Pain from Spain

In 2008 (as senator) and 2009 (as president), Obama told Americans on no fewer than eight occasions to "think about what's happening in countries like Spain [and] Germany" if you want to know about his model for successful, pro-growth "green jobs" policies, and what we should expect here as he fundamentally transforms America into something more like a European social democracy. This audaciously challenged European economists and energy policy experts, who had a better idea what the real score was, to keep quiet. They didn't, and first revealed Spain's policies to be economic and employment disasters. Soon enough, Germans, Scots, Italians, and others also weighed in on their own supposed miracles whose fiscally devastating reality would become so obvious and embarrassing that Obama, after tailoring his speech to substitute one country after another as they were exposed, finally gave up the speech altogether. But not the policies, which as the reelection year of 2012 cranked into gear he revived to push as economic boons. This time, apparently, it will be different.

This first shoe to drop came in March 2009, when a research team from Madrid's King Juan Carlos University produced a detailed, substantive, heavily sourced, two-method paper using official EU and Spanish figures even where they appeared to be inflated, to avoid claims of invention. Titled "Study of the effects on employment of public aid to renewable energy sources,"[5] the paper concluded that Spain's "green jobs" program was an acute economic failure, creating some temporary jobs at enormous per-job expense while propping up unsustainable "bubble" industries and costing far more jobs by incurring spectacular debt. Think Solyndra, on a nationwide scale.

By revealing the truth about Spain's increasingly mythologized "green jobs" and renewable energy experience, the study threatened the prospects for Spain's companies to be bailed out by the United States should we repeat their country's policy mistakes, as Obama demanded. This led to political and union attacks in Spain on the researchers, including slander, cries of their being "unpatriotic" for letting the cat out of the bag, and trying to get them fired.

Things weren't much better here, given that the study embarrassed the White House, prompting uncomfortable media attention and a question about the issue posed to then-spokesman Robert Gibbs at a press conference (which in turn only generated more attention in Spain). So Obama replaced Spain with Denmark in his speech. Soon Danes produced a study through the thoroughly establishment think tank CEPOS.[6] This paper also revealed tremendous costs and that Obama's claim about Denmark's "renewables" experience, too, was steeped in mythology. Only once the subsequent German study[7] was published was the jig plainly up, and the viscerally nasty attacks largely subsided.

Incredibly neither Obama nor his speechwriters considered the prospect that Spaniards, Germans, and Danes would respond to a naïve and uninformed pretense so boldly and serially perpetrated by the highest-profile U.S. political figure. Did he think they would not notice? So much for worldly. Did Team Obama believe that the entirety of his European base would give him a pass? Whatever the mistaken assumption, he learned his lesson, as the Spanish study left a mark. "Green jobs" soon became a punch line and it was back to the talking-point drawing board.

What did not change was the major component of his planned re-design of the U.S. economy, of creating and supporting phony industries while "bankrupting" (Obama's word) energy sources that worked in order to give "new sources" like windmills, etc., the chance they'd flubbed since being introduced as competitors to fossil-fueled electricity

a mere 120 years before ("new"?). So the administration, clearly pan-
icked, prepared to strike back. More to the point, their cronies demanded they do so. So the crew that campaigned on change pulled out
the oldest play in the book—attack the messenger. The U.S. government
responded to foreign academics, for assessing the impact in their own
country of their own government's policies, by going after them.

Internal emails acknowledged that the way they deployed a public
agency was unprecedented, further illuminating the political nature of
this abuse of taxpayer resources in support of cronyism.

The liberals dispatched a taxpayer-funded agency (DOE, through
NREL), to publish a product that the agency's staff admitted among
themselves was not the sort of thing they actually did. But they did it
nonetheless, amid political demands to strike back at antagonists who
had embarrassed the politicos, and rescue their allies in taxpayer-dependent industry with an authoritative-sounding governmental imprimatur.
Their response was a five-page talking-points memo posing as a technical
assessment assailing the Spanish economic study the accuracy of which,
they could not hide, was becoming more obvious each month. It was an
ideological hodgepodge of curious and unsupported economic claims
published under the name of two young non-economist wind advocates
working for the federal government.

These taxpayer-funded employees offered green dogma in oddly stri-
dent terms. Emails obtained using FOIA show, however, they got more
than a little help from their friends in industry and the pressure groups.

Their effort was on its face suspect, not just for the substance of it.
As the administration's flailing became obvious, I wrote on *National Review*'s "Planet Gore" blog:

> In the face of some recent pushback—for example, from the studies
> out of Spain and Denmark referenced in this space on numerous
> occasions—the windmill welfare queens over at the American Wind
> Energy Association (AWEA) have been cranking up the snivel vol-
> ume to eleven.
>
> Reading the group's press releases it does seem that they even had

a hand in getting the President of the United States to sic a taxpayer-funded agency on a foreign academic study about a foreign country's experience with its own policies, because said academic team and its writings threaten the welfare if the word gets out.[8]

Thanks to FOIA, we now know that the latter assertion was correct. Emails show the Obama administration produced this denunciation at the behest, and with the active participation, of the Union of Concerned Scientists and lobbyists for "Big Wind." The latter also served as the administration's "cutout" or conduit to the left-wing Center for American Progress, ostensibly shielding their collaboration.

Sounding the Alarm, Among Friends

The appointment of Cathy Zoi was an early coup for the liberal activist world seeking a beachhead in positions of responsibility in the Obama administration. As TreeHugger.com gushed, providing a stellar personnel analogy, "First President Obama snatched up Van Jones from Green for All to be Special Advisor for Green Jobs, Enterprise and Innovation at the Council for Environmental Quality. And now he's hired Alliance for Climate Protection CEO Cathy Zoi to serve as Assistant Secretary for Energy Efficiency and Renewable Energy in the Department of Energy, pending her confirmation."[9]

Such staffing moves would not actually prove difficult, with Center for American Progress chief John Podesta serving as the cochair of the Obama-Biden transition. He promptly filled the administration with his team and, importantly, positioned the rest to serve as outside advisors to and assets for the Obama team. Free from, say, the Freedom of Information Act.

But their communications with colleagues on the inside would still be subject to FOIA and surely the target of troublemaking taxpayers. Given her pedigree, and the subsequent billions in "stimulus" booty going to the kinds of businesses invested in by Al Gore and employing her husband (who later moved in-house to one of the green lobby groups), Zoi was a logical recipient of FOIA requests. And therefore a logical one to deploy evasive tactics.

We already know that senior officials regularly avoid using their government-issued email accounts—their order was to put nothing in writing, almost ever. This is not to say that they didn't use their government accounts at all; as noted previously, in March 2012 I obtained correspondence between Zoi and senior partners in Solyndra's consulting firm affirming very close bonds. They were, after all, her consultants when she was working for the movement on the outside, too, running Gore's group. For example, she asked the Glover Park Group consultants over for dinner a few times.

Zoi also asked for some examples of work that might help her push the shared campaign from her perch on the inside: "copies of energy and climate ads and reels"; "a representative, cool selection of state ads would be good. Plus the reel Carter [Eskew, Democrat consultant/strategist and Gore campaign pooh-bah] did just following Live Earth . . . ," the latter being a request for a fund-raising video promoting the 2007 fiasco of energy-hogging concerts in the name of the anti-energy agenda. She also sought "the Martin ad 'Al Sharpton and Pat Robertson,'" in which those two energy policy mavens shared a couch touting the global warming agenda à la the ad with Nancy Pelosi that helped sink the USS *Gingrich*. And she also asked them to provide her some specific anti-coal ads.

This is the assistant secretary of energy, mind you, who was later briefly in line to oversee fossil fuel programs, until someone somewhere apparently decided that this confirmation fight was not one to pick.

Another email she received I noted in the opening pages, from former "senior member of the Kerry/Edwards Rapid Response War Room"[10] Jason Miner, boasting to her of his Vegas circumstances. Miner rubbed it in that at that very moment he was poolside at Caesars having a drink with Zoi's twenty-something "Senior Advisor" Udai Rohatgi (a 2005 poli sci grad who voters elevated from a perch as "Email production Manager at Obama for America," presently wielding the lofty slot of Senior Advisor and Staff Director in the Office of the Under Secretary of Energy).[11]

Rohatgi no doubt picked up his own tab, not leaving it to Solyndra's outside advisors. Though I suppose ultimately we all split the bill, given Solyndra was a bust living on the taxpayer's largesse, whose much larger bill cost us dearly thanks to political relationships working the way they were intended.

On the more substantive matters Zoi left few tracks. Yet I did find, in the stack of documents responsive to my FOIA request for information about the Spain hit job, one email she wrote. It nicely ties a bow on some behavior that, if it involved Republicans not Democrats and oil not windmills, would have kept the *New York Times* and *Washington Post* giddy with self-satisfied umbrage, as heads rolled and possibly even elections were decided as a result. This is thanks to the candor expressed in the email traffic until what they had gotten themselves into began to become clear, after Congress became interested, at which point correspondents became even more guarded, writing essentially to seek face-to-face discussions.

Zoi's telling email revealed the origin of high-level, political involvement in this seedy affair, and went in its entirety as follows:

> From: Cathy Zoi
> Sent: Saturday, June 27, 2009 6:21 PM
> To: [four DOE staffers]
> Subject: New NREL wind/jobs study about to pop—
> ready for Monday?
> Importance: High
>
> Heard 2nd hand that Rob Gramlich has a new wind/jobs study
> that could counter George Will's crappy op ed of this week. How
> close are we? Can we get it out now?[12]

Will's op-ed was actually substantively sound, if politically inconvenient, exposing Spain's reality and therefore prolonging the Obama administration's headache. But the rest of the "High-Importance" missive is a little difficult to square, given that Gramlich didn't actually work for the Department of Energy. He of the "we" was in fact the chief lobbyist for

Big Wind, AWEA, broadly populated by Spanish wind giants and other foreign firms trying to sell the United States their windmills. With no little success, incidentally, since such foreign-based companies received 80 percent of Obama's stimulus money for such projects[13]—helping forestall their home countries' green bubbles from bursting.

Which of Your Stories Is the Truth?

The first sign of something fishy came when NREL responded to media inquiries by claiming that the paper asserting the Spanish study was nothing worth paying attention to was entirely DOE's idea, while DOE's Office of Congressional Affairs wrote to a Senate office conducting oversight to claim that it was all NREL's doing. I pointed out this red flag in my FOIA requests to both DOE and NREL:

> We note that one of two co-authors of the above-cited NREL paper, which paper attests that "This report was prepared as an account of work sponsored by an agency of the United States government," is on record in an E&E News story announcing of the project, "DOE requested the analysis be performed."
>
> However, DOE Congressional Affairs is on record saying the following:
>
>> NREL initiated the report on their own as part of their ongoing analytical role to assess emerging issues and monitor external studies and develop internal memos or external documents to address research that is at odds with DOE/EERE scientific understanding.
>>
>> We therefore seek documents revealing the origins of the effort and clarifying the alternating, mutually exclusive claims of NREL saying DOE told me to do it and DOE telling Congress that it was all NREL's idea, fully aware of DOE's extant protestations to congressional offices that the above-cited paper is of like kind with other NREL products

(noting here that no paper DOE cites is comparable on any
level [citations omitted]).

The question "Which time are you lying?" came to mind, though it
was not at all clear that the answer could not be "both." The records I
received reveal great internal concern among high-level DOE political
appointees when similar questions were pressed, and a resistance to putting the answer in writing. They conclude with emails citing late-night
phone calls to get the story straight, and calling—again with "High
Importance"—a meeting at 9:00 a.m., September 22, 2009, in the office
of Zoi's chief operating officer, Steven Chalk, to "huddle up" face-to-face
and get things straight.

The emails also make plain that this huddle involved the Department
of Energy's coordination with Center for American Progress (CAP),
Union of Concerned Scientists (UCS), and AWEA. The "rent-seeker"
cronies and the ideologues wanted the administration to produce an
attack that would serve all their interests. The administration was eager
to oblige, with NREL getting cold feet only as the unseemliness of what
they were doing sank in later. By then it was too late, and high-level
political appointees under pressure from the industry lobby forced the
lower-level activists to finish the job.

Incredibly, during my tussle over obtaining these records, DOE withheld responsive documents exchanged between it and the pressure group
CAP and lobbyist AWEA on the grounds that these are "inter-agency
memoranda." This is the oft-abused "pre-decisional" defense commonly
employed against FOIA requests when seeking to withhold certain
communications among agencies or including, for example, paid consultants. Using that exemption here, DOE apparently implies that wind
industry lobbyists and Soros's Center for American Progress are—for
legal purposes—extensions of the government. The rest of the document
production revealed this to be one of the more honest public representa-
tions by the administration in the affair.

As a routine matter, congressional offices typically get somewhat more
respectful service than FOIA requesters, although the Issa Committee's

investigation showed the Obama administration giving Democrats and Republicans rather different treatment. Wisconsin Republican representative James Sensenbrenner Jr. wondered how this NREL memo masquerading as analysis was hatched, if for no other reasons than NREL didn't do this sort of thing. He wrote to Zoi with five specific questions about how and by whose instruction this paper was produced. It took more than three months but, on January 6, 2010, Zoi wrote back with a one-paragraph reply failing (or refusing) to answer any of the queries.

However, the documents I uncovered reveal that her office was fully aware of the answers to these questions but had elected to keep the information to itself. The questions raised about green jobs did seem to threaten the vast increase in Department of Energy spending on the Obama/AWEA agenda also shared by the ideologues at CAP and UCS. Team Obama poured cash into energy efficiency and renewable energy with abandon. One such program at the department skyrocketed from a budget of $1.7 billion in 2008 to $18 billion in 2009.

Particularly given that numerous progress reports and discussions of this NREL paper were copied to an aide in her office obviously tasked with keeping tabs on the effort, the episode reflects quite poorly on Zoi's candor.

Spinning a Tangled Web for Windmill Welfare Queens

EERE's Chief Operating Officer Chalk responded in writing to concerns about this tangled web of special interests, ideologues, and lobbyists converging within the federal government. In his letter to Representative Sensenbrenner, Chalk gave a nod to EERE's "ongoing and pre-existing relationship with AWEA" as not unique, but common, just "one of many trade associations that NREL work with. . . ." If true, then Obama's DOE is vastly worse than even these documents portrayed. Consider these emails that put new meaning in the term "taxpayer servant." Servant to some particularly politically helpful companies, anyway, in an industry better known for receiving tax dollars than paying them:

"AWEA policy people are quite concerned about a recent report published in Spain. . . ."—May 12, 2009, email from Eric Lantz of NREL to seven colleagues, including the PR shop

"[W]e need to come up with an appropriate response to these criticisms soon. I just spoke to a few people at AWEA about this and they are discussing it this afternoon."—Reply to all that same day from NREL's Suzanne Tegen

"Sounds good, David. The AWEA folks are wondering what we'll do, so if this is our plan, I'll let them know."—May 14, 2009 email from NREL's Tegen to colleague David Kline

Then Chalk got too cute, writing "NREL had no direct contact with either the Center for American Progress or with the Union for Concerned Scientists related to the Spanish Study." As the Institute for Energy Research (IER) noted, "Mr. Chalk was very careful with his language. It doesn't say that NREL had no contact with the Center for American Progress or the Union of Concerned Scientists, but rather they had no direct contact. Mr. Chalk had to be so careful with his language because they obviously had contact. And according to the documents Mr. Chalk included as an attachment to his letter to Congressman Sensenbrenner, NREL employees used employees at AWEA as their conduit, a middle man, so to speak, to get input from CAP. In an NREL employee's words: 'Liz (Elizabeth Salerno is an AWEA employee), would you send this [draft of the NREL rebuttal] to the CAP folks?'"[14]

Numerous records produced under FOIA by NREL show that the administration sent their draft for comment and assistance to AWEA and, through them, sought CAP's input. Indeed, despite other discussions of a joint response, at no point did anyone suggest openly affiliating with CAP, with whom communication was obviously discouraged and about whose involvement all emailed discussions cited AWEA as the go-between.

EERE and NREL emails revealed they indeed worked studiously

with CAP through intermediaries, knowing that correspondence to and from CAP—the administration's well-known outside arm—was a sure FOIA target (if not apparently understanding we might also seek or otherwise obtain correspondence mentioning CAP). These included, for example, emails discussing having the memo "leaked"[15] because, while they could get the same effect as publishing it, one administration aide cautioned that this favor for Big Wind and the ideologues at the political boss's insistence isn't, after all, NREL's function. Someone might notice that. This suggestion also came with a request: "Is it okay if we send our response to colleagues at AWEA and CAP? We promised it to them many weeks ago. . . ."

Colleagues, and editorial reviewers of our work? Yes. "Direct contact?" Absolutely not.

Another email also shows that Elizabeth Salerno, AWEA's manager for policy analysis, provided NREL with three sets of industry talking points and the CAP response. See? From AWEA. No "direct contact" with CAP there.

On June 9, NREL, via Tegen, sent three AWEA officials a draft administration response to the troublesome Spaniards, asking for review and input. She asked Salerno, "Liz, would you send this to the CAP folks?" Again on June 16, 2009, we see Tegen writing to AWEA and UCS asking, "Liz, Jeff, were you able to get any information from the people at CAP as to whether they could review it?" Both emails kept Zoi's office in the loop by copying Avi Gopstein. Gopstein was the Science Policy Fellow for the American Association for the Advancement of Science (AAAS, and which, as we will see from their interventions in the UVa case, is now really an ideological activist group) placed, by chance, in Zoi's office.

DOE did not produce to me whatever input or responses AWEA and UCS provided.

DOE's claim to Congress to have "had no direct contact with CAP" was insulting for the brazenness of daring Congress to sanction such cheek. But focusing only on this aspect of Chalk's tap dance ignores that IER's characterization of it was far too generous, to be sure. By emphasizing NREL (vs. his department, DOE), and "direct contact," Chalk engaged in some rhetoric of a part with the meaning of "is" and how one can never really be "alone" with anyone in the White House. Yet still his statement is not true, as a reading of the emails shows. It is true that AWEA was often the conduit between DOE and UCS, too. But the emails released proved that DOE *and specifically NREL* did correspond directly with UCS about the matter.

One of the records produced by NREL under FOIA revealed that, at the very beginning of the affair, a "rebuttal" was first emailed around by the AAAS fellow in Zoi's office, Avi Gopstein. In his opening missive Gopstein cited the need for a rapid response as a priority. Copied were EERE's chief operating officer, deputy assistant secretary, and director of strategic planning and analysis.

Two days after Zoi's email asking when DOE could issue the response that she had heard about from Big Wind and described as being Big Wind's, the gentleman at NREL in charge of the pushback indicated more anxiety. In a beaut of an indictment of the scheme and the shabbiness of DOE's operation, he wrote:

> As you probably saw from an email from Maureen, EE-1 has asked about the "NREL Report" on the Spanish report. FWIW I agree with Suzanne that what we have is more of a memo than a report; a good critique of the Spanish report, but a memo—no research was done really. Please advise how you would like us to proceed in responding to EE-1 request: Form? Memo from whom to whom? (We don't have formal request to NREL from EE-1, just the chain of emails citing said request). Review, signoff, etc.? Given guidance, we'll proceed to make it so.[16]

The clumsy repetitive use of Zoi's handle (EE-1) seems to labor to not betray a rule against giving away even whether EE-1 is a she or a he (given the CIA's code name for bin Laden's Pakistani redoubt of AC1, possibly they're also living out their Walter Mitty avatars by aping the really cool kind of spies). And notice the amusing sneer quotes in the original, referring to what Zoi styled as AWEA's report, calling it "the 'NREL report.'"

So this shows how you, the taxpayer, came to underwrite a project of political appointees, ideologues, and industry to "counter" (per Zoi) research by foreign academics assessing their own nation's domestic policies falsely hailed by Obama as a success to be followed here. But without actually doing any research. Just repeating dogma, to deny an increasingly apparent reality.

A Smear Is Born

Despite all of this scheming, it was not at all clear that NREL/DOE would ultimately release anything on the subject because, as they agonized over, it was just not the kind of document that NREL produced. This was a hurdle they revisited often, looking for ways around the problem of so many influential parties demanding it.

The proposed open collaboration among DOE, AWEA, and UCS with a sub rosa role played by CAP was subsequently forwarded around NREL by Tegen for input. This call for such overt action to defeat the enemy was too egregious a red flag, with Tegen's NREL colleagues sounding a note of caution immediately. An email from Kline warned, "I recognize this is not a lobbying piece per se, but contributing directly to an AWEA and UCS communique [*sic*] could raise eyebrows." So they sought to hide the collaboration.

The email thread in which Tegen asked for a call with their industry buddies began with UCS sounding a call to arms among this Bootlegger-and-Baptist (and bureaucrat) coalition on May 13, 2009, and seconded by AWEA's Salerno. "It is critical we respond, this thing won't die and its [*sic*] doing a good job of undermining our green jobs message. If we put together a call with [Center for American Progress, still not copied on any correspondence that copies the administration, showing good discipline], can ucs [*sic*] participate on a comprehensive response?" This is damning.

On the bright side this email carried a hilarious tail to the thread, with UCS's Jeff Deyette—as part of a direct correspondence with NREL's Tegen, which DOE's Chalk said never occurred. Responding about the call to collaboratively assail the academics writing about doings in their own country, Deyette wrote "Yes, of course. Send around some time options, and we can get on a call. Does anybody have a copy of the study that we can look at?" Yeah, let's go after that study! Oh, and I'd better see it first . . .

On May 29, NREL's Tegen wrote to a larger group of DOE/NREL colleagues, "And we are working with AWEA (who is working with UCS and others) to put out a response to this report," which she called "methodologically unsound." Given events that were then unfolding, later developments, and the obviously dogmatic insistence of that swipe, I'm not sure she read it any more than the UCS guy who nonetheless agreed to go after it. Incidentally, when White House spokesman Gibbs was asked about the study and dismissed its findings, on follow-up questioning he admitted he, too, had not read it.[17] The Spanish government did, however, and in recognition acknowledged the study's findings internally and changed their law.[18]

On June 3, NREL officials internally agreed that "we will pass to [Zoi's Sherpa] Avi Gopstein . . . as well as colleagues at AWEA and the Political Economy Research Institute at UMass (authors of other Green Jobs analyses) for external review." The University of Massachusetts (UMass) group was the outfit UCS used to put an academic label on its arguments. So, external peer review of a paper written at the request of industry and axe-grinders, by industry and axe-grinders.

In a June 29 email, NREL's Eric Lantz indicated to colleagues that "Cathy Zoi heard from somewhere that this response was put together and is very interested in seeing it." Despite several such missives, there is no evidence that Zoi ever did actually look at it. In fact, the contrary seems to be the case according to her professed ignorance, despite her office's Gopstein being kept in the loop. So this email seems to mean that she was interested in seeing it go out. As she had written to her team.

But cautions continued to flow. "[T]here has been some question raised about whether this response/commentary deserves 'technical report' status as no new analysis was actually conducted for the work. . . . Is there a formal memo or briefing publication category that this can be put under and/or what are the implications of designating it as a technical report," which it plainly wasn't. It was not the sort of effort for which they even had a category, but more a political hit, if one that higher-ups wanted performed. As the Institute for Energy Research responded, "In other words, never mind the economic analysis, just find a way to discredit the findings because it's getting traction."[19]

By August 11, 2009, Tegen was still noting, "We just normally don't respond to reports like this," but said that "EERE is asking for it."

EERE was indeed asking for it, however you wish to take that. A June 29 email indicated that EERE's wind program manager "Megan McCluer heard about our 'response' from Cathy Zoi. I have no idea how Cathy Zoi heard about it—maybe from someone at AWEA?" Maybe. I like the sneer quotes but, calm down, stop using her name. "Anyway, they would like to see our response ASAP. At least that's my impression."[20]

McCluer came to DOE from wind turbine manufacturer Clipper Windpower, a company that pushes man-made global warming alarm.[21] Imagine a former Big Oil employee in a Republican administration's Department of Energy pushing an unconventional, political paper out the door, in collaboration with conservative advocacy groups, pretending to be substantive while defending (not too convincingly) the oil industry after embarrassing revelations it really did cause global warming? That's such a damning scenario that Al Gore sought to manufacture it for his own uses, including in his various speeches and his movie—a rare Oscar-winning documentary whose main claims were tossed out of court as unsupportable.[22] He chose as his bogeyman former American Petroleum Institute lawyer Phil Cooney, who went to work in the George W. Bush administration. Gore selectively constructed a narrative in which Cooney behaved like the administration principals in this situation. (Historical fun fact: it was Cooney's trash that I learned by chance Greenpeace was also taking each week back when they were taking mine, hoping to similarly concoct a sinister relationship.)

Later in the same day the McCluer email was sent, NREL's David Kline sent around to colleagues a "link to George F. Will piece that is evidently causing a stir at Forrestal and elsewhere." Forrestal is the DOE headquarters building in Washington, D.C. I think we know where "elsewhere" is, thanks to the one Zoi email DOE produced to me.

By June 30, the pressure from Zoi seemed to be taking its toll on the foot soldiers. Kline wrote to Tegen, "I think we can get what we need to get done via email. We'll stress with all the reviewers that Zoi"—breach-of-protocol warning, things might be getting hairy but that's still "EE-1" to you when putting things in writing—"has asked for this and see how quickly we can get it out of here."

In early August, Tegen updated her boss, indicating the lobbyists were also getting antsy. "Hi Doug [Arent], AWEA has asked for an NREL response." Oh, then by all means provide one.

On August 12, NREL senior officials worried among themselves, "Our DOE sponsor and the cognizant DAS [deputy assistant secretary] both have the report. They expect us to release it and are 'concerned' that we have not."[23]

It finally went out the door days later.[24] And it was not substantively compelling, despite this intense effort. Facts do still matter. This lack of heft is also possibly due to it being a political document; and, after all, Spain's government, despite its own political denials, as a matter of law and policy acknowledged the study's findings.

So in this we see a formal product of the United States government going after, and being quickly deployed for further hit jobs on, foreign researchers for studying their own system, which our president had falsely called an economic success story. It was begun in a panic by industry, and was published nominally by a government technical research body. It was produced clearly at the behest of political forces, kicked around internally but a source of concern for so patently being not something the agency actually did.

Then higher-ups got wind of it from an industry lobbyist who was eager to see it go out, and they, too, became interested in seeing it go out.

So your money was spent in the name of cramming down ideologically driven, dishonestly sold, and economically destructive policies that would cost you ever more money, with net economic harm and debt to linger for decades.

In an editorial titled "The Big Wind-Power Cover-Up," *Investor's Business Daily* wrote that what was exposed here "amounts to an authentic scandal in the league of Climate-gate."[25] These revelations surely helped derail the "green jobs" push and set the context for ready public comprehension of the Solyndra debacle. In that respect, possibly it had a similar impact on this industry as Climategate did on the rest of the global warming industry, if with less prurient revelations of unethical behavior and thuggery.

But although these revelations helped slow the "renewables" agenda, draining the public fisc and harming the overall economy to benefit politically selected actors that otherwise would hardly exist, it did not completely doom the enterprise. By mid-2012, congressional Republicans had again teamed with Democrats in a joint effort to revive the expired wind production tax credit, at which industrial wind has suckled for twenty years on wealth transfers in the name of "jump-starting" a supposed "infant industry" that is getting a tad long in the tooth to pull that one off. It failed, though not by nearly enough, such that Republicans again immediately joined Democrats on legislation to revive it as well as talk of a "lame duck," post-election push to renew this corporate welfare.

Of course, even Climategate needed a Climategate 2 leak, more FOIA requests and even litigation as follow-up. And since the "renewables" rent-seekers are still at it, and Obama vowed in his 2012 State of the Union speech (and subsequent road show) to "double down" on the boondoggle, we're still probing for more smoking guns to remind the public what is really going on.

7.

Artless Dodgers: Liberal Scheming to Dodge Disclosure, from the UN to the Obama White House

Phil Jones of England's University of East Anglia knew he had a problem. The fifty-something director of the school's Climatic Research Unit (CRU) had, like others, grown fat off the American and British taxpayer for years while riding the biggest gravy train to hit Big Academia in ages.

Recently, however, curious researchers had begun asking for information he kept, which information was a principal basis for proposed massive economic restructuring in the United Kingdom, United States, and throughout the developed world.

This was information that he either could not produce or—as one intemperate, subsequently leaked email indicated—would do whatever he could do to avoid producing.

The first signs of trouble had come the year before when researcher Warwick Hughes first sought temperature data, custodianship of which was still Jones's claim to fame. This would soon be supplanted by his central role in a scandal arising from this custodianship. Jones plotted this course by first putting Hughes off for half a year then, in a February 2005 email, revealing his hubris and/or disdain for the scientific method with a sneering reply, "Why should I give information to you when all you want to do is find something wrong with it."[1]

Now others wanted a peek at "his" data, which actually were underwritten by American and British taxpayers and owed to the interested public under England's Freedom of Information Act, which had recently gone into effect.[2] This was in fact one of two transparency laws now causing anxiety among secretive academics and bureaucrats, both allowing taxpayers to inquire into what support Jones and others had for their claims, and the economic restructuring grounded in those claims.[3]

With an odd mix of smugness and panic, Jones wrote to Michael Mann at the University of Virginia that same year, "If they ever hear there is a Freedom of Information Act now in the UK, I think I'll delete the file rather than send to anyone."[4] Later that same month he wrote to two U.S. academics, complaining of such inquiries, "Don't any of you tell any body that the UK has a Freedom of Information Act!"[5]

In the same confession to Mann, Jones reaffirmed his makeup, vowing, "We also have a data protection act, which I will hide behind. Tom Wigley has sent me a worried email when he heard about it—thought people could ask him for his model code. He has retired officially from UEA [University of East Anglia] so he can hide behind that." Here Jones signaled his future exchanges about the lengths to which one should go to avoid scrutiny, which included asking Mann, by then at Penn State University, to contact another colleague Jones could not reach for the purpose of getting him to delete emails that might be subject to FOI requests.

Later Jones also wrote, "Data is covered by all the agreements we sign with people, so I will be hiding behind them."[6] This claim of safe harbor proved to be one that Jones's employer would be unable to substantiate, once some persistent taxpayers brought his and UEA's stonewalling before a tribunal—a proceeding from which they kept Jones curiously far away, although he was a natural candidate to testify.[7]

Jones, the entire global warming industry, and the scientific establishment so heavily dependent upon public financing for their escapade were, as these boasts indicate, very big into hiding things from the public paying their freight. This included hiding data behind whatever excuse would do, hiding inconvenient data from their publications, hiding inconvenient research from the public through professional thuggery, and what became the notorious "Mike's Nature trick . . . to hide the decline" of temperatures.[8]

Can't have temperature decline. It had been decided—by them, really—that temperatures had steadily risen, that this would continue, and that this was man's fault; for this reason, they argued, their gravy train must continue and society must accept a specific policy agenda. This is "the cause" Mann repeatedly wrote of in several leaked emails. Given this cause's stunning economic and other impacts, doubt, if allowed to exist, could only mean delays, thoughtful discussion of the evidence, and possibly worse for said gravy train and agenda. Doubt was therefore not acceptable. Neither was scrutiny. Which would lead to doubt.

The Tom Wigley whom Jones referenced in his email to Mann about hiding behind laws is an Australian, who may have retired from UEA but now lives more directly off the U.S. taxpayer, working for what is essentially the federal government at something called the National Center for Atmospheric Research (NCAR). NCAR is one of thirty-nine Federally Funded Research and Development Centers (FFRDCs), all sponsored by a government agency, in NCAR's case the National Science Foundation. It is like, say, the better-known FFRDCs Lawrence Livermore, Los Alamos, or Oak Ridge national laboratories, or the aforementioned NREL—all subject to and which comply with FOIA—but which somehow has to date dodged such accountability. NCAR is housed in a federal facility on federal property, and subsists almost entirely—95 percent with de minimis exceptions like renting facilities on occasion—on tax dollars, specifically budgeted by Congress in appropriations legislation.

One can be forgiven for thinking NCAR sounds a lot like a government agency. It did, at least, to journalist David Harsanyi and me, and we both requested some of its records under FOIA. NCAR refused to provide them, claiming that it is not an agency of the federal government. We'll see about that, as time and resources permit, given that it will take litigation; preferably, some in Congress will demand that remaining at the taxpayer trough means agreeing to squeal like the rest of the litter.

Regardless, Jones, Wigley, and various peers discussed other ways of shielding data from people who apparently would "find something wrong with it."[9] Or from people whose lives, Jones admitted in one email, were to be significantly altered if these proclamations out of his operation, NCAR, the University of Virginia, and other taxpayer-dependent and increasingly activist institutions had their desired policy impacts.[10]

So Jones wrote to a sympathizer at a United Nations body seeking a solution to nosy porkers who had found out about these FOI laws and dared try to use them, seeking access to information they paid for. This led to a chain of events to subvert American and British law that went straight to the Obama White House and appears on track to be resolved by a federal court in Washington.

In 2010, findings by the Department of Commerce's inspector general, discussed below in detail, began to emerge. It turned out that I was not the only party who had been on the receiving end of patently unlawful ruses to subvert FOIA by career activists at the National Oceanic and Atmospheric Administration (NOAA). The move amounted to these activists simply pretending that, when they were busy on taxpayer time in taxpayer-funded offices on taxpayer-funded computers, doing a job specifically tasked them as part of their taxpayer-funded position, why, they really weren't working for the U.S. taxpayer at all. No, they were really working for the United Nations. And, so the claim went, these documents they held weren't government records, but UN records free from FOIA.

As a result of this phony construct, NOAA claimed that no such records responsive to the requests existed. We don't have them! when in fact they do is a familiar refrain and, curiously, here it was invoked about the same kind of documents, and indeed many of the exact same documents, as we also sought from the University of Virginia, which had employed a similar claim that also failed under scrutiny. Later, like NOAA, they admitted to authorities the records existed. It is also what the University of East Anglia told researcher Steve McIntyre. Until they admitted to authorities the records existed.[11]

This claim, the first of three excuses employed when these NOAA-employed activists working at NOAA were finally questioned further by an authority—a federal inspector general—was nonsense, having absolutely nothing to support it. It was just helpful make-believe to avoid producing things under FOIA that they'd rather have kept private. The stunt merely affirmed, along with some already leaked emails, that a wide network of bureaucrats and other activists were working to keep secret the public records relating to their past efforts aimed at justifying a "fundamental transformation" of the nation's economic and governance structures.

These records they were protecting, like those Jones and company were worried about hiding or destroying, were already created, sitting on U.S. and other government or otherwise FOI-covered computer servers. But what about going forward, as they continued with their enterprise, now that the FOI nooses appeared to be tightening? What to do about documents and communications they would still have to create?

The bane of these schemers, Canadian mathematician and expert in statistical analysis Steve McIntyre, was among three others who had received the same routine before me. McIntyre directed me to a patch-work of clues suggesting that Jones et al. and these federal bureaucrats had teamed with the UN Intergovernmental Panel on Climate Change (IPCC) in an active campaign to seal off this threat of FOI requests from bothering them again.

They would circumvent transparency laws which were conditions of receiving public funding by avoiding creation of this nagging paper trail where possible and, in an inspired move, create electronic safe houses where they could work presumably free from prying eyes.

To do so required White House blessing. I detail their acquiescence elsewhere. For now, consider the scheming that led to that step.

Can't Spell Uncooperative Without UN

The IPCC is the UN's intergovernmental global warming advocacy and, supposedly, scientific body (whose website affirms it performs no scientific research, but it does issue lots of proclamations). It asserts that one of its three hallmark principles is an "open and transparent" process.[12] But it doesn't even pretend to practice that.

As University of Hamburg professor Richard Tol, who has firsthand experience as an IPCC lead author, writes, "The IPCC pretends that its authors operate in their personal capacity, even if people work on their chapters in their bosses' time."[13] They do this very deliberately to try to avoid the consequences of many of its participants being representatives of national governments, doing their job paid for by the taxpayer through the national governments, not the UN. Period. Further, as we argued in the UVa case is inescapable, IPCC participation is the sort of work-related activity that schools encourage and consider when considering tenure. As such, the academics participating do so in their capacity as academics with their employer, in pursuit of their professional responsibilities for their employer, and there is no possibility that emails on their university account, provided for university-related business, are not university emails.

I also suspect that a quick check of expense accounts would show that academics do not pay out of pocket but seek reimbursement for any related expenses not paid for by the IPCC, just as much as the governmental and pressure group participants do. Regardless, academics and bureaucrats participate in their professional capacities.

The IPCC nonetheless continued this pretense that its work is therefore confidential and not subject to distribution or unauthorized viewing,[14] even after the Obama White House, in word if not in deed, had thrown the UN under the bus in the face of pressure from congressional oversight to defend that outrage. Specifically, the Obama White House ultimately acknowledged that any document obtained by government employees in the course of their IPCC work is subject to FOIA and other transparency laws.

The IPCC's defiant ignorance of their claimed transparency began with the group's response to a 2006 request to see reviewer comments for its upcoming Fourth Assessment Report (the doomsday proclamations that it exists to produce). Facing the threat of an adverse outcome, producing negative precedent on top of its embarrassment, the IPCC

relented, even if it was in stages, falling back from one position to another, each representing a guilty look on their rhetorical faces. This took
the form of a series of excuses: the information is already available on
the Web (even if they couldn't quite direct the requesters to it); it was
deleted; it was created in the participants' personal, as opposed to official
capacities (a brazen and unsupportable nontruth); it will be made available at a library at Harvard University during restricted hours, by appointment and at least one week's advance notice, with limited copying
permitted due to copyright restrictions.[15]

It turned out the IPCC had ritually ignored inconvenient reviewers,
proving it was in no sense "peer-reviewed," as the media liked to say in
promoting the group's pronouncements as authoritative and justifying the demanded policies. This stunning truth emerged only after the
resistance to such requests proved damaging by their clumsiness, and a
successful McIntyre-led campaign to compel disclosure.[16]

The resistance and these methods indicated there was something to
hide, and so begat numerous FOI requests of IPCC authors, like Jones
and those at NOAA. That the IPCC adapted to the campaign for actual
transparency revealed a dawning awareness about these requests. It was a
wake-up call: they were exposed under FOI laws and their enterprise was
probably on borrowed time.

Even stranger behavior began, consistent with the disgraced Jones's
entreaties to do something about this threat of meddling taxpayers
looking into the IPCC's business—that business being taking taxpayer
money to produce and hype papers demanding imposition of a retro-
grade agenda of energy scarcity. In a retort coordinated with authors
who, like Jones, were subject to FOI laws came the claim that releasing
emails would prejudice relations with the UN.[17]

Then came the infamous "we lost it" claim from Jones about other
information that seemingly prompted the Climategate leaker to expose
the game. That, of course, only caused more scrambling, not just to
rationalize away nasty, past behavior but to insulate themselves from
having to comply with the inevitable, continuing requests this exposure
begged.

And so, as night follows day, came the claim that "we aren't covered."

* * *

All of this was set in motion by FOI requests a year and a half before the Climategate leaks, as revealed in an email from Phil Jones to NOAA's Thomas Peterson. On July 29, 2010, Jones wrote saying that he had persuaded a Swiss who headed up the IPCC's Working Group I ("the science"), Thomas Stocker, and the IPCC brass to raise FOI issues at the next IPCC meeting, in Bali:

> I have got the IPCC Secretariat and Thomas [Stocker] to raise the FOI issues with the full IPCC Plenary, which meets in Bali in September or October. Thomas is fully aware of all the issues we've had here wrt Ch[apter] 6 last time, and others in the US have had.[18]

Remember, those "others in the US" are, like Jones and all taxpayer-funded IPCC authors, performing official duties when contributing to the IPCC. This shows them trying to find a way around laws covering their work.

Peterson, a leading authority for the alarmist cause, had popped up as a central figure in Climategate emails to or from his NOAA address, as well as emails I received under FOIA from NOAA directly. In writing to him, Jones was referring to the heartburn caused to IPCC participants by past and ongoing FOI requests to national government agencies for IPCC-related records. He took care to note the problems that IPCC-related FOIAs were causing fellow travelers in the U.S. government, most particularly Peterson's colleagues at NOAA.

These problems were made manifest by the exposure in Climategate of specific disgraces, such as scheming by Jones et al. to keep an unhelpful paper out of the IPCC report, and the IPCC breaking its own rules in its efforts to rebut that same research debunking the "Hockey Stick." That was the improper behavior "with regard to Chapter 6" the last time the IPCC issued one of its reports.[19]

It was toward the same end goal of engineering an IPCC response heading off future FOI requests that Jones—a Brit funded for years out of the U.S. Department of Energy—pleaded with Stocker to do something about the FOI threat as an IPCC cochair. McIntyre's scrutiny of Stocker's public handiwork and Jones et al.'s leaked emails revealed the plan, put into place, to create unofficial, password-protected websites on which U.S. government employees could perform official business, on taxpayer time and computers, but presumably without the condition that the taxpayer be able to get his hands on the records created, received, or possessed in the course of such duties.

The plan began to take shape in IPCC documents produced after an October 2010 meeting of IPCC Working Group I in Busan, South Korea. This was the first meeting after a report, prompted by Climategate, of the InterAcademy Council (IAC), a consortium of national academies of science of a number of countries that reviewed the IPCC's processes and procedures, excoriating the body for its myriad deficiencies.[20] Into the Busan document, which alternated between an homage to transparency and insistence that there be none just yet, Stocker placed a suggestion that "closed electronic fora could be established when needed."[21]

Remember, this document nominally reflected the proceedings of the meeting that took place between October 11 and 14, 2010. However, by October 8, Stocker had in fact already established "closed electronic discussion fora" for WG1, evading emails and national transparency laws.

> In order to enhance communication among the chapter authors between the meetings, chapter-specific internet fora will be available which are only accessible to the members of the chapter teams and confidentiality is protected by user-specific passwords. Additional information on the chapter forum, as well as other electronic resources provided by the TSU [Technical Support Unit] in support of the writing process, will be presented during the First Lead Author Meeting.
>
> For direct conversations among two or several chapter authors, telephone conference facilities such as Skype are recommended. The TSU is looking into the possibility of offering WebEx via the IPCC Secretariat.[22]

So, secure websites and videoconferencing instead of email and other documents, escaping exposure to FOI requests—or so the presumption went.[23] These other steps IPCC was "looking into" were in fact done deals. The IPCC also published confirmation of a secure website for WGII participants to gather electronically in lieu of distributing documents, which when received would also be subject to disclosure to the people who paid for them. In a submission to a May 10–13 IPCC session in Abu Dhabi, it stated that "a password-protected Author Portal was launched on 17 August 2010 to provide an array of tools to [participants] in support of the assessment reports—including, but not limited to, draft repositories, WebEx teleconferencing and document sharing. . . . This closed web site serves as the primary means of communicating logistics to writing team members."[24]

So, raise "the issues [they've] had," Stocker did, forcing through an IPCC declaration that it was exempt from its member nations' FOI laws. House Science Committee chairman James Sensenbrenner and Investigations Subcommittee chairman Paul Broun (R-GA) informed the White House that they were now aware and none too happy about another fact, that the IPCC had also posted other claims that it would keep materials from the public,[25] including the U.S. taxpayer, who paid for much of them and was expected to pay more dearly if the IPCC succeeded in roping the United States into its agenda.

Later, in 2012, the British government disavowed the practices Stocker slipped into effect, in a letter to a curious member of Parliament in which they implausibly called the chicanery "likely a drafting error." It claimed "the IPCC is aware of the issue and intends to address it"—here we go again with that euphemism—"at the next opportunity."[26] Preliminary indications were that yet again this would mean "addressing" not the problem that was caught, but the problem that was their getting caught.[27]

UN Claims Authority to Waive U.S. Law

Phil Jones had counseled colleagues as part of the effort to hide information, "The FOI line we're all using is this. IPCC is exempt from any countries [*sic*] FOI—the skeptics have been told this. Even though we (MOHC, CRU/UEA) possibly hold relevant info the IPCC is not part our remit (mission statement, aims etc) therefore we don't have an obligation to pass it on."[28]

This was a stunningly arrogant and impossible proclamation. These are the laws that it had been subject to all along, as a condition of its funding, over which it has no claim to authority. As University of Hamburg's Tol reported from an IPCC lead authors meeting in San Francisco, properly analyzing the ploy:

> [T]he IPCC member states have ruled on freedom of information legislation. Specifically, it has been decided that FoI does not apply to IPCC material. This is false. FoI is national legislation. These laws can only be interpreted by the relevant courts. These laws can only be changed by the relevant parliaments. The civil servants that speak on behalf of their countries have no right to usurp FoI legislation, and the IPCC has no say in this matter.[29]

Tol's report came just on the heels of the late-November "Climategate 2" sequel by the anonymous leaker styling himself "FOIA2011," which leak provided an email affirming the establishment of unofficial computer servers to enable the IPCC to hide from FOI laws, with an assist from the Obama White House. They'd created safe houses of sorts, private servers on which to conduct the taxpayer's business. They would avoid emails going forward[30] and, they thought, have a place to hide future deliberations.[31]

Private servers were created for all three IPCC Working Groups, each housed in the home country of the representative leading the group (WGI in Switzerland; WGIII, the "green economy" group, in Germany;[32] and the one that we know the White House has accessed,[33] for WGII, housed at private Stanford University on hardware owned by the Carnegie Institute for Science. This is discussed in detail in the next chapter).

With no cited or apparent legal basis but with the active participation of the Obama administration, the IPCC took the initiative to "clarify" coverage of "IPCC activities . . . in relation to requests under national Freedom of Information legislation."[34] And so Stocker, speaking for the group, claimed, "[T]hey are therefore considered to be specific closed fora for predecisional documents."[35] Use of the passive voice—"are considered" (by whom?)—implies more authority than is available for an IPCC declaration. Notice also the IPCC invoking the precise language of the most commonly abused FOIA exemption ("predecisional," refuge of a bureaucratic scoundrel, exemption 5, discussed later), intending to influence or purporting to reflect authoritative judgment about application of the United States' FOIA.

This is the same accountability-loathing crowd that seeks diplomatic immunity for its nondiplomatic enterprises, particularly in the field of its "green" projects (from the Kyoto Protocol's governing infrastructure to its "Green Climate Fund," through which they hope to transfer $100 billion per year from rich countries to developing nations in the name of global warming).[36]

Its absurdly grandiose pronouncement reflects the desperation of the mission and the knowledge that it would not survive public inspection. FOIA covers agencies of the United States government. Federal agencies invoke the "pre-decisional" exemption under FOIA, which applies to work produced, sent, or received by covered agencies reflecting the deliberative process for official products of covered agencies (it also covers attorney work product, attorney-client privilege, and other privileged work, none of which applies to federal employees contributing to the UN IPCC).

Sure, the IPCC enjoys substantial direct and indirect underwriting by the U.S. taxpayer. But as a body "established by the United Nations Environment Programme (UNEP) and the World Meteorological Organization (WMO)," and "an intergovernmental body [that] is open to all member countries of the United Nations (UN) and WMO,"[37] headquartered in Switzerland, it is not an agency of the U.S. government, or any other.

However, records produced, sent, or received by U.S. government employees as part of their IPCC-related work are agency records covered by FOIA, as the national government participants remain representatives of those governments, performing official duties. This is well established. For example, a federal inspector general (and now even the White House, after this was exposed) concluded that U.S. government employees participating in IPCC activities are not officially detailed, delegated, or seconded to the UN but remain U.S. government employees—and records produced, sent, or received by them are produced, sent, or received by U.S. government employees.[38]

Yet the public record is clear that these electronic fora—still accessed presumably using government computers, on government time, always as official communications in pursuit of official duties—were established to supplant official channels of communication in order to evade national transparency laws.

And as part of this, with the assistance of academics and political ideologues on a mission, the IPCC claimed to wave away, by proclamation, the legal considerations making these records subject to FOIA.[39]

This is not within the IPCC's powers and it does not alter application of U.S. law. Yet the Obama White House assisted this, only to admit the truth when the scheme was exposed, adding further texture to its ostentatious claims of transparency.

Other U.S. Government Agencies Help Out

In the name of their "cause," there is a manifest proclivity among activist career bureaucrats and political appointees to hold little regard for inconvenient laws, and an ability to find moral equivalence between their own unethical, unlawful, and even criminal behavior and others' purely legal FOIA requests. The precise role of U.S. government agencies in this broader campaign, however, remains unclear due to stonewalling a series of FOIAs designed to discover the truth.

We see one tease, however, in a particularly revealing email from Phil Jones to his colleagues Tim Osborn and Dave Palmer about upcoming IPCC machinations at the 2010 Bali meeting, the one for which Jones had persuaded Stocker to get the IPCC to solve their problem with overly curious researchers and taxpayers (emphasis added):

> Subject: FOI—the issue with IPCC that is going to the Commissioner
>
> Tim, Dave,
>
> I've spoken to Renate Christ who is head of the IPCC Secretariat in Geneva. I've given her a note about what we want, but we won't get a response by our August deadline.
>
> What will happen though is that the whole issue of National FOIs/ EIRs will be discussed at the next full IPCC plenary meeting in Bali in October. This is not a meeting that many scientists will go to. IPCC have got lawyers involved from their sponsoring UN organizations (UNEP and WMO). *They have been alerted up to the issue by us and by others (mainly from US organizations like NOAA, DoE).* They will come to a ruling then.
>
> I know this doesn't help us for this request, but hopefully future IPCC-related FOIs/EIRs will be easier to deal with.
>
> It seems as though they are taking the issue seriously. I did tell them that the various FOI acts probably differ slightly, but they seem to be aware of that.
>
> Cheers,
> Phil[40]

Got it. The IPCC meeting won't be scientists, it will be bureaucrats and lawyers. Huddling to keep what the taxpayer is paying for from the taxpayer. The Obama administration is doing its part. So this move to subvert U.S. law has the blessing and active participation of the U.S. government.

Jones couldn't contain his damning outbursts, also offering for the record:

I hope I don't get a call from congress! I'm hoping that no-one there realizes I have a US DoE grant and have had this (with Tom W.) for the last 25 years.[41]

Any work we have done in the past is done on the back of the research grants we get—and has to be well hidden. I've discussed this with the main funder (US Dept of Energy) in the past and they are happy about not releasing the original station data.[42]

Work on the land station data has been funded by the US Dept of Energy, and I have their agreement that the data needn't be passed on. I got this in 2007.[43]

He had earlier written of his DOE patrons, "They are happy with me not passing on the station data."[44] So DOE has some explaining to do and, it seems, some records to turn over. Therefore in November 2011 I filed a request seeking the correspondence Jones referenced between him and his funding patrons, specifically both offices within DOE that had funded him. This generated some media heat,[45] and three and one half months later, on the Ides of March 2012, DOE mailed their response: "no responsive records."

How could this be? Simple. The bureaucracy has decided as a matter of policy that emails sent in the conduct of federal government business are not necessarily "federal records" requiring preservation, meaning they somehow do not rise to the level of "evidence of the organization, functions, policies, decisions, procedures, operations, or other activities of the Government or because of the informational value of data in them."[46] Right. They only cover things like spending taxpayer money and encouraging grant recipients to refuse access to what we paid for.

Instead, emails are regularly destroyed (unless by chance first caught up in a FOIA request prior to disposal). Those emails that an employee deems a "record" requiring preservation and not deletion—at their discretion, as the parties with the greatest incentive to delete embarrassing or incriminating information—are only to be deleted after copying them to a record-keeping system, and ultimately stored at the National

Archives.[47] I discuss this obvious conflict of leaving this to each employee later.

For perspective on this decision to not keep emails unless an employee specifically asks them to be maintained, days later a headline in the *Washington Post* read, "Data on citizens to be kept longer." Personal information about the governed will be kept longer, now for five years, "even if they have no known connection to terrorism."[48] But not information, particularly email, showing what their government is up to.

One agency that also claimed "no records" in response to FOIA requests on related information is, as noted earlier, NOAA, which for years had led the United States' involvement with the IPCC. NOAA's Dr. Susan Solomon played a central role in these machinations, as Stocker's predecessor. As cochair of the IPCC Working Group I she was the lead U.S. representative to the IPCC. For context as you read on, know that she sees carbon dioxide (what you exhale, plant food, but emissions of which are also a proxy for that bane of environmental activists, reliable, abundant fossil fuels) as an energy by-product akin to nuclear waste.[49]

Amid the fallout from the leaked Climategate emails affirming some oft-rumored behavior by government employees and taxpayer-dependent scientists, including among other things destroying or concealing records from discovery, Oklahoma Republican senator James Inhofe wrote "preservation letters" on December 2, 2009, to Solomon, Lawrence Livermore National Laboratory's Benjamin Santer,[50] and, for good measure, Michael Mann. All had appeared in several Climategate emails.

Inhofe wrote to them all, citing penalties for destroying official records unlawfully, and stating in pertinent part:

> Agency/organization official records include records either made or received under Federal law or in connection with the transaction of public business. All official records, regardless of their form, belong to the agency/organization rather than the person or persons who have custody, and they are to remain in the custody of the agency/organization until there is official authorization for disposal. Correspondence designated "personal," "confidential," "private," or

"restricted," but which relates to the conduct of public business is an official record. Records created as a result of daily activities, e.g., calendars, appointment books, schedule logs, diaries, and other records documenting meetings, appointments, telephone calls, trips, and other activities that contain substantive information relating to official activities not documented elsewhere, are official records and subject to the provisions applicable to official records. While state laws may differ, many have coverage similar to Federal law.

It is worth explaining Inhofe's reference to that which is "not documented elsewhere." Climategate revealed copying and removal of records from FOI-covered equipment or premises after destroying the original. When this is done but a copy is maintained elsewhere, it remains the government's copy (just as in the case of federal government employees using a personal email account or computers for official business, or private servers to house them, though none of us envisioned such moves at the time Senator Inhofe wrote this).

The Climategate leak also revealed other questionable practices, so Inhofe sought assistance from the Department of Commerce's inspector general, given Solomon's roles there and with the IPCC. What Inhofe did not know at the time was that NOAA had denied a series of FOIA requests for IPCC-related records that were routed through and thereby died with Solomon.

Commerce's IG wrote, "We found a reference in the CRU emails to a FOIA request submitted to NOAA in June 2007, related to the IPCC, which, upon further investigation, raised questions about NOAA's processing of the request. . . . NOAA received and responded to these requests over a span of three weeks, informing each requester that '[a]fter reviewing our files, we have determined that we have no NOAA records responsive to your request. If records exist that are responsive to your request, they would be records of the IPCC and as such can be requested from the IPCC. . . . ' Contrary to NOAA's assertions, we found that it did not conduct a sufficient search for records prior to responding to these FOIA requests."[51]

The IG report states that the requests made it no further than Solomon, with she and a colleague serving as gatekeepers.[52] "[T]he [other] NOAA scientists with whom we spoke indicated that as a result of their participation in WG1 as authors and/or editors, they may have possessed responsive records, but were never apprised of the FOIA requests. As such, they did not search for and forward potentially responsive records for agency processing, as is required under FOIA."[53] Here we see the abuse invited by tasking those having an interest in hiding records with searching for and producing records and, for the higher-ups among them, with determining where requests will be forwarded internally.

Like those FOI requests centered in the United Kingdom sparking so much scandal, these requests sought documents showing discussions about producing the IPCC Assessment Reports. Although any objective analysis made plain that these records were covered by FOIA, NOAA career staff devised arguments as to why IPCC-related records should not be released. The most devious part was claiming, without anything to support it, that they were not agency records but instead belonged to the UN.

None of the first three requesting parties confronted with the claim challenged it,[54] and the requests fell by the wayside in the face of this refusal, until NOAA pulled the same stunt with me in mid-2010.

Solomon explained her rationale for not considering the records for search or production when they obviously were the target of the FOIA requests. It was grounded in a claim "that she had been detailed from NOAA to the IPCC from 2002 to 2007."[55] Further, after the fact, she consulted with an Office of General Counsel attorney for a determination, who "noted that he had been led to believe by [Solomon] that she was officially detailed to the IPCC."[56] But investigators "found no evidence that any of the employees, including [Solomon] were formally 'detailed' to the IPCC."[57] Also, the attorneys serially disputed Solomon's story given to investigators.

In short, Solomon and her superior chose, ostensibly on grounds that didn't pass muster with the IG, not to look for requested records because they viewed them as the UN's and not the agency's (that is, the taxpayers'). Together they disputed the claims by NOAA lawyers about whether this behavior was on their own instigation or because of advice received by agency counsel (who state they did not provide the advice attributed to them). This presents us with two activist employees saying one thing, and not one but two lawyers, who stand to lose their licenses to practice if caught lying to investigators, saying another.

The game began to unravel after my February 2010 FOIA request seeking numerous categories of records relating to Solomon's role in the IPCC, Mann's selection as a lead author almost right out of school, her discussions about the "Hockey Stick" and Climategate, her involvement in efforts to discredit contrarians whose work was slowing the agenda, and other topics.

Several months after my request I spoke by telephone with a NOAA FOIA officer assigned to the matter, Marie Covard, who informed me that the responsive records had been identified and segregated. The delay, she said, was because they had to sort which were "agency records" covered by FOIA and which were "UN records."

I had recently won on administrative appeal with NASA after they used a similar claim to withhold emails created on official time (only to then refuse to provide the emails at issue, requiring us to sue them). So I immediately memorialized this conversation by email, challenging the notion that the agency could refuse access by claiming records on these absurd grounds:

Dear Ms. Covard,

This is to confirm our telephone conversation in reference to the February 19, 2010, Dr. Susan Solomon FOIA, of Wednesday the 26th at appx. 10:50 am. In our discussion you indicated a request for an extension would soon issue, on the grounds that the appx. 8,000 pages of responsive documents compiled so far require sorting for determining which are agency documents and which are "IPCC documents." As I noted, particularly given the president's serial pronouncements of transparency and a bias toward disclosure (as is also inherent in the FOIA Act), NOAA should err on the side of determining that records created on taxpayer resources and taxpayer time, in pursuit of official agency duties—in this instance, serving as a U.S. governmental representative to the IPCC—are agency documents and should be released. This is consistent with FOIA precedent.

In one item CEI [the Competitive Enterprise Institute] is presently litigating, noted in yesterday's news here *http://www.washingtontimes.com/news/2010/may/26/nasa-accused-of-climategate-stalling/*, we also affirmed what seems to be fairly black-letter FOIA interpretation. There the agency affirmed on administrative appeal that records similarly created, if *not* in that case for a body to which the staffer was appointed by the federal government, were agency records. So as to avoid unnecessary delay and of the sort that would certainly appear to run contrary to the president's own, repeated emphases on disclosure and transparency, I suggest that the present case is materially stronger. The "IPCC documents" are agency records on the grounds, inter alia, that in producing or receiving them Dr. Solomon is acting in her position with NOAA, on behalf of NOAA and otherwise USG, largely or entirely on taxpayer resources, and the documents should be released.

One week later, after what I presume was huddling over the unexpected unpleasantness of someone calling NOAA out on this practice of stopping requests in their tracks, Covard wrote back, in pertinent part:

I would like to clarify one statement in your email below, in which you stated the extension was needed, "on the grounds that the appx. 8,000 pages of responsive documents compiled so far require sorting for determining which are agency documents and which are 'IPCC documents.'" The 8,000 pages of responsive documents we have found so far are currently being reviewed, but there is no question that these documents are NOAA documents; none of the 8,000 pages we have located thus far are IPCC documents. NOAA is still in the process of searching Susan Solomon's files.

Here NOAA neither confirmed nor denied its position, taken for years with several parties, but instead effectively abandoned it, as it was clear they would be forced to defend the indefensible. Yet by this time NOAA had been "searching Solomon's files" for months and had already informed me the search was complete, and admitted they had located the responsive records. This search began to resemble O.J.'s quest to find the real killer, with two more years of bumbling, defiant refusal to turn over records they had plainly stated were found, subject to FOIA and set aside after their excuse became, in Washington parlance, no longer operative. Despite—I am told by agency counsel—the chief information officer going out to Solomon's home to search her personal computer and email account once the lawyers got involved, NOAA continued stonewalling me and a congressional committee that also found this of interest.

They initiated a series of document productions, both to me and the House Science Committee, ultimately giving the latter more than thirty-eight thousand pages of the records I requested while outrageously holding on to the key emails, in the name of "respecting the scientific review process and the expectations of confidentiality that underlie the scientific activities that are the subject of" my FOIA request (and those requests by McIntyre et al. that NOAA was now finally forced to satisfy).[58] That language reflects neither an exemption under FOI nor a legitimate basis for withholding information from Congress. They seemed to be buying time for IPCC authors, particularly including Michael Mann, whose emails, many of which NOAA was copied on, were the subject of court battles.

That language is, however, now apparently code among this particular movement for telling people they'll have to fight long and hard to obtain public records, as it reflects the same legally meaningless pose struck by UVa and Mann to oppose releasing emails.

And so chairmen Sensenbrenner and Broun pushed NOAA again, noting:

The Committee does not recognize this as an acceptable exemption for withholding records. Moreover, "federal courts, when considering Congress's broad investigatory power to obtain documents containing confidential or other proprietary information, have expressly held that executive agencies and private parties may not deny Congress access to such documents, even if they contain information whose disclosure to the public is otherwise statutorily barred." Additionally, "courts have held that release of information to a congressional requestor is not considered to be disclosure to the general public and once documents are in congressional control, the courts will presume that committees of Congress will exercise their powers responsibly and with proper regard to the rights of the parties."[59]

However direct and compelling, as well as indicating that a subpoena could be arranged if necessary, NOAA was not moved. These were documents related to a key liberal "cause" and so once again the liberals just weren't that into transparency. The stonewall continued.

8.

Technological Trickery, Exposed: The Scandalous Epidemic of Hiding Public Service on Personal Email Accounts

T here is overwhelming authority in law and regulation that, with exceptions for incidental activity, government employees may not use official assets—their taxpayer-funded time, computer, car, credit card, office, phone, etc.—for unofficial purposes.[1]

There is so far a paucity of authority, but only common sense, governing a new twist now made urgent by systematic abuses by Obama officials in their conduct of public business.

I and others such as Landmark Legal Foundation have established that high-profile, controversial Obama appointees did leave enough emails to be produced under FOIA to reveal key details of their clever activities. Yet we also did enough requests to know that, in the relative scheme of things, their email use was quite limited. The stunning discovery that it was Carol Browner, of all people—whose document-destruction during her last stint came as a parting gasp thanks to a Landmark Legal suit—who also ordered a secret account created that not even her own agency (EPA) knew if she used shows that this mind-set of defying transparency laws drives liberals to extreme measures. Also, a seemingly smart defensive move of avoiding their government email accounts looks pretty stupid when we realize the implausibility of their having gone without email, and that they instead turned to private accounts for official correspondence, hoping to hide it.

The Browners and Zois of the Obama administration showed a

certain discipline in mailing habits while they were federal employees, knowing the targets they were for scrutiny, and the potential for scandal each of them represented for their own reasons, all related to the appointees being career liberal activists. And each likely deployed a "Sherpa," an underling in their orbit who would communicate on their behalf on as much as possible (Browner's edict creating the secret email account allowed for her Sherpa to also access it when so ordered). But it's now level ground, acknowledged (if then disregarded) by even *Mother Jones* and the *New York Times* that Obama appointees use private email to conduct official business. What they have egregiously ignored is just how widespread the practice seems to be.

Worse, this is particularly true of the White House, from which one would expect the greatest compliance if only because of Democrat hysteria over several Bush White House aides having been shown to have used Republican National Committee email accounts for what was arguably political activity. But instead, to no similar outcry, a former Google executive then employed in the White House "unwittingly revealed his frequent e-mail contacts on his [social networking service] Google Buzz profile in February [2010],"[2] showing he was regularly in contact with his former employer, including on policy matters, and regularly used private email accounts to conduct official business.[3]

Lucy Dalglish, executive director of the Reporters Committee for Freedom of the Press, was quoted in 2012 as saying, "Any time public business is being done electronically, whether its [*sic*] public or private email, the public should have a record. When you use private devices to do public business you remove public accountability."[4] But she was specifically commenting on an inquiry about a Republican, Mitt Romney, having done it. More on that in a moment.

Relevant laws and regulations were of course drafted before today's widespread use of and dependence upon email and personal electronic equipment such as smartphones or computers. Interpretation of the law hasn't fully kept up with the advances in technology, or with the decreasing respect for the law by taxpayer-funded ideologues on a mission. One career government attorney working on these matters readily agreed to me that use of private email and computers to perform official business is widespread; he confided that these laws are "way behind" the use of technology. However, there is no doubt that federal employees are expected, and instructed, to copy their official email accounts with any messages on private accounts that relate to official business. But this leaves compliance exclusively in the hands of those who have already decided a private email account was the better choice. This inherent conflict provides some hint about just how widespread compliance is, or is not, in practice.

As the House Committee on Oversight and Government Reform has noted, "The technological innovations of the last decade have provided tools that make it too easy for federal employees to circumvent the law and engage in prohibited activities."[5] Putting aside for the moment that official records on private accounts are likely rarely turned over, addressing current electronic record practices the GAO wrote in late 2010 that "almost 80 percent of agencies were at moderate or high risk of improper destruction of records; that is, the risk that permanent records will be lost or destroyed before they can be transferred to NARA [National Archives Records Administrator] for archiving or that other records will be lost while they are still needed for government operations or legal obligations."[6] Per GAO, "The Archivist referred to these results as 'alarming' and 'worrisome'; in a subsequent oversight hearing, the director of NARA's Modern Records Program testified that the findings were 'troubling' and 'unacceptable.'"[7]

Amusingly, in 2012 one liberal media outlet jerked to attention over a public official's having used private email, after numerous stories in recent years had already noted, in dicta, that the practice by Obama appointees was widespread. What worried the *Huffington Post* wasn't the Obama administration, however, but the revelation that in 2006, as the headline panted, "Mitt Romney Used Private Email Accounts to Conduct State Business While Massachusetts Governor."[8] We'll see if *HuffPo* maintains this concern as these practices become more broadly known, though their umbrage despite Obama administration practices leaving them unmoved provides some hint at the answer. Their author wrote,

"Private email accounts used by public officials to perform their public jobs are effectively off limits to review by citizens, watchdog groups, political opponents, and news organizations because they're often used secretly. Free accounts from commercial providers also are more vulnerable to hackers who exploit easy-to-use features to reset email passwords."

The media in general had so far shown no interest in the implications of or even further pursuing such stories for what else they might indicate about the federal government, what with 1600 Pennsylvania Avenue being under new management. So there may be little room for making this an issue as the most transparent administration in history, which clearly is no such thing, seeks four more years. One item, which as I write this I am the first to report and could change this, is Obama campaign manager Jim Messing having used his AOL email account as a federal employee to arrange Big Pharma's deal to help cram ObamaCare down America's throat.

That could elevate the discussion, given the road map of outrage and oversight prepared by Democrats against Karl Rove and others, discussed below, which Republicans ought to use to shame even the establishment press into giving some attention to what was after all previously declared to be an egregious offense worthy of inquiry, lawyers, and serial condemnations dripping with as much spittle as invective. But how legally explosive might the reality of widespread use of private email accounts for official business prove to be? That is a pertinent question for the following reason: in response to the Google alum's impermissible practices, "A White House spokeswoman said [private] e-mails are not subject to the FOIA."[9]

To the extent she was saying (as she obviously was) that emails on private email accounts are not subject to FOIA, that is simply not true, although the issue requires formal resolution by the courts. What we learn in legal "discovery" as we seek to obtain private email abusing public office in this way will go great lengths toward framing the extent of the problem.

I expect this will prove a big legal problem for the White House, or some career activist in government or at some public university, once we find the appropriate test case (two are in the works). As one consultant notes, "If you work for a government agency there is a good chance that your communications are subject to some sort of Freedom of Information rules. In either case, sending official information on your personal account would place it outside of the controls in place to protect and retain email communications. Doing so is not only a compliance violation, but also gives the appearance of a willful and intentional attempt to circumvent the system and covertly hide your communications."[10] It also seems unlikely to work, except of course for those government employees who destroy all such emails.

But for that reason, that these employees have exclusive control over the account, it is another story altogether whether we ever get emails that authorities have no practical way of preserving or maintaining the integrity of.

The principle that should and, upon judicial review, surely will govern is an obvious one: conducting official business on a private resource doesn't make the business any less official.

Because of pressure by public advocates, laws are beginning to catch up to the email age, which adaptation even President Obama has formally acknowledged must accelerate (if only for emails and social media communication held on government computers).[11] When Congressman Henry Waxman (D-Beverly Hills) became so exercised over learning that Karl Rove and some other Bush White House employees frequently used email accounts provided to them from the Republican National Committee (RNC), particularly when dealing with or about lobbyist Jack Abramoff, he launched an investigation and many proclamations for others to follow. His report was rife with indignation that, while these senior officials obviously used email extensively, only a relatively few emails were preserved.[12] Even though the emails were on private accounts, Waxman flatly declared them to be "presidential records."[13] In many cases, he's right, even if the White House and the bureaucracy implement the law in a way disagreeing with that conclusion (as you'll see, a glaring problem is that emails are only "records" when an employee suggests they be so preserved).

More recent developments indicate that this chain of logic and application of the law do not apply regardless of political affiliation.

The Waxman investigation's report cited to precious little legal precedent to support its umbrage, merely asserting that a failure to sufficiently preserve presidential records is a potential violation of the Presidential Records Act. Just as would be failure to abide by the Federal Records Act (FRA), a similar law applying far more broadly, and across the federal government.[14] One federal court described the FRA in this context in a 1999 opinion styled *Public Citizen v. Carlin:*

> The Federal Records Act is a collection of statutes governing the creation, management, and disposal of records by federal agencies. The [1943 Records Disposal Act, or] RDA portion of the FRA establishes the exclusive means by which records subject to the FRA may be discarded. . . . The RDA requires an agency to get the approval of the Archivist before disposing of any record. [Internal citations omitted].[15]

As a result, each agency has adopted detailed record retention, preservation, and disposal schedules to comply with government-wide rules established by the NARA. "The mission of the National Archives and Records Administration (NARA) is to safeguard and preserve government records, ensuring continuing access to the essential documentation of the rights of American citizens and the actions of their government. However, in today's environment of fast-evolving information technology, this important mission is increasingly challenging. At the same time that paper and other physical records continue to be created in large numbers, federal agencies are creating vast and growing volumes of electronic records."[16]

They have also said it is impractical to preserve them all, which questionable statement only begs further problems. It is up to the head of the agency learning of possible destruction or removal of records to notify the archivist and initiate action against the employee; if he does not within a reasonable period of time, the archivist "shall" ask the attorney general to do so. (Criminal penalties, including fines or jail time for the unlawful destruction of records or documents, can be found in 18 U.S.C. Section 2071.) Particularly with Eric Holder in charge, do not hold your breath about this occurring for these sorts of violations.[17]

NARA's regulations imply that it is up to the agency whether to allow the use of private emails for official business (which NARA and agencies nonetheless generally discourage), on the condition that the emails be preserved. Sort of. "Agencies that allow employees to send and receive official electronic mail messages using a system not operated by the agency must ensure that Federal records sent or received on such systems are preserved in the appropriate agency recordkeeping system."[18] Thus agencies are discouraged but clearly not prohibited from allowing employees to use private email accounts or personal computers, on an honor code, despite the obvious conflict of leaving it to the employee to decide what to turn over and also other sound arguments, for example that this constitutes unlawful use of voluntary or personal services banned by the Anti-Deficiency Act.

This all begs the question, what is a "record"? With the scandal brewing and my, and my colleagues', intention to obtain judicial resolution making a public debate over this likely, here is how the government record-keeping system is supposed to work.

Per the Federal Records Act, the National Archives is responsible for oversight of agency records management programs and practices, and archiving temporary and permanent records documenting the activities of government. Emails are to be kept in, not as, record-keeping systems. They are subject to deletion.

NARA issues guidance for records management programs and disposition (destruction or preservation). Each federal agency must "make and preserve records that (1) document the organization, functions, policies, decisions, procedures, and essential transactions of the agency. . . . These records, which include e-mail records, must be effectively managed."[19] The term *records* has a distinct, extensive definition, the keys to which are that the document arises "in connection with the transaction of public business," and either is preserved, or is appropriate for preservation, being "documentary of the organization, functions, policies, decisions, procedures, operations, or other activities of the Government," or "because of the informational value of data in them."

GAO writes, "As the definition shows, although government documentary materials (including e-mails) may be 'records' in this sense, many are not."[20] Further, it is up to a particular office to rule whether certain types of documents are or are not "federal records" under the Federal Records Act (or to not bother to take a position at all, which is the same as declaring them not federal records). This is one more way to avoid creation of a "record." In that case documents received or even downloaded may permissibly be destroyed. While it is not precisely a good-faith move, given what we already know it is hardly out of the question.

Indeed a reading of the act immediately presents the angles that, history indicates, the federal activist would find too tempting to pass up. For example, the wiggle room in the definition of "documentary" material, or the delineation of when "preliminary drafts" or "working papers" need not be preserved is catnip to this particular crowd. Those happen to be the very notional loopholes (real or imagined), in this law adopted by the United States Congress in 1950 and amended for relevant purposes in 1974, which were posited by Phil Jones et al. when they first sought to duck public requests. In fact, Jones et al. sought to hide this same class of records we have discovered are being housed on unofficial, private computer servers to put them beyond the taxpayer's reach.

But setting the general policy is in the particular agency's discretion, and agencies leave that discretion as regards individual correspondence to . . . the individual employee. The same one who inherently has a conflict in deciding which correspondence, relating to official business but conducted on an account other than the one assigned for official business, should be turned over for possible preservation.

Further, what constitutes a "record" for FOIA is even broader, which disparate definitions ensure that covered records are regularly destroyed (as I have experienced). Which often are sought because inappropriate or revealing behavior is suspected. So the system is rife with conflicts, designed to fail, and is proving a failure as we see liberals, of all people, abusing the daylights out of it. Because at present it mostly presents them a threat, not an opportunity.

Per NARA, "[A]gencies are required to establish policies and procedures that provide for appropriate retention and disposition of electronic records. In addition . . . agency procedures must specifically address email records: that is, the creation, maintenance and use, and disposition of federal records created by individuals using electronic mail systems."[21] Similarly, they must ensure employees are aware of the rules.

But while "not all e-mail is record material [and] Agencies may destroy nonrecord e-mail,"[22] it remains the case that "records" may still be created on private email accounts, regardless of whether they are ever declared such by the employee or turned over to the agency; if they are never declared a record, even if by definition they are, they are never captured by NARA records disposition requirements. This is similar to the problem that, if the employee chooses to not volunteer them, they are never captured by FOIA.

The government offers an entire decision tree of factors for determining whether an individual email is a "record." It would be simpler at the front end to declare that emails sent or received on the account provided and assigned for official business are official business, and therefore records.

But this would mean the feds have to keep everything, so discretion is afforded to employees as the easiest course for the government, even if it is the riskiest and least transparent for the taxpayer. In short, government wants the benefits of email but not the responsibilities to the taxpayer that come with it. This frees them from storing all email traffic, which the government says it cannot do. Possibly the government has gotten too big? (It is also possible the government could ban email until the government figures out how to store it; we did manage to have an awfully big government before email.) This system is cherished by "the system" because its built-in conflict ensures the employees are the ones who sort their messages, as opposed to someone else tasked with ensuring compliance with the law.

Specifically as regards private accounts, "Agencies are also required to address the use of external e-mail systems that are not controlled by the agency (such as private e-mail accounts on commercial systems such as Gmail, Hotmail, .Mac, etc.). Where agency staff have access to external systems, agencies must ensure that federal records sent or received on such systems are preserved in the appropriate recordkeeping system and that reasonable steps are taken to capture available transmission and receipt data needed by the agency for recordkeeping purposes."[23] "Must." Though they don't.

Those agencies claiming, when asked by the GAO, that their employees are prohibited from accessing outside email systems on government assets also acknowledged that they did not bother explaining to employees the procedures required in the event the employees nonetheless did so,[24] as is only reasonable to assume the employees will.

In truth, there is no regime of transparency rules to protect the taxpayer, illustrated further by these assertions to GAO.

- EPA "[o]fficials also told us that employees could access Web-based e-mail systems for limited personal use, but that they were not permitted to use these for official business."[25] Meaning: no agency employee will volunteer such emails when they exist.

- The Federal Trade Commission's "CIO [chief information officer] told us that agency staff cannot directly access external Web-based e-mail through the agency's Web browsers, and agency employees have been instructed not to use such systems for official FTC business. However, this official said that agency employees may use the commission's remote application delivery environment to obtain limited access to external Web-based e-mail as a convenience."[26] In other words: They can't. Unless they want to.

- Only one of the four agencies surveyed by GAO had its systems configured so that staff could not access external email applications.[27] Affirming that there is no rule.

Emails are either records (documenting agency business and worthy of preservation), temporary records, transitory records (can be disposed of in six months or less), or nonrecord materials. Whichever they are is determined by the agency, first generally by class and characteristics, and then on a document-by-document basis by the employee.

This explains how, for example, the National Science Foundation could be telling the truth when providing a "no records" response to my FOIA request seeking correspondence reflecting the development and staging of a colloquy between an NSF aide (a former staffer for a Senate liberal) and Michael Mann, helping justify Mann's refusal to turn over other records underwritten and then sought by the taxpayer. I had copies of some of the orchestrating emails that were responsive to my request. They had been kept by other systems to which Mann had forwarded them. NSF claimed "no records" existed, as apparently they had destroyed theirs.

Congressman Waxman established for us the deeply held principle that using private email to conduct official business, and destroying or not turning over such records, violates the requirements of PRA (or FRA) and is a serious matter, as are efforts to evade the law. It is likely that the response to a direct FOIA request for work-related Gmail will be an assertion by the staffer, who after all was seeking to avoid transparency, that he did not create or else discarded all such emails. Barring the ability to inspect the equipment or accounts, that will be the end of the affair. Enforcement is up to the agency or our highly politicized attorney general, and therefore no remedy for violations is likely. This is not to say we cannot exact a cost for this behavior by making the White House publicly fight to block such an effort to obtain these presumably hidden communications, and/or by demonstrating to the public that the emails have been systematically deleted and the laws ignored.

Until we obtain judicial recognition that such subterfuge will not be permitted to undermine laws, which must be adhered to as a condition of public employment (whether or not that is enforced), we will have to direct public attention to these self-discrediting practices. Then comes formal recognition that private email accounts used for public business clearly creates the sort of record the laws expect agencies to preserve, and court order compelling production to the public as such, with sanctions if the emails are "disappeared." As you will read, this process is already well-advanced in the United Kingdom.

Private Emails, Public Access

Any administration, not to mention this uniquely self-congratulating one, must comply with record-keeping laws. We know the use of personal email accounts to conduct official business begs the question of whether such records are "federal records" for FRA purposes and, similarly, fall under the broader "agency records" for production under FOIA (assuming they haven't been voluntarily provided by the agency, or deleted). If the answer is yes, as appears to often be the case, then we should prepare for a wave of revelations exposing appointees and bureaucrats who thought they had found a way to beat the system and hide what they didn't want us to see. Such records plainly relate to one's government position and whether or not sent, received, or held on an official computer would be subject to FOIA.

Unfortunately the Obama administration has brazenly denied this truth, flying in the face of express policy and the law's clear intent, if taking advantage of the fact that no court has yet compelled production of such records, thereby formally and inescapably catching the law up with technology and practice.

But should these emails also be subject to preservation, under PRA or FRA, such that the agency must obtain them from the employee and keep them where they will not be deleted?

Following the argument of one authority cited by Waxman, the answer is of course yes.

[T]he White House policy from the first days of the Bush Administration has been clear: use only the official e-mail system for official communications and retain any official e-mails received on a nongovernmental account. A February 26, 2001, memorandum from

Alberto Gonzales, Counsel to the President, to White House staff stated:

> e-mail is no different from other kinds of documents. Any e-mail relating to official business therefore qualifies as a Presidential record. All e-mail to your official e-mail address is automatically archived as if it were a Presidential record, and all e-mail from your official e-mail address is treated as a Presidential record unless you designate otherwise. . . . [I]f you happen to receive an e-mail on a personal e-mail account that otherwise qualifies as a Presidential record, it is your duty to ensure that it is preserved and filed as such by printing it out and saving it or by forwarding it to your White House e-mail account.

The February 2001 White House Staff Manual similarly stated:

> Federal law and EOP policy require the preservation of electronic communications that relate to official business and that are sent or received by EOP staff. As a result, you must only use the authorized e-mail system for all official electronic communications.[28]

Experience shows that employees using private email do not arrange for systematic forwarding of copies to their government email account for proper retention and preservation according to the rules. After all, these employees made the threshold decision to use an account other than the one assigned for official business.

One White House office caught at this practice reaffirmed that forwarding was mandatory: OSTP director John Holdren issued a May 2010 memo to all staff, which stated in pertinent part:

> In the course of responding to the recent FOIA request, OSTP learned that an employee had, in a number of instances, inadvertently

failed to forward to his OSTP email account work-related emails received on his personal account. The employee has since taken corrective action by forwarding these additional emails from his personal account to his OSTP account so that all of the work-related emails are properly preserved in his OSTP account.

If you receive communications relating to your work at OSTP on any personal email account, you must promptly forward any such emails to your OSTP account, even if you do not reply to such email. Any replies should be made from your OSTP account. In this way, all correspondence related to government business—both incoming and outgoing—will be captured automatically in compliance with the FRA. In order to minimize the need to forward emails from personal accounts, please advise email senders to correspond with you regarding OSTP-related business on your OSTP account only.[29]

That's about as self-serving a spin as is possible on the truth that OSTP learned this because a private citizen had discovered the employee's egregious violations on his own and brought it to OSTP's attention in a FOIA seeking more evidence of the impermissible behavior. But also note that a computer automatically capturing email in compliance with the FRA does not mean it is preserved. If not declared a "record" by the agency, it gets destroyed anyway.

Already, one litigant has cited the Federal Records Act (without success) to object to alleged use of personal emails to conduct government business, although the court offered little discussion of the argument when moving beyond it.[30] So the issue remains untested. But game it out. Say you suspect that an agency is using unofficial equipment or accounts to meaningfully perform official business with outside interests, as I do in several instances and have recently proved in two others; barring a lucky stroke of an email leaking, any evidence of this would only be on the respective private accounts or computer resources. The agency then responds to a FOIA request claiming that no responsive records exist, having found none on government computers or accounts. If you appeal or sue, you are left to argue that, on information and belief, you conclude this practice is occurring and that a reasonable search requires searching private email accounts, computers, etc., as appropriate, which you suspect have been used for such purposes (for the moment, let's not presume the employee deletes all such emails from his private account).

Your only hope in this case is a diligent administration attorney managing the appeal who demands a search and an attestation under penalty of perjury, as well as a secretive employee who forgets to delete the records before the announced search of her private email or computer takes place.

Otherwise, an agency or court could reasonably reject that claim out of hand, so long as it is mere, unsubstantiated suspicion. But what if we demonstrate it is a reasonable one? It is possible to show a rational basis for this belief. Begin with the history of administration officials using private email accounts or unofficial computers, and creating unofficial electronic safe houses trying to duck these laws, all detailed in these pages. Further, we know that many federal government employees work from home, requiring official work on a private computer, and as discussed later, this is often promoted by the government, which therefore must also search that equipment.

If no responsive records are found by what the agency claims is the necessary reasonable search, and it is implausible that they do not exist, at that point it is entirely reasonable for a court to order a search of private accounts and equipment, or at minimum first require that employees, or (less optimal) a senior manager, attest whether employees have engaged in such behavior. They should have been asked to do this at the administrative appeal stage, but often they are not. Although some appeals are mishandled, I have also encountered precisely the sort of reviewing attorney one would want in this instance, focusing only on how the law treats his client (which is the agency, not the taxpayer).

You should insist upon a sworn assertion as to computer and email account use, preservation or deletion history, and search. An agency is required to undertake search efforts "reasonably calculated to uncover all relevant documents" and "cannot limit its search to only one record

system if there are others that are likely to turn up the information requested."[31] Reasonable means that "all files likely to contain responsive
materials . . . were searched."[32] The D.C. Circuit Court of Appeals has
held it was "inconceivable" that no drafts of documents produced from
the agency's office or related correspondence existed, ruling the search
inadequate on those grounds.[33] So at some level of suspicion about
these activities in individual cases, a "reasonable" FOIA search requires
a search of private email and/or computers, as the evidence indicates, an
affidavit regarding their use, or both.

As you'll see, this is where liberals, including in the White House, appear to be vulnerable, and not only as regards email.

In addition to substantial evidence of private email use for official
business, we know about or, in other cases, are fairly confident of this
strategy extending to the use of private computers. Before laying out
these details, consider the Obama administration's future as it is unfolding in this context in the United Kingdom, where something that
Waxman was on to, if apparently motivated by politics (keep reading),
is blowing up in the face of public servants who thought they were too
clever to be bound by such promises and conditions as a Freedom of
Information Act.

Gee Whiz, My Gmail Is Public: Public Business on Private Email Is Still Public

As 2011 drew to a close, an ominous item appeared in the London
Telegraph, hinting in the penultimate paragraph at an outcome await-
ing senior Obama administration officials who seem to believe they are
outsmarting the law in order to keep their dealings as public employees
secret. Reading almost as if it, like the email it quoted, was drafted hur-
riedly on a handheld device, it noted:

> In September Dominic Cummings, Michale [*sic*] Gove's chief po-
> litical adviser, was reported to ahve [*sic*] told colleagues that "i will
> only answer things that come from gmail accounts from people who

i know who they are. i suggest that you do the same in general but thats obv [*sic*] up to you guys—i can explain in person the reason for this."[34]

Cummings's reason was of course to avoid creating an official record. But as we now see, this depends on keeping secret the ways that you are keeping secrets, a tangled web indeed. If this activity is discovered, logic will in the end prevail: transparent efforts to subvert transparency law do not make official business any less official.

It is fitting that the United Kingdom's government has been forced to confront this matter before we are in the United States, given that the most high-profile effort encountered to exempt records produced by national government employees originated in Britain. Old Blighty's information commissioner (an individual whose job is something of a cross between a FOIA appeals officer and our Office of Government Ethics) ruled that email sent from private accounts by high government officials should be disclosed. This came in response to a September 2011 Freedom of Information request seeking details of emails sent by the Secretary of State for Education Michael Gove to certain named individuals. With a twist. The request identified the secretary's private email account from which it sought records, revealing that "the education secretary had used an undisclosed private email account—called 'Mrs Blurt'—to communicate with advisers."[35]

One press account noted, "The Information Commissioner, Christopher Graham, confirmed today that all official correspondence is subject to disclosure laws. He issued the warning after the Department of Education claimed that emails between Michael Gove and his advisers 'do not fall within the FOI Act.'"[36] Which is precisely what the Obama White House claimed, with similar accuracy, when asked after the OSTP official was caught using his Google account to conduct public business.

After ruling on the requester's appeal (he had been denied by the department via its Obama-esque effort to escape coverage) the Information Commission Office (ICO) spokesman said, in a statement:

The Information Commissioner has issued his decision in the case involving a request for information in an *email sent by the Secretary of State for Education on a private email account*. The Commissioner's decision is that *the information amounted to departmental business and so was subject to freedom of information laws, being held on behalf of the Department for Education*. The Department is now required either to disclose the requested information (the subject line of the email and the date and time it was sent) or issue a refusal notice in accordance with the FOI Act giving reasons for withholding it.[37]

The decision notice details that the covered emails involved Gove and four specified correspondents. One was an employee of the Department for Education, two of whom were not employees, but "Special Advisors" to the department. This was relevant because one argument to avoid producing the records was that the exemption should derive from their status as non-employees. (These "provide a Minister with political advice and assistance where it would be inappropriate for traditional civil servants to be involved. Special advisers are personal appointees of the Secretary of State employed as temporary civil servants.")[38]

That he was corresponding with non-employees mattered not. The correspondence still related to official business and, since the owner of the (private) account was a public employee, the emails were the public's. "It is information if it 'amounts to' public authority business, or whether information was 'generated in the course of conducting the business of the public authority'" and is thereby "held by" an agency.[39] This is akin to FOIA's coverage of "agency records." So we see this decision does not turn on any particular aspect or distinction of the British FOIA in contrast to the U.S. or other laws, but because the records sought reflect the conduct of official business.

In responding to the requester, the department "informed the complainant that following a search of the department's electronic records it had established that it did not hold the requested information." Five days later it acknowledged that this meant "a search for any information falling within the scope of the request had been conducted on the relevant 'official email account' by a member of the Secretary of State's private office."[40]

The requester appealed, with the benefit we do not always have, which is possession of evidence that presumably only the parties to the correspondence have: "a copy of an email ('the email') dated 29 December 2010 and which appeared to have been sent by the Secretary of State Michael Gove to Dominic Cummings, amongst others. The email was sent from a private, non-departmental email account."[41]

He argued that the contents of the email were responsive to his FOI request and that failing to identify them violated the department's duties under the FOI law. "In its response to the Commissioner the DfE explained that it had not searched any private email accounts when it received the request and that only the Secretary of State's official account was searched. The request was specifically for 'information from the Secretary of State's accounts' excluding 'emails sent on his behalf by a private secretary' and therefore no further email accounts were searched."[42] Once the requester let the cat out of the bag on appeal that he had a copy of responsive email not turned over, if sent from a private account, the analysis took on a new character. The record's existence could not be denied, just whether its provenance and location meant it was not a public record.

The key to determining that was "the purpose of the email and whether the majority of the contents of the email amount to the business of the department."[43] To ascertain these, one looks at the sender and recipient(s) of the email; the relationship indicated the record was likely official, and the content confirmed this, which the requester was fortuitously able to demonstrate. If he had not, the party hearing the appeal would have been ruling on a hypothetical and far less likely to come down as he did.

As such, in all FOIA requests, where appropriate, I include in my letter that I seek the described information on all accounts assigned or available to the official, and any unofficial account(s) on which the official conducts or has conducted official business during the period covered by the request, noting that the individual and the agency must turn over responsive emails held on such accounts. The agency will presumably pass that notation along when notifying the party to search for and provide responsive records, though it does not have the ability to ensure such emails are not then deleted. Only at the appeal stage, with a diligent administrative counsel handling the appeal, will the staffer be asked to attest to his use of other accounts. Even an honest answer "yes," however, will not ensure that the records are not deleted and made available.

This British ruling, when fully understood here, should terrify Obama political appointees, given the practices that we know are occurring and that administration lawyers and FOIA officers confirm to me are widespread.

The commissioner said of his ruling that "It should not come as a surprise to public authorities to have the clarification that information held in private email accounts can be subject to Freedom of Information law if it relates to official business," because "[t]his has always been the case—the Act covers all recorded information in any form."[44]

As the *Telegraph* also wrote, quoting the commissioner's public comments:

> The statement has reportedly worried many civil servants, many of whom communicate more informally using private webmail accounts believing they were exempt from the Freedom of Information Act. Campaigners have claimed Gmail and other services are used to conduct official business without public scrutiny.[45]

The commissioner opened his opinion the same way a U.S. court no doubt will when finally asked, which is by recognizing "that this is a novel issue and one which may not have been anticipated when the Freedom of Information Act was passed."[46] He concluded his ruling by repeating that sentiment, and (note: the commissioner writes his opinions in the third person) that (emphasis added):

> 28. . . . In his recently published guidance on official information held in private emails, he acknowledges the practical difficulties

public authorities face when the need to search private email accounts is identified. *The Commissioner is conscious that in this case, he has only been able to reach a decision because the email was sent to him by the complainant.* He has acknowledged in this decision notice that officials at the DfE were not aware of the full contents of the email until the Commissioner forwarded it to them. Although he has some sympathy with the officials dealing with this matter in these circumstances, consideration of the means by which the email came into the hands of the complainant is not within his remit. He notes, however, that the authenticity of the email sent to him by the complainant has not been disputed.

29. The use of private email accounts instead of departmental accounts for the conduct of official business is a matter of concern to the Commissioner for a number of reasons. Adherence to good records management practice should be encouraged to promote data security, to preserve the integrity of the public record and to ensure effective compliance with access to information obligations.[47]

Notice his recognition that this practice was only caught because one of the emails leaked. Also catch his sympathy lying with the civil servants who will need to search Gmail, AOL, and Yahoo accounts—not with the employees who feel pressures due to the FOI law and seek to hide their official business there. Taxpayer servants who retreat to private email accounts, which is reasonably presumed to be an effort to dodge disclosure laws to which they have agreed to comply, are not victims when found out.

The commissioner also refers readers to his guidance, "Official information held in private email accounts: Freedom of Information Act," which is "intended to clarify the legal status under FOIA of information relating to the business of a public authority held in private email accounts in particular, but also other media formats," noting that to be "an emerging area of FOIA compliance."[48]

So here is the precedent applying the basic principle that official business remains official business, no matter how you skirt the law and hide it from the taxpayers. "Information held in non-work personal email accounts (e.g., Hotmail, Yahoo, and Gmail) may be subject to FOIA if it relates to the official business of the public authority. All such information which is held by someone who has a direct, formal connection with the public authority is potentially subject to FOIA regardless of whether it is held in an official or private email account. If the information held in a private account amounts to public authority business it is very likely to be held on behalf of the public authority in accordance with" the act.[49] "It may be necessary to request relevant individuals to search private email accounts in particular cases."[50]

It also is necessary to have them swear out the relevant details of searching for, preserving, and deleting those records.

"Ministers and officials are not banned from using private email for government business as long as they disclose it. However, it is illegal to conceal information concerning government business from those seeking public documents under the FoI Act."[51] The message was clear: use these accounts all you want, but they are not a safe house from scrutiny.

In the United States, federal government employees are expected, according to agency policy, to forward all such emails to their government-issued accounts, or otherwise to make and maintain copies for the agency's access, with paper copies being the gold standard of record preservation according to government attorneys. When employees are *specifically* instructed that this expectation also indicates that destroying these emails constitutes an unlawful act, we will have made progress. And we should expect to see a spike in texting by government employees. Until this redoubt, too, is eliminated.

And it will be. Consider the ICO's phrase "[r]elevant information in other forms." There, as with our federal FOIA law, "'information . . . means information recorded in any form.' Therefore, official information recorded on mobile devices, including text messages on mobile phones, or in any other media, may also be considered to be held on behalf of the public authority" (ellipses in original).[52] Similarly, the United States Code's definition of "records" for purposes of maintenance and destruction "includes all books, papers, maps, photographs, machine readable materials, or other documentary materials, *regardless of physical form or characteristics, made or received by an agency of the United States Government under Federal law or in connection with the transaction of public business and preserved or appropriate for preservation by that agency* or its legitimate successor as evidence of the organization, functions, policies, decisions, procedures, operations, or other activities of the Government or because of the informational value of data in them" (emphasis added).[53]

Then of course some other effort to defeat the law will be experimented with, for the reason that government employees are trying to hide their written records, which the laws require be made, behavior exhibited in exaggerated form by liberals who have turned the notions of transparency and disclosure on their heads now that they control the institutions subject to transparency laws.

When this is pressed in the courts we should expect a similar outcome here as is found in the British ruling, whose language also sounds familiar having read the Waxman report. So, of course, we ought to expect bipartisan agreement on the outrage of these evasive and otherwise improper practices.

We ought to expect this in a world less disingenuous than exists in Washington, I should say. In the real Washington, Waxman received evidence obtained by Consumer Watchdog (in 2010) of White House staff using private email accounts to do official business, the very behavior that Waxman had declared during the Bush administration to be the stuff of legal violations requiring investigation. When, in 2012, I asked committee majority staff (now Republican) about the state of play of the inquiry prompted by the evidence obtained by Consumer Watchdog, they had no idea that any such evidence had been transmitted to the committee, or that such a request for investigation was made. Two staff including one counsel indicated they had no knowledge or record of the committee having been informed of this call for a similar inquiry.

We know that the then-chairman decided against replicating his umbrage about charges involving the Bush White House, when confronted with proof of Obama's White House engaging in the practice. In fact, it looks as if liberal Henry Waxman sat on it.

Applying existing law and common sense that should have governed throughout, this recognition in the United Kingdom nonetheless signals big changes there, and big trouble for the Obama administration. As one British media outlet put it, "It would seem that as the UK has followed the US in its freedom of information laws, so our politicians seem to have also followed their Washington DC colleagues in their attempts to evade the law,"[54] with the latter assertion linking to a Waxman outburst about . . . using private email accounts to avoid creating a record.[55] Which bombast he then holstered when presented a demand for investigation of the same activity by the Obama White House. One that he, with some irony, apparently elected to not disclose to his colleagues on the committee.

And, of course, these principles also extend to using nonofficial equipment like computers to defeat transparency laws, which, as discussed elsewhere here, is also occurring.

Other shoes began to drop immediately. "Civil servants were unable to find specific messages, circulated between Mr Gove and his advisers, when asked to retrieve them under the Act,"[56] wrote another story titled "Michael Gove aides 'destroyed government emails.'" Another's subhead intoned, "Civil servants have been warned that using private email accounts for official business in an effort to dodge Freedom of Information Act requests is a criminal offence."[57]

Team Obama should take note that, in addition to a failure to offer good-faith service to the government being a violation of ethics laws, barring unique circumstances this practice can also rise to the level of a criminal offense here in the States. It just won't be prosecuted so long as Eric Holder is attorney general.

9.

Using Private Computers to
Keep Official Business from Prying Eyes

O ther problems besides FOIA exist for secretive White House employees and, arguably, throughout the U.S. federal government. These are the record retention and preservation statutes of the Presidential and the Federal records acts. These, probably as much as FOIA, have spawned the creativity by Obama appointees and others in government to avoid transparency. We know about Obama White House aides systemically arranging meetings off campus to avoid creating the required record of their activities, and using private email accounts to avoid capture and preservation of any records created privately, even though any given email is by no means certain to be classified by their office as a "record."

But the threat of retention and preservation apparently triggers other means to escape disclosure, which is to avoid the documents from ever appearing on one's official computer.

One approach around that for the activist bureaucrat or political appointee committed to keeping his activities secret would appear to be simply accessing records on an off-site computer (a laptop, home or public library computer, or one at a congressional office or agency employing a friend not likely to receive FOIA requests for the same kind of records). Still, under the law that should nonetheless qualify the documents as being "received by" an employee, and therefore still subject to capture under FOIA. That is, if the kind of record has been ruled on by that office as being a "record."

Regardless, in character and under the law, using a private computer is equivalent to using private email accounts to conduct official business, whether sanctioned or not. The benefit such efforts possibly offer is that the activity is unlikely to be discovered and so, like using a private email, a government employee may have plausible deniability about whether records being sought do or ever did exist. Of course, it is even possible that an agency discovers that work is being performed in this fashion and still allows employees to get away with it. Keep reading.

But government employees would never do that. Right?

Wrong. I have confirmed that federal employees are using private computers to conduct official government business, even quite possibly White House business, free from ready capture by federal document preservation systems. This is not only the logical conclusion in some cases, but has also been admitted to me, orally by administration counsel, and in a different case altogether in a filing by the Obama administration in federal court. Ironically, the latter was done to excuse the administration's failure to produce emails exposing improper employee activism on taxpayer time. But, in so doing, they admitted to allowing employee abuses that may, as with private email accounts, prove terribly embarrassing and even scandalous in the end. As they should. But, no doubt, not without a protracted legal battle. As the case that revealed that practice is proving to be, mired in court for two years and counting.

One other example that may provide the precedential case involves the discovery of how the administration helped create the already-described electronic safe house with the UN and left-wing activist groups expressly to get around FOIA.

Using personal equipment or accounts, clearly discouraged by policy and regulation, gives the taxpayer no guarantee that the required paper trail or otherwise any record of the activity will be created, except what is on their private equipment. It again leaves matters subject to an honor system. GAO writes that "in a decentralized environment, it is difficult to ensure that records are properly identified and managed by end users on individual desktops (the 'user challenge')."[1] This of course extends to and is compounded by use of personal or otherwise unofficial equipment. GAO concluded that no matter how stringent the technology, this can always be circumvented "without commitment from agencies." This commitment does not exist.

Further, the practice of using unofficial computers is discouraged except when it isn't. There are employees using unofficial computers for a substantial portion of their work and not subversively, but often and with the government's approval. EPA, for example, aggressively encourages telecommuting, promoting "Earth Month" and seeking to reduce employee "carbon footprints."[2] Other agencies encourage employees to do so, providing employees "RSA tokens" (authentication security measures allowing external access to internal, for example, email systems), implying the use of private computers to conduct official business. At EPA, these tokens proved too large an expense, with so many employees working on public business on private computers, that the agency switched to a Web-based system enabling the practice.

Yet with exceptions involving classified and similar information, federal employees generally are not expressly prohibited from working on private computers or accounts. Instead, when they do they are expected under each agency's record-retention policies to retain and preserve all such records, copying the agency on the records or at minimum making them available. This can be in electronic format but to this day paper copies are considered the ideal.

From my experience and interviews with government FOIA specialists and lawyers, the practice seems to be that when an employee does preserve records, that does not equate with regularly turning over copies. Unless they inform the agency of their behavior, this record is beyond the government's reach. "NARA found that almost 80 percent of agencies were at moderate to high risk of unlawful destruction of records."[3] That these are employees who in many (but not all) cases first chose to step outside the rules to do something that is discouraged, and which is just what one would do to avoid disclosure of his activities, indicates a low likelihood that they will inform their superiors and provide the government full and accurate copies if the records are the sort likely to be subjects of FOIA requests.

There is a government-wide record preservation schedule and then individual agency schedules with different retention periods for different sorts of information. In other words, how this is done in practice is often on an agency-by-agency basis, but all employees agree to be aware of, understand, and obey these schedules.

In so subjective a system and with few bright-line rules, and with so much left to the employee who has the incentive to blur or cross what lines there are, this system invites trouble. This is particularly so with the Obama administration, hyperpoliticized and having shown such disdain for transparency and disclosure laws that we can identify systemic practices to subvert them.

And now we know the invitation for mischief was irresistible.

That this is going on, and abusively, is not supposition. I raised the prospect with an administration lawyer opposite me in a FOIA case, noting my past experience, current suspicions with the White House, and the unfolding British scandal with Gmail. He responded by admitting awareness of the practice, that it is not isolated, and even that in the case we were working on the government had sent a chief information officer to the home of a senior official to review her computer and private email account after we had elevated our pursuit of certain controversial records to involve lawyers. These are records that the same employee had denied existed, knowing they did but creating a reason to not consider them, tens of thousands of pages of which the agency was now compiling to provide me and Congress to satisfy the request.

Consider the White House signing off on use of private computer servers brought online for the purpose of subverting IPCC-related record production, and possibly (the White House answers, often overdue, have been slippery) executed in a way that foils document preservation regimes.

After I learned of those private computer servers the Obama administration had agreed to use, I sought all records viewed on them, arguing that any such record, no matter where stored, was received by the agency in question at the time it was viewed and therefore was subject to FOIA. If they had to go to the server to pull it, or provide me the username and password, I wanted those records.

Two agencies stonewalled me, cold: NOAA, and the State Department, the latter taking more than four months simply to send a letter acknowledging the request but to date, after three-quarters of a year, it still has produced no records. The third, the White House Office of Science and Technology Policy, was responsive after I drew media and congressional attention to their specific involvement.

That is because this was an office that required watching. For whatever reason, upon taking office the Obama administration yanked the lead on American involvement in the IPCC from NOAA (our career employee friends who have so much difficulty with IPCC-related FOIA requests), moving it to the Executive Office of the President. OSTP was led by the controversial Dr. John Holdren, dubbed by some, in keeping with the times, Obama's "science czar," who drew interest for his cooling-, then warming-, but always anti-population enthusiasm.[4] His strange history is a varied one[5] and includes noodling about sterilizing the incorrigibly fecund population through the drinking water supply[6] and arguing against having "too much energy."[7] Apparently there's a downside to needing fewer workers for tasks of drudgery and manual labor (if you wondered what inspired Obama's musings about the havoc wrought on employment by ATMs and airport kiosks).[8]

So let's not assume Holdren would be appalled by using private servers or otherwise private computers to avoid public scrutiny of the "cause," to which he was a fully paid-up subscriber.

After I publicized this, two Republican chairmen in the House of Representatives, James Sensenbrenner, vice chairman of the Committee on Science, Space and Technology, and Paul Broun of its Subcommittee on Investigations and Oversight, wrote Holdren asking for an explanation. Holdren wrote back on November 17, 2011, and acknowledged the existence of the servers ("Author Portals") and more, stating in relevant part:

> These portals are used . . . to distribute information to authors and reviewers. . . . The portals are also used to share documents, such as drafts of technical reports, among authors and reviewers. . . .

If a U.S. government employee accesses a document through the
Portal, a copy of the document is downloaded onto the employee's
Federal government computer. If a U.S. Government employee
wishes to share a document with other authors or reviewers via the
Portal, the document must be created or modified on a Federal government computer and then uploaded to the Portal. Thus, all documents downloaded from or uploaded to the Portal remain on the
employee's Federal government computer, where they are subject to
applicable Federal laws, including the Freedom of Information Act.

The good news is that, with the plan having been exposed, this statement represents the Obama White House openly disputing the IPCC's
unilaterally conjured exemption from FOIA for work by federal employees contributing to these doomsday reports designed to influence
national policy, and coerce agreement to regimes like the Kyoto treaty.

The actual candor of this disavowal remains to be seen and will be
resolved by further pressure to release records as the IPCC goes through
the motions of its next end-is-nigh proclamation designed to influence
U.S. economic and energy policy, due out in 2013. Regardless, this
statement must be read in the context of being written after the off-site
servers had been discovered, and recalling the servers' origins. While
expressing earnest fealty to the law it resolves nothing about how the
law is actually being complied with, but instead begs several more questions. The one clear answer Holdren gave came in a later correction to
his denial[9] that anyone at OSTP had accessed these servers, admitting
in a January 30, 2012, letter that in fact one had done so[10] after OSTP
provided me a partially redacted "email communication between OSTP
and the [IPCC]" under FOIA exposing this.

The second point of importance in Holdren's statement to Congress
is that any record viewed on OSTP computers would be captured; and
so long as they are not destroyed, as he implies they are not, they would
be subject to (though not necessarily produced under) FOIA.

That abounds with problems. First, there is nothing to stop a U.S.
government (USG) employee from accessing such documents on other

than a government-issued computer; there is not in fact, as is implied, any systemic protocol either informal (written) or formal (enforced; for example, if the system only allows access from confirmed USG computers). We know this for reasons including that most authors and reviewers are not USG employees, and they presumably are not precluded from accessing the servers. Many come from left-wing pressure groups. In fact the one OSTP staffer whom I established, through FOIA, had been assigned a username and password came to OSTP from an activist group called Climate Central, Inc., for which he served as . . . an IPCC lead author. The green-group contributor and contribution became the White House's.

Another question Holdren begs is whether OSTP has made a determination as required under the FRA that such documents when viewed and captured are (or are not) "federal records" documentary of the organization, functions, operations, or other activities of the government, or because of the informational value of data in them. If not, then by implying that records downloaded are preserved Holden's letter was misleading. He needs to clearly state whether there is a policy prohibiting their being erased, or whether he required, and ensured, that they were retained. I have asked for a clear answer, and as of this writing still await it.

Here is why. In the one email OSTP coughed up, the IPCC correspondent "Dave" (last name redacted) provides OSTP Senior Policy Analyst Philip Duffy with a username and password to access the servers. (Although I specifically asked for the password and username in my request, it was redacted; I did not appeal but may specifically request it later, setting up a rollicking battle.) An attached thread to the message (the original email from which it is excerpted was inexplicably not provided) includes a confirmation from Duffy that "the portal resides at Stanford on hardware owned by Carnegie."[11] Carnegie refers to the Carnegie Institute for Science, a private, if federally funded, nonprofit group.

The server itself, therefore, is presumably beyond FOIA's reach, which was its purpose. Documents downloaded from it are not, unless

OSTP refuses to declare them "records" and promptly destroys its copy each time. I plan to continue requesting whatever documents have been downloaded, again setting up a battle over their tactics to keep secret what is publicly owned.

This email established that Holdren's aide, a former pressure-group activist who apparently "won . . . the 2007 Nobel Peace Prize"[12] (but not really), asked for and was given access to the server. However, OSTP gave me a "no records" reply to my request for any records viewed on this server. OSTP's subsequent story to the House chairmen and then to me when I pressed the issue was that the aide only obtained the user-name and password to see what the fuss was all about after my FOIA and subsequent congressional interest, but he didn't really view any re-cords. OSTP thereby informed me and Congress that no one at OSTP is actually working on the 2013 IPCC Fifth Assessment Report presently being developed.

"[O]n OSTP computers."

This is entirely possible, though with each new request we will see how long this is maintained; at some point it will be implausible and we will have no choice but to conclude they are either using personal computers or have still refused to decide if these are "Records," or have decided they are not and are destroying their versions.

As to the first possibility, in response to my follow-up, OSTP denied that this activist in the Obama White House used a personal computer to perform this particular official business of accessing the off-site server.

It is appropriate to recognize that agencies will on occasion say excul-patory things, and take positions to avoid producing records, that upon scrutiny cannot be backed up. However, this came in reply to an appeal, handled by counsel, which at least at other agencies (where there are more career lawyers, as opposed to political appointees) is when employ-ees are asked to attest to such questions. Their response did not indicate such formal attestation was obtained.

We know this White House's history and even culture of circum-venting transparency and disclosure laws. We know they participated in setting up a private server to conduct official business on this topic, expressly to avoid FOIA. We know that at least one OSTP employee has sought and been assigned a username and password for this server, while confirming the server was privately owned and managed.

And we also know that some federal employees, including those working in the same field, use nonofficial equipment to perform official work, and that the government declares this beyond its reach.

So I admit that I am skeptical. And the FOIA requests of OSTP will continue as the IPCC process continues. It remains entirely possible that we will continue to be told that a project on which the U.S. taxpayer is spending millions and millions of dollars, highly discredited as it has been in recent years for unsupportable claims and deceptive behavior, is not actually receiving any participation from the lead federal office tasked with providing the United States' contribution to help shape the project and its products.

Now that we have discovered the effort to move records to off-site, private computers, I'm not sure there's a good answer for the Obama White House on this one. But something that has a solid ring of truth to it will suffice.

They Swear They're Using Private Computers for Official Business

That political appointees and career activists in government would use private computers is in keeping with tactics we have uncovered, from the use of private emails, hiding meetings with lobbyists, using handles and cutouts as already described, to the fact that they went along with creating such a supposed safe harbor to intentionally evade FOIA.

But I happen to have an affidavit admitting to this specific practice. This was provided me by NASA in September 2010 in a FOIA lawsuit we filed at the Competitive Enterprise Institute to obtain records of a scientist who was running a third-party activist website promoting an ideological agenda on taxpayer time. (This was again in the context of "global warming," as many of my findings have been, since my work has concentrated on energy and environmental policy; the preponderance of these examples in one area likely indicates their widespread enjoyment, unless of course there is something uniquely sneaky about global warming and anti-energy ideologues . . .)

The administration attested in federal court that the career employee/ activist was using a nongovernmental computer to perform this work as well as certain official duties. They did so in order to defend their failure to provide certain emails to and from the employee's email accounts relating to this activity, saying that because the emails were written or accessed on this unofficial computer, under their system this made the official emails beyond the administration's reach.

Yeah, they said that. And as a virtue, somehow.

So to claim that NASA was reasonably searching for responsive records, they admitted the very practice taking place in one global warming activist's taxpayer office—NASA's Goddard Institute for Space Studies (GISS), run by Al Gore advisor and alarmist extraordinaire James Hansen—that one could reasonably suspect is taking place in another such bastion of climate agenda activism, John Holdren's OSTP. By pure coincidence both individuals are activists in the same field: the blogger, Gavin Schmidt, hired by Hansen as his protégé, and the OSTP aide hired away from a green pressure group.

The affidavit, by GISS's Associate Chief Larry D. Travis, attests in pertinent part:

> Dr. Schmidt uses two separate computers on which he conducts his work for NASA. . . . One computer Dr. Schmidt uses is a laptop computer that is owned by NASA. . . . The other computer is a desktop computer owned by Columbia University. Dr. Schmidt purchased this computer with National Science Foundation grant monies he received while he was an employee of Columbia University, prior to his becoming a civil servant with [NASA]; . . . [T]he [Space Station Program or SSP] contract providing IT support to GISS covers service for this computer. Nevertheless, Dr. Schmidt maintains this computer; SSP does not regularly service Dr. Schmidt's computer and no SSP contractor has administrative privileges on the computer. Dr. Schmidt's email correspondence is stored on his

Columbia desktop computer [NB: that's the private one, paid for not by Schmidt but by the taxpayer, to which he does not allow NASA access]. Dr. Schmidt accesses his Columbia University email via an Internet browser on the computer. Dr. Schmidt does not download his Columbia email messages to his computer; rather, they are located on a remote Columbia mail server.[13]

The reference to the Columbia University email account goes back to the issue that official or work-related business performed in any way remains official. It's just that we see here a way around it: refuse the government access to the account and the computer you use to access it. In its pleadings with the court, NASA has described this as "the non-NASA computer,"[14] "a computer that the Agency does not own, to which the Agency has no right of access, and for which no Agency official or contractor has administrative privileges."[15]

NASA's boast is that official records can be and are accessed by private computers, and that this not only corrupts the agency's ability to properly comply with FOIA, it erodes the agency's record retention and preservation. Elsewhere in the affidavit NASA states that the computer Schmidt uses is

a desktop . . . which Dr. Schmidt uses to send and receive all of his email from the @giss.nasa.gov, @nasa.gov, @columbia.edu, and @realclimate.org domains. See Travis Decl. ¶ 18. Dr. Schmidt has never given administrative information technology ("IT") privileges for either computer to the IT support services contractor that serves Agency personnel. See id. Thus, the email sought here is relayed to and resides on a computer that the Agency does not own, to which the Agency has no right of access, and for which no Agency official or contractor has administrative privileges. Moreover, there is no central mechanism by which GISS IT personnel can obtain access remotely to email sent to or received by a GISS email user; instead, the only way to reach such email would be via directly accessing the hard drive of the computer on which the user accessed his or her GISS email. See id. at ¶ 12b.[16]

This is outrageous, as is the fact that it is condoned. NASA is hereby knowingly sanctioning a corruption of responsibilities to create, retain, and preserve documents, both for the Federal Records Act and for FOIA. This ain't rocket science. But we do know it is with NASA's sanction.

Moreover, as Dr. Travis explains, even with respect to the emails from the @giss.nasa.gov and @nasa.gov domains, these have not been integrated into an agency record system or file.

> Once a[n agency] employee accesses his or her [agency] email via his or her personal computer, those emails are no longer located on any server at [the agency]; in other words, the act of accessing a specific email deletes that email from the 'spool' on the server. [The agency] does not currently have (nor has it had in the past) a centralized backup of [agency] email traffic." Id. at ¶ 12b. Moreover, even if the Agency did have a centralized backup of emails from the @giss.nasa .gov or @nasa.gov domains, emails sent or received by Dr. Schmidt pertaining to his work on the RealClimate blog would not be integrated into an Agency records system or file. . . . [17]

NASA's point was that its own system has gotten so far out of their control that, well, an entire class of records cannot possibly be deemed "agency records" and so they have no obligation to search for or release them because the truth is while they may relate to official business, gosh, their employee won't let them see them. And as is inherent in the system, the approved process has largely destroyed them.

One could not hope to find a more explicit acknowledgment—or, more accurately, series of admissions, enthusiastically volunteered in an effort to get out of one frying pan (producing incriminating emails) into an apparently bigger fire—that employees use unofficial computers for official duties and keep the records accessed on these computers away from the prying taxpayer eyes by skirting FOIA. They even use them to access official email accounts in a way that destroys the record.

So, liberals are using unofficial computers to perform official work and shake off the nagging system of information access and document retention designed to let the public know what their government is up to. We know they're doing it, and they've said so in court. They boasted of it. It matters not that this admission came as a way to avoid FOIA. This tipped their hand as to a tactic that likely would have gone unnoticed, and might well lead ultimately to bigger disclosures, and revelations.

When these means of evading relevant laws are resolved by the courts, as they must be given the apparently widespread nature of their employment, it surely will be determined to be a futile, desperate gasp. Unfortunately, this particular case is languishing, with no action to move it forward to the merits, and so relevant abuses are allowed to escape resolution. Which sometimes happens.

As we have already been forced to argue to the Obama White House and expect to soon argue in court, conducting public business on private phones or computers doesn't make the business, and therefore the records, any less public. This particular example is simply an extreme case of flaunting disregard for this principle, particularly given NASA's brazenness of sanctioning it and invoking the abusive practices as an expedient excuse to not turn over records produced on taxpayer time and resources.

10.

It's Academic: Campus Activists Want Your Money, Not Your Scrutiny

Research published in 2012 indicated a long-term decline in trust, specifically by more educated conservatives, not of science but of "the people running the institutions" of science. As succinctly captured by University of Tennessee law professor and Instapundit blogger Glenn Reynolds, "The reason is the use of science as an argument-from-authority for bigger government. If scientists want more trust, perhaps they should try not to be tools."[1] Sage advice. The truth is that these taxpayer-dependent advocates have, in direct proportion to the riches flowing from us to them, increasingly soiled their own nest with scandal, regularly in service to ideology or just more taxpayer money.

And now they want exemption from scrutiny. Because scrutiny hasn't been serving them too well. Sounds to me like, if anything, they need more.

But, tools will be tools. This research into public trust was conducted after those revelations in 2009 and 2011 of widespread and organized efforts by British and American academics to destroy emails and other records being sought by FOIA requests, or to copy, delete, and remove copies off-site to similarly keep them from prying eyes. These revelations in turn led to the broader effort by Big Science and their doppelganger Big Academia to block other requests from being honored and, looking forward, to escape coverage from FOI laws. With their enablers in other

leftist circles, including political ones, they've circled the wagons to declare the application of FOI laws to, and even antifraud statutes requiring release of, "their" records outrage.

Do not allow their frothing to obscure the progression: requests for
documents led to scandalous practices to hide and destroy the records
that, when exposed, led to more requests for records that, if fully revealed, threatened to derail their lucrative ride on the taxpayer's back.
At that point, official academia manned the ramparts, discovering their
repressed concerns over, for example, FOI laws, sublimated until then
with the comforting knowledge and experience that those laws were only
used to cause trouble for those who threatened their franchise.

Exposure of miscreant behavior led to calls for exemption from exposure for the first time, despite legislative inquiry, drafting, and enactment,
then implementation of the FOI laws and the passage of many years
without complaint. Academia had now been burned by the taxpayer
seeing what the taxpayer was paying for, and the grandees decided it was
time to say what had to be said: We're different. Laws are for you, not for
us. Keep the money coming. But take your "strings" and stuff them.

With the arrogance and strained relationship with rationality we have
come to expect of academics, they are now campaigning (including in
the UVa lawsuit to which I am co-counsel and, I suspect, one or two
more we will file soon out of necessity) to expand their status as a politically preferred class. They demand we extend the preferences granted
them, now all the way to exemption from requirements applying to
other taxpayer-funded realms.

As noted, this first came to our shores from England, if hardly with
a stiff upper lip. Instead it was a response to the scandal being centered
there, at a taxpayer-funded university subject to FOI but unlawfully
withholding records under that law. We've already seen warnings to the
House of Commons by two universities, Nottingham Trent University
and London's University of the Arts, that the wrong kind of people with
motives not shared by academics using FOIA was a prospect so horrify-
ing that the law should let those schools refuse to give information to
people they don't trust.

In our litigation with UVa, the following gratifying exchange occurred right up front in the April 2012 hearing, throwing a wrench in at least one party's plans for the day:

THE COURT: Let me interrupt you a second.

MR. FONTAINE: Yes, sir.

THE COURT: Modern American debate seems to require us to accuse adversaries of improper motives. We see that in the public forum all the time. What if, for general purposes, all of those bad motives are true? How does it affect the legal right to FOIA protection? Are we—do we have a purity of heart test before we apply FOIA's legislative acts?

MR. FONTAINE: No, Your Honor, the law on that is quite clear. It is not really the Court's function to try to weigh the motives.

THE COURT: Well, then, why are you arguing that to me?

Within days of the court putting a stop to ad hominem employed to distract from the substance, a reporter for the liberal *Los Angeles Times* named Neela Banerjee emailed me and my colleague David Schnare stating that she wanted to write about us, and reiterating the arguments that the court had firmly instructed counsel were not relevant. It seemed that, if the courts will not allow themselves to be used in such fashion, the media were perfectly willing. This was for a story with a deadline just days away, she said. Months later, no such story had run. Possibly the reporter's editors showed different judgment. Possibly, as is reasonable to conclude, this had an errand-boy aspect to it.

Apropos of nothing in particular, I note an email sent by Michael Mann to Phil Jones in August 2007, which I provided to Banerjee as a courtesy in one of my responses to her interest, along with some wonderful excerpts from our trial transcript that I admit made writing the sort of piece she indicated she was working on a little less easy to credibly do. That Mann email stated in pertinent part:

I have been talking w/ folks in the states about finding an investigative journalist to investigate and expose McIntyre, and his thus far
unexplored connections with fossil fuel interests. Perhaps the same
needs to be done w/ this [troublesome researcher, Doug] Keenan
guy.

I believe that the only way to stop these people is by exposing them
and discrediting them.[2]

Substance obviously wasn't going to work. So maybe he was right.

Amid these and related efforts by academics, sanity gamely sought
recognition, in the form of the United Kingdom's information commissioner, Christopher Graham (he who affirmed that using private email
accounts will not succeed in keeping public business secret). "'Is academic research really threatened by the prospect of premature release of
data sets? Are ministers living in fear?' Graham asked a government com-
puting conference [in February 2012]. 'The Chicken Licken version of
the FOI that the sky is falling is just that: it's a folktale—and the trouble
with folktales is people start reacting to what they think is the case even
when it isn't.'"[3] Later that month the British government rejected these
cries for special treatment.[4]

Other glimmers of hope emerged. One came in a public forum styled
as "Data debate: Is transparency bad for science?" sponsored at Imperial
College, London. This, too, obviously was prompted by the emerging
specter of FOIA-driven transparency breaking out all over the land, as
was written into the law to no protest just a few years prior. High-profile
participants included *Guardian* columnist and green zealot George
Monbiot, philosopher/academic and appointed member of the House
of Lords Baroness Onora O'Neill, and one scientist, David Colquhoun
(who impressed with his stance, "Give them everything!").[5]

O'Neill's discourse contained a typical curiosity about whether, really,
the unwashed are sufficiently competent to deserve seeing public records
that they paid for, if held by academics. This seemed to unnerve even
Monbiot, by "seeming to introduce the idea that maybe data should be

tailored to the competency of the receiver. This rightly outraged George who asked Onora whether she meant that data should only be available to someone deemed 'competent.' Onora denied that was what she said but explained herself by repeating the same idea. Not a good tactic."[6]

Meanwhile, Back in the States

The U.S. faction stepped up their contribution to the movement when requests for information picked up steam here, pulling threads exposed by that scandalous Climategate leak of records, many of which were subject to federal and state FOI laws as well as the United Kingdom's. After a series of open letters and organized appeals they received an assist from the scientific establishment's loftiest quarters, with *Science* magazine prominently featuring a letter signed by 250 members of the National Academy of Sciences titled "Climate Change and the Integrity of Science." Published on May 8, 2010, it opened, "We are deeply disturbed by the recent escalation of political assaults on scientists in general and on climate scientists in particular."[7]

Requests for information that the taxpayer paid for, shining light on the development of arguments being used to demand more money and sacrifice from the taxpayer and bestow more authority and importance to government and academia, were "political assaults." Left uncharacterized was the unique status academics had already been granted by the political class, as well-fed protectorates of the state. Is this not a political assault on the taxpayer? They weren't saying.

Although the letter identified not one party who is "harass[ing]" them or behind "the outright lies spread about" scientists (which lies were also left unspoken), it takes little imagination to discern which activities got their goat. After all, these and similar types had already campaigned against, most prominently, the Virginia attorney general's request for records under a taxpayer protection, antifraud statute, my own request for the same records, and requests by me and others for IPCC-related records under various FOI laws.

With what soon proved to be uniquely satisfying irony, the lead signatory on the letter was Peter Gleick, a "MacArthur Genius" prize winner residing at the Pacific Institute in Oakland, California, which institute he founded. A year and a half later Gleick was exposed as having assumed a false identity to obtain private records of a group with whom he disagreed and, according to forensic analysis, "more likely than not" having created a fake document,[8] all while claiming that an unidentified whistleblower had provided it to him.

All of these signatories were the sort of "leading lights" the *Wall Street Journal's* Anne Jolis wrote about when describing other "caviling" by such cheerleaders for and sometimes active participants in a movement "brainstorming to pressure journals and review boards to suppress work that challenged their theories, trading tips on how to avoid public-information requests and planning how to present their findings so as to best further 'the cause.'"[9]

Yet here these professional passengers on a taxpayer-financed gravy train portray themselves and colleagues as victims of "political assaults," invoking Joseph McCarthy as you just knew they would. Assuming authority grounded in credentials, which, if it exists, is politically derived, they style opposition to them as illegitimate for being political. Meanwhile, evincing a lack of self-awareness that seems to be required in their field, they made plain to the rest of us that this authority they proclaim is not merely to proclaim truths, but is a political authority.

But, they insist, let's keep politics out of this, shall we? The poor dears would actually occupy a very different station in life but for the grace given them by politics.

And the opening paragraph of this same piece was of course a political appeal demanding enactment of policies, openly calling on "policymakers and the public to move forward immediately . . . [against] the unrestrained burning of fossil fuels," the supposed horrors of which they also insisted they need not make the case about. Removing any doubt possibly remaining, *Scientific American* senior editor Gary Stix later published an editorial titled "Effective World Government Will Be Needed to Stave Off Climate Catastrophe," calling for creation of "a new set of institutions [that] would have to be imbued with heavy-handed, transnational enforcement powers . . . capable of instilling a permanent crisis mentality lasting decades, if not centuries," begging the ultimate question, "How do we create new institutions with enforcement powers way beyond the current mandate of the U.N.?"[10] (Hint: start by not boasting that that's what you're doing.) Not to be outdone, *Science* magazine then ran a similar article, tellingly under the heading "Policy Forum" and boasting more than twenty authors, titled "Navigating the Anthropocene: Improving Earth System Governance."[11]

But, by all means, keep those horrid politics away from us. Hmm.

In their deflection, projection, and self-pity the open letter signatories also lost sight of their own agreement to external (public and political) oversight as a condition of their professional livelihoods, regardless of how much they may personally disagree with such constrictions as laws and conditions on taking public monies. The law may be the law, and agreed conditions may be agreed conditions. But, darn it, they insist that we stop looking into their claims—the claims' substance, mind you, in which they ground their claimed authority—and instead just accept their demands of economic policies, impacting us all and for generations, despite the further debilitating fact that such policymaking is out of the realm of any plausible expertise they might claim or imply.

Who needs "ask not what your country can do for you," or, "Mr. Gorbachev, tear down this wall," when in the mirror you see Bill Murray saying, "Back off man, I'm a scientist"?

Transparency is for schmucks, and besides, science can police its own ranks. They wrote, "Like all human beings, scientists make mistakes, but the scientific process is designed to find and correct them." Always beginning sometime tomorrow.

Of all we have learned since emails first leaked in November 2009 about the specific scandal from which they here are seeking to evade consequences, one lesson is indisputable, and that is that they are not interested in self-policing in any meaningful sense of the term. They will drum out critics, seek to have them fired, block their ability to publish, initiate all manner of nasty campaigns against them to avoid criticism, making object lessons of those who dare. But beyond risible "mistakes were made" vagaries, it's always time to move on, with the only reforms necessary being whatever must be done to avoid getting caught again.

And, like a lucrative football program with errant coaching staff, they will whitewash their own scandals. In fact, as noted below, Penn State proved this by responding to the scandal in its football program and Michael Mann's troubles in almost identical fashion. The key is to "move on."

They want the money. They do not want the strings, like transparency and accountability.

Academics Under Siege?

Other outbursts included an unintentionally hilarious letter to the president of the University of Virginia by the American Association of University Professors, the American Geophysical Union, and the Union of Concerned Scientists calling on the university to back out of a court-approved agreement and protective order to turn emails over to me and my colleague Dr. David Schnare, both bound to abide by the order as officers of the court.[12] Here we see more projection, as they argued we could not be trusted to keep with professional standards.

The agitated academics referred to UVa's efforts to fight release of "personal email correspondence and other documents from Dr. Michael Mann and more than thirty other scientists." So addled by a need for special treatment, the faculty temporarily lost possession of their logical faculties. These were of course by definition not personal emails, which the authors implicitly acknowledge by also asserting the correspondence was among scientific peers, about science. Going after others personally doesn't make such efforts "personal."

Regardless, showing true academic insight, they also stated that releasing the records—as the law on its face requires, and as was agreed to as a condition of their employment, meaning they took taxpayer money with a promise to abide by this—constitutes "harassment and intimidation." Just for them, of course. Not for the rest of those schlubs covered by FOIA, who of course are expected to be held to their promise. It's not like these academics advocate lawlessness or anything. Just special treatment when it threatens their sweet deal.

These activists, some with PhDs and therefore cloaking their activism as academia, found it "troubling that the agreement would allow ATI lawyers, including the very individuals who filed the open records request," those being me and Schnare, to read the records. There they go again with that whole *wrong kind of people* argument. Then, with equal persuasive force, they cited a *Washington Post* editorial—the one saying precisely the same thing, that people like Horner, well, we're not so sure they should have the same access under the laws—as evidence that the emails are probably exempt anyway. This is what one does when one has no legitimate argument, which, if it existed, we would have heard by now.

Even releasing records under a protective order, allowing review for purposes of identifying which emails whose claimed exemption we challenge in order to seek the court's ruling, "will send scientists at public institutions a message that communicating frankly with colleagues carries significant risk." Verily, one need not be an academic to see the obvious outcome: You are hereby charged with frankly communicating with your colleagues. Surely that's in the law books somewhere. Probably near the back. Or, possibly, what is being "frankly communicated" (as in, confessions are "frank communications") determines whether one puts one's self at risk.

This is a guilty conscience speaking, in code not exactly requiring a Cray supercomputer to decipher, admitting that the sort of communication that's there just might be like those that had been leaked or released under FOIA already, revealing hidden temperature declines, organized efforts to destroy and otherwise conceal covered records, and, worse, plots to retaliate against academic scientists on the basis of their work. (That means violating their "academic freedom." Remember that.) And this is the nominal basis for rewriting the laws designed to let the taxpayer know how his money is spent.

Such thinking proliferated in all the usual quarters, and then some. The AAUP had first joined a letter by twelve signatory groups including the American Civil Liberties Union of Virginia, People for the American Way, and, naturally, the Ornithological Council (apparent birds of a feather with ACLU and PFAW). They wrote the university several months before the other letter, flatly and accurately stating in their opening paragraph that we sought "a broad array of materials produced and exchanged by Professor Mann in the course of his work as a professor and scholar working on topics related to global climate change."[13] So much for "personal" emails. Oh, what a tangled web we weave . . .

They then gave the real game away, "urg[ing] the University of Virginia to follow Chancellor [Biddy] Martin's lead [at University of Wisconsin] in balancing the interests in public disclosure against the public interest in academic freedom, which the University of Virginia has recognized in its faculty handbook as 'an essential ingredient of an environment of academic excellence.'" Such a lofty balancing test they demand! On one scale rests a law, passed by the people's elected representatives to provide (all) taxpayers access to the records of institutions they pay for, including these. On the other is something in the UVa faculty handbook (but ignore the rest of the handbook, forms, policies, and rules making plain that these emails are subject to FOIA). Shades of the Left's recent confusion about "judicial activism."

Academic Freedom to Violate the Academic Freedom of Others

If "academic freedom" were a special privilege found in the Constitution, we by now surely would have had its presence identified from behind the emanations or penumbrae shielding it all these many years. Instead, as is ritual for our friends on the left who see Senator McCarthy under their bed where they dream dreams of manning the trenches of Madrid, they pointed to a 1950s case rejecting a loyalty oath for campus faculty (*Sweezy v. New Hampshire*, 354 U.S. 234 (1957)). "Sweezy" rolls off the woollier academic set's tongues as smoothly as *¡No Pasarán!*

More recently, and inconveniently, the federal court of appeals for the 4th Circuit (which includes Virginia) wrote the one opinion squarely on point. This case, *Urofsky v. Gilmore,* involved other Virginia college professors demanding to view porn on their university computers—science! Research! I get it for the articles!

That court wrote that, when it comes to "the speech of state employees in their capacity as employees"—as the ACLU et al. authors clearly admit is the case when Mann sent and received the work-related emails we sought—"[i]t cannot be doubted that in order to pursue its legitimate goals effectively, the Commonwealth must retain the ability to control the manner in which its employees discharge their duties and to direct its employees to undertake the responsibilities of their positions in a specified way."[14]

This translates to the present context thusly: The legislature decided to cover you under FOIA. Which is one reason you agreed that you had no expectation of email privacy. Deal with it. You want to plot against academics whose work debunks yours? Don't do it in writing. Otherwise, expect to be outed and people to obtain the rest of your opus.

Still, the *Sweezy* mythology dies hard, as academia seeks to wriggle out from under a law framing their privileged role, as at least in some respects, being the same as anyone else's. So it is worth noting the *Urofksy* opinion's lengthy discourse dismissing the promiscuous invocation of "academic freedom" without serious consideration for what that means.

Which is what liberals do. Jonah Goldberg's 2012 book, *The Tyranny of Clichés,* nails our leftist friends for a particular ritual, employed in many different forms but always to duck openness. His thesis, argued as usual with devastating effect, is that in order to disguise or simply avoid scrutiny of the substance of their demands, liberals "hide ideological claims in rhetorical Trojan horses, hoping to conquer terrain unearned by real debate," "reducing arguments"—which often aren't really arguments, hence the desire to avoid them—"to bumper stickers." He cites, for example, "diversity is strength." I nominate "Forward."

The tactic fits snugly here. Liberals are regularly engaged in rebranding campaigns to avoid embracing that they are liberals, but Goldberg's case applies equally to the left's campaign against transparency, advanced, with no sense of irony, in the name of free speech.

This is beautifully captured by their wrapping the bunting of "academic freedom" around this campaign in the UVa FOIA case to exempt and protect their redoubt of activism at public academic institutions from scrutiny—academia being one of the liberals' main vehicles for advancing their agenda, enabling claims that their prescriptions are no less than what physical and social science demand.

Letting the public see what they pay for in the name of research and education, which is too often political campaigning and ideological bilge from universities turned politically activist institutions—where no one forces liberals to work and where taxpayers cover the freight—is an "assault" on a constitutional right. Check back later as they are still trying to locate it in the actual Constitution.

There are reasons, becoming more apparent with each episode, why President Eisenhower's farewell address warned not only of the "military-industrial complex," but of something else:

> The prospect of domination of the nation's scholars by Federal employment, project allocations, and the power of money is ever present—and is gravely to be regarded. Yet, in holding scientific research and discovery in respect, as we should, we must also be alert to the equal and opposite danger that public policy could itself become the captive of a scientific-technological elite. It is the task of statesmanship to mold, to balance, and to integrate these and other forces, new and old, within the principles of our democratic system—ever aiming toward the supreme goals of our free society.[15]

Prescient. As my colleague David Schnare writes, "university faculties have always been closed, exclusive and highly self-protective tribal societies, [and] few tools exist to peek behind the ivy-covered walls. For public universities, state Freedom of Information laws offer citizens the means to see how these public servants spend the people's money. The tension is between the right of citizens to monitor the work of their employees and the need for faculty to be able to conduct research without undue interference before it is published."[16] Sure, faculty require a free ability to be curious without undue interference—including from politically preferred movements—such that "emails about research should not be subject to FOIA prior to publication of the research, but should be available upon publication"; but claiming some publication may result some day is a stall not a sufficient basis to deny the taxpayer the information he paid for and deserves. Treating them like they really are like others living off of the state gives academics "the incentive they need to be ethical and otherwise professional, while both the public and other scholars have the opportunities to learn and extend knowledge. Faculty should embrace this."

They don't. And their yelps of "academic freedom!" as somehow resolving or even stating anything material is more code for a liberal argument they don't want to admit making, in this case "freedom" to use taxpayer dollars the way they wish, unburdened by scrutiny meaning free from accountability. That kind of "academic freedom."

What makes it more insulting is that the evidence already in the public domain shows the protagonists in the UVa Climategate affair using public resources for despicable, organized efforts to engineer adverse professional consequence for those academics and scientists who dared publish challenges to "the cause." That constitutes a violation of their challengers' "academic freedom" far more than my asking to see emails discussing spiteful campaigns of retaliation.

The *Urofsky* court wrote that "the wisdom of a given practice as a matter of [university] policy does not give the practice constitutional status."[17] "Significantly, the [Supreme] Court has never recognized that professors possess a First Amendment right of academic freedom to determine for themselves the content of their courses and scholarship, despite opportunities [for the Court] to do so."[18]

As with statutes, who needs court opinions when they aren't helpful? Big Science and Big Academia have taken it upon themselves to shrilly, hypocritically, and incoherently claim a First Amendment right to "academic freedom," which extends to (actually) violating that same right of problem academics who apparently don't have the same right. But whom, by disagreeing with the right kind of academic, are apparently just asking for organized retaliation.

Advanced Stages of Denial

Not to be outdone, the American Association for the Advancement of Science board of directors issued a hysterical statement in June 2011. With great rhetorical hand waving about "[r]eports of personal attacks on climate scientists, including harassment, legal challenges, and even death threats," the letter itself most focused its attentions on the two actions that weren't unsubstantiated rumor, but instead real: the Virginia attorney general pursuing some pretty dense smoke to decide whether there existed the fire of fraud, and FOI requests.[19]

Specifically alarming them were my requests to UVa as well as to NASA for the required ethics filings of the lucratively compensated public servant and activist, Al Gore advisor James Hansen. They pointed to the menace of us actually filing a lawsuit as outrageous. But we wouldn't have had to if NASA had complied with the law—as the lawsuit forced them eventually to do, without going to trial, when NASA's lawyers and the Office of Government Ethics finally told them they needed to cough up the documents already (if just when Hansen was annoying the White House).

According to a press release touting AAAS's indignation:

"AAAS vigorously opposes attacks on researchers that question their personal and professional integrity or threaten their safety based on displeasure with their scientific conclusions," the Board said in the statement, which was approved on 28 June.

Scientific progress depends on transparency, the Board said, but "the sharing of research data is vastly different from unreasonable, excessive Freedom of Information Act requests for personal information and voluminous data that are then used to harass and intimidate scientists."[20]

It's not all that scientifically advanced to invoke threats to safety and personal attacks and then neither provide nor even reference any supporting information. In fact, FOI laws have recently revealed universities not only to have lied about what they did and did not do in the face of scientific scandal,[21] but to have recklessly encouraged hype over this very same if fictitious campaign of death threats against academics that AAAS alludes to, which had gained international attention and condemnation for a reprehensible menace to civilized society that . . . wasn't.[22]

More substantively, how did my simply replicating—once—a FOI request for records of an academic scientist, which for all intents and purposes was identical to requests that had been previously employed repeatedly with nary a word from AAAS, become excessive and unreasonable? It's basic science, really. A nonexcessive, reasonable level of FOI activity by people like me is some number less than one.

AAAS concluded, "we are concerned that establishing a practice of aggressive inquiry into the professional histories of scientists whose findings may bear on policy in ways that some find unpalatable could well have a chilling effect on the willingness of scientists to conduct research that intersects with policy-relevant scientific questions." But it was the actual "practice" of doing this that AAAS expressed no concern over, when it was engaged in by a group with which AAAS has no problem— Greenpeace. These posturing partisans also had nothing to say about evidence of scientific thuggery and disgrace, revealed in the principals' own words about fudging results, organizing efforts to destroy and otherwise conceal covered records, and (real) plots to retaliate against academic scientists on the basis of their work (Climategate). They only realized they had a problem when we asked for the "context" we were told would explain it all away.

Further, notice how using laws precisely as they were written and designed in order to follow up on real scandal is "aggressive inquiry into the professional histories of scientists," beyond the pale. At least by this they, too, agreed these were professional, not personal, histories. Although one cannot always choose one's opponents, one often lucks out with the process of self-selection.

As if all of this were not enough, the threat posed by asking questions appeared so grave that *Nature* magazine piled on. *Nature* is considered the world's most prestigious scientific journal, if one implicated far too often in promoting fashionable and lucrative notions of the scientific establishment. In a November 2011 editorial prompted by my group's lawsuit for the UVa records, *Nature* argued that taxpayers should just pay for work and keep their questions to themselves.[23] Be satisfied that self-policing and oversight are being handled by people and institutions flagrantly exposed as not interested in or up for the job in the very episodes prompting *Nature* to rush to their defense. The best response to that is, if you do not like the deal that comes with living off coercively obtained taxpayer money, live off something or someone else.

All that this boisterous arrogance represents is the left-wing academic complex playing to type. Sort of a Hollywood, Al Gore–style "we're different, so we deserve different standards" shtick. Not a serious argument. And, like their transgressions, which they demand be exempted from scrutiny and exposure, it should be given the seriousness it deserves.

The heavy-handed activism of academic interest groups like AAUP and AAAS, and numerous ad hoc coalitions, affirmed that American academia, like their European counterparts, suddenly sees a grave threat in having FOI laws applied to them, as they agreed in return for the taxpayer support and cushy lives. Academics sign up for this when accepting their job. At the University of Virginia, that is literally true, where faculty sign the "Use of Electronic Communications and Social Media: Certificate of Receipt."

Until their "reforms" are locked in, universities are proceeding to manufacture reasons to bar people they do not like from accessing public records. Which tells us to use FOIA more often.

How's That Self-Policing Working Out? Fox, Meet Henhouse

Despite academics and scientists demanding exemption from transparency laws on the grounds not only that they're special, but that they are also fully capable of self-policing, the truth is that they have proved they cannot be trusted to do so. In that respect, they're certainly not special. It is now common for those who hold documents paid for by the taxpayer to refuse to turn them over to the taxpayer when asked. As discussed in these pages, this has been demonstrated through, for example, a congressional investigation of the Obama administration's handling of FOIA, a federal inspector general inquiry, and my own experience as well as that of others. All reveal senior officials charged with responsibly carrying out their obligations under the law engaging in activities subverting the law, not apparently by accident, with the overriding consideration of keeping information hidden.

Similarly, we know that universities will go to great lengths to avoid producing documents to allow external scrutiny, but also self-policing. For example, at no time in its fight against the commonwealth's attorney general or in its litigation with my group, the American Tradition Institute, did the University of Virginia ever assert it had conducted an inquiry into the allegations of misconduct. Not once. They just refused to turn over the related records. Despite damning evidence of what occurred in its name, on its watch, the efforts to examine the supposedly exculpating "context" were sneered at, mischaracterized, and fought. But never investigated.

The reason was simple. I am reliably informed the UVa Board of Visitors raised the issue of conducting an internal inquiry given all that had emerged, and the intense public interest in getting to the bottom of it. The idea was rejected because the administration could not guarantee that the findings would not be subject to FOIA. Draw your own conclusions.

Meanwhile they watched in court as Mann, who went on from UVa to Penn State, continued to say he had been "exonerated," with neither Mann nor the university ever acknowledging that his litany of juries consisted of parties other than UVa, the sole institution with the ability to inquire into and even exonerate his actions there.

Even if true, these claims had no bearing on whether the emails were subject to FOIA, as our judge satisfyingly pointed out to Mann's counsel in April 2012:

THE COURT: Let me ask you the flip side of that coin.

MR. FONTAINE: Yes, sir.

THE COURT: What if the investigations had revealed misconduct by Mann? Would that affect the FOIA ruling here?

MR. FONTAINE: No, it wouldn't, Your Honor.

This placed a close second among the day's top moments to the court's calling a halt to the odd reliance on ad hominem arguments already excerpted.

One could only believe exoneration occurred, either specifically or of the broader Climategate revelations about academic scientists' other behavior, by diving down the rabbit hole to escape the reactions, pre–wagon circling, to those revelations which were in full context and the principals' own words. Greenie columnist George Monbiot wrote in the *Guardian*, "Pretending that this isn't a real crisis isn't going to make it go away. Nor is an attempt to justify the emails with technicalities. We'll be able to get past this only by grasping reality, apologising where appropriate, and demonstrating that it cannot happen again."[24] Never happened. Instead, wagons were circled and the make-believe "no there there" campaign kicked off.

Clive Crook, generally sympathetic to the cause, wrote in the *Financial Times* how this demonstrated "[t]he closed-mindedness of these supposed men of science, their willingness to go to any lengths to defend a preconceived message," and that "[t]he stink of intellectual corruption is overpowering."[25] Yet UVa apparently showed no curiosity about determining what happened there and fought all others' attempts to do so. (Further, a former professor who maintains close ties to the school informs me that the Department of Environmental Sciences defiantly recommended in the spring of 2012 to give Mann a chaired professorship, a request that as of this writing I am told still sits on someone's desk.)

Certainly, the basis for these damnations by allies doesn't get exonerated without some serious wishful thinking, whopping spin, and a slathering of whitewash. All of which were present in abundance.

However, Penn State purported to have scrutinized Mann's behavior. Of course, PSU had no remit to inquire about the behavior in question occurring at UVa, even if it wanted to (unlikely given how it avoided coherently scrutinizing some particularly central activity in question while Mann was at Penn State). It is relevant that this is the same school that exonerated itself in a whitewash over its football program's sex-abuse scandal before having that exposed, under the same now-ex-president presiding and who rushed to similarly attest to the Mann inquiry panel's thoroughness, later exposed as farcical.[26] Both involved charges that, if found meritorious, could lead to a loss of revenue and stature for the respective department in question, and the school. In both cases the school asked itself if it did anything wrong and risibly claimed that an objective inquiry found the answer was no.

Both moves suffered under the weight of time and scrutiny. Fallout from the football program stumble was immediate. Fallout from the Mann misstep is delayed but does seem inevitable.

Putting aside for the moment "Mike's Nature trick" to "hide the decline" in temperatures, and other questions about his research and retaliation against critics, a key question involved Mann's response to a request made to him by Phil Jones. That was for Mann—while Mann was at Penn State—to ask a colleague named Eugene Wahl to destroy some records that might be sought under FOI laws. Penn State's lack of even the most rudimentary curiosity about that count made its effort facially absurd. This was one major reason it was mocked even in sympathetic media quarters.

But I also know of evidence provided by a principal in the inquiry process indicating that it was a whitewash.

Excuse the cryptology here, but for now I have reason to presume that the person is working toward a comfort level with how and when to make the truth known. That will play itself out. But the person's written statements certainly seem to ice the cake on what this transparently deficient inquiry was, and was not. Here is the backstory.

In many venues including his participation in our litigation with the University of Virginia (railed against by numerous apologists as our suing Mann,[27] though it was he who sought to enter our lawsuit, to which he is officially an "intervenor," so the ignorance of this claim is difficult to forgive as anything but fevered ranting), Mann strenuously claims to have been investigated and exonerated by numerous inquiries; left-wing groups call him the "much-vindicated Michael Mann."[28] This is a spectacular invention, as the supposed inquiries were on their faces no such thing. For example, no one has ever been able to review the evidence the entire academic and scientific establishments are fighting to keep private—the supposed "context" that would set everything straight, and precisely the evidence necessary to be considered by anything claiming to be an inquiry at least of the key period after he published his discredited work. Which is when he was at UVa.

Had Penn State appeared to be conducting an actual inquiry, one thing experience has taught us is that it would have been the subject of howling by the usual suspects. In fact, *Sweezy* would have been less irrelevant in that case, involving a tribunal with potential professional consequences depending on its conclusions. They would have said about any such effort what they say about our FOIA request and about the Virginia attorney general's inquiry. But they didn't. For reasons that are now obvious but which it almost seems they knew at the time.

Consider that the panel claimed that "Dr. Mann produced upon request a full archive of his emails in and around the time of the preparation of [the IPCC's Fourth Assessment Report]."[29] Really? But, wait, isn't an investigative panel obtaining his emails somehow a violation of his "academic freedom," a grave threat to science, etc.? Not really. But the lack of hysterical refusal to be scrutinized (quite the opposite, in fact, according to the PSU tribunal) does give a hint as to the legitimacy of Penn State's initiative. Had it represented an inquiry panel, posing potential consequences, looking into his emails, Mann has proved he would not have turned over his emails if asked. With my request for the UVa emails, under FOI law and with no ability to sanction him, he and many others launched every weapon they had to obstruct us. But not here.

The contrast between that and the silence over a supposed investigative panel with disciplinary consequences, and the response to the prospect of others obtaining similar records, are red flags about Penn State's undertaking. It is almost as if it were understood, going into the exercise, that neither Penn State's nor any other of the supposed inquiries was a serious endeavor. And on their face, both during the proceedings and upon reviewing their products, this proved to be the case. Further, it seems that the supposed PSU exoneration was influenced and possibly even guided from behind the scenes by someone claiming to have recused himself, because he was conflicted. For example, consider that PSU chose not to question certain principal but inconvenient witnesses.

All of this was apparent the moment the school's report issued. First, it stated that Mann was asked the following (emphasis added):

> *"Did you engage in, or participate in, directly or indirectly,* any actions with the intent to delete, conceal or otherwise destroy emails, information and/or data, related to AR4, as suggested by Phil Jones?"[30]

Here Penn State referred to Jones's request to Mann, "Mike, Can you delete any emails you may have had with Keith re AR4? Keith will do likewise. He's not in at the moment—minor family crisis. Can you also email Gene and get him to do the same? I don't have his new email address. We will be getting Caspar to do likewise." To which Mann replied in pertinent part, "I'll contact Gene about this ASAP."

Pretty comprehensive, pretty clear. Except that the panel's question does not seem to have been sincere, given their acceptance of Mann's less-than-complete response, conjuring images of Inspector Clouseau:

> Finding 2. After careful consideration of all the evidence and relevant materials, the inquiry committee finding is that there exists no credible evidence that Dr. Mann had ever engaged in, or participated in, directly or indirectly, any actions with intent to delete, conceal or otherwise destroy emails, information and/or data related to AR4, as suggested by Dr. Phil Jones. Dr. Mann has stated that he did not

delete emails in response to Dr. Jones's request. Further, Dr. Mann produced upon request a full archive of his emails in and around the time of the preparation of AR4. The archive contained e-mails related to AR4.[31]

No credible evidence given two things, the first being that Mann answered, No, I did not directly participate in activities. *We inquired whether he did A or B. He says he did not do A.*

They say he also provided the described, select archive of his (Penn State) emails. How the university knows it is a "full archive" of the described emails is apparently from Mann's word. If it was complete, how they reached this conclusion is again somewhat hard to fathom. Because Mann was in fact in email contact with Eugene Wahl in a way that confirms engaging directly or indirectly in actions intended to have emails deleted, concealed or otherwise destroyed. More on that momentarily.

We will never know, it seems, what was in the emails Mann provided. However responsive his reply, or not, and however complete the email archive was, in fact, the panel lapped it up. Possibly it was the busy grant-preparing season.

Because simply by taking the obvious and necessary step of interviewing Mann's alleged correspondent, Eugene Wahl ("did you engage or participate indirectly in any actions with the intent to delete, conceal or otherwise destroy emails?"), Penn State would have answered its question. Without taking this step, no effort can even be called an "inquiry." Choosing not to take this step makes a mockery of the proceeding and disqualifies it from being called an inquiry or exoneration. Penn State chose not to take it, for its own reasons. That was their call. They hoped it would pass muster. And Mann et al. use it rhetorically, even if our UVa court has asked for such claims to please stop.

But a federal inspector general wasn't in on the game and took the step of asking Wahl. The result exposed both Mann and the parties who chose not to interview Wahl, who had moved to that hive of taxpayer activism and FOIA noncompliance, NOAA. When finally asked, Wahl told the Department of Commerce's inspector general that he did delete the emails.

And why would you have done that? The excerpt from the report is as follows:

> CRU email #1212073451. In an email dated May 29, 2008, in which the Director of the CRU [Jones] requested a researcher from Pennsylvania State University [Mann] to ask an individual, who is now a NOAA scientist, to delete certain emails related to his participation in the IPCC AR4.
>
> This scientist explained to us that he believes he deleted the referenced emails at that time.[32]

As McIntyre wrote:

> Previously we knew (from the Climategate emails) that Mann had told Phil Jones that he would ask Wahl to delete any emails on AR4. Now we know that Wahl "believes that he deleted the referenced emails at the time." Now this does not prove that Wahl deleted his emails on or about May 29, 2008, as a result of receiving an email from Mann asking him to do so—it might have been a coincidence. But—contrary to Penn State findings—it is certainly prima facie evidence warranting an investigation.[33]

McIntyre wrote this even before learning of internal shenanigans.[34]

We now know Wahl acknowledges he did delete the specific emails after receiving Jones's request. That request was in an email. A request whose purpose was to get Wahl to delete the emails. Forwarded to Wahl, by Mann, in response to Jones's request to Mann to "email Gene and get him to do the same?," that being "delete any emails" of a certain sort, to which Mann replied, "I'll contact Gene about this ASAP." And did so. And Gene says he deleted the emails at that time.

How this did not rise to the level of direct involvement with activity

designed to delete emails is, presumably, because Mann simply forwarded the request. Which was from Jones. So, really, Mann never asked
Gene to delete the emails, once again just like you can never be "alone"
with someone in the White House.

This of course assumes that the record of Mann contacting Wahl
"ASAP" was found in the emails he volunteered to an inquiry panel. Because we know that they couldn't be bothered to interview Wahl. Among
others central to anything resembling an inquiry.

So, that's not an inquiry. It is not a credible exoneration. It is not
self-policing. It was a whitewash, according to the belatedly developed
first-person words of a principal (read on). This was on its face so bad
that even sympathizer Crook wrote, in the *Atlantic* magazine:

> The Penn State inquiry exonerating Michael Mann—the paleocli-
> matologist who came up with "the hockey stick"—would be difficult
> to parody. Three of four allegations are dismissed out of hand at the
> outset: the inquiry announces that, for "lack of credible evidence,"
> it will not even investigate them. [Crook then excerpts the incredu-
> lous Richard Lindzen of the Massachusetts Institute of Technology,
> quoted below] . . . Moving on, the report then says, in effect, that
> Mann is a distinguished scholar, a successful raiser of research fund-
> ing, a man admired by his peers—so any allegation of academic im-
> propriety must be false.[35]

After citing other language of the report for mockery, he then brings the
hammer down:

> In short, the case for the prosecution is never heard. Mann is asked if
> the allegations (well, one of them) are true, and says no. His record is
> swooned over. Verdict: case dismissed, with apologies that Mann has
> been put to such trouble.[36]

Particularly given that the panel did not follow its own guidelines in
constructing this supposed exoneration,[37] it is reasonable to conclude

that Penn State swerved around the obvious necessity of an interview with Wahl (and others like McIntyre, whose dealings with Mann directly led to Mann's exposure) because the panelists, or someone above them, wished it to avoid such conversations. Indeed, criticisms immediately came from those interviewed, like MIT's Lindzen, according to the investigators themselves in the final investigative report, and as what may have been a subtle warning of the scandalous pressure or the behind-the-scenes orchestration that was going on:

> When told that the first three allegations against Dr. Mann were dismissed at the inquiry stage of the RA-IO process, Dr. Lindzen's response was: "It's thoroughly amazing. I mean these are issues that he explicitly stated in the emails. I'm wondering what's going on?"
>
> The Investigatory Committee members did not respond to Dr. Lindzen's statement.[38]

It was more of a question, really, but the committee members were to be the ones asking (and ducking) the questions here. However, as one person involved wrote privately to someone not interviewed who should have been, in one of the riddle-like emails that led finally to a private admission of what transpired, "You were not contacted for a reason. Recuse but not excuse!"[39] Other evidence elaborated upon this, to the effect that someone initially involved with the Mann inquiry had claimed to recuse himself from the proceeding, while not in fact excusing himself from the effort. This person is, to this day, a professional associate of Mann.

By now it is clear that publicly funded science and academia will do what they see as necessary to avoid public scrutiny. This even extends to refusing to have a law applied to them that they agreed was a condition of their living off the taxpayers. And, apparently, far more.

Liberal academia does not believe you are entitled to any reasonable review or scrutiny of how it spends your money, even if it is on campaigns designed to enhance the role and power of government and academia and cost you much, much more.

With all that FOI laws have allowed us to expose in just the past two years about the conduct of academics and their administrations, it is no wonder that liberals don't like FOI laws applying to their pet taxpayer-funded projects. Academia wants to be freed from the constraints of scrutiny and accountability, constraints that they agreed to as a condition of taking our money. Far from behaving like people deserving of special treatment, even exemption from laws (for reasons still not clearly articulated), they seem to be the worst offenders, in need of more adult supervision than even the rest of government.

11.

FOIA: What It Is and How It Works

The federal Freedom of Information Act and state FOI laws allow the public to obtain full or partial disclosure of agency records, so long as the records are not protected by a specific privilege. That is to say, unless a record falls within a specific exemption, it is presumptively yours. This has not come without a fight from the bureaucracy, so the law is no stranger to judicial interpretation, even at the Supreme Court level. And with extremely rare exceptions the federal government has prevailed in FOIA cases it chose to fight all the way.[1]

Basically FOIA provides an agency, absent "unusual circumstances," twenty business days from the date it receives a reasonably specific request for records (which translates to a calendar month) to determine whether to withhold any records under an identified exemption and to notify the requester of its decision. States typically afford the agency between five and ten days, up to fifteen although some states simply say the response must come within a reasonable time. These statutes establish the procedural and substantive process by which citizens request and agencies provide information. The federal law outlines mandatory disclosure procedures and grants nine specific exemptions to the requirement that "records" be produced. Precedents in interpreting the federal law, broadly speaking, translate to application of state laws.

The court has established a series of principles in favor of transparency that guide basic FOIA practice. Among these are that "[t]he basic purpose of FOIA is to ensure an informed citizenry, vital to the functioning of a democratic society, needed to check against corruption and to hold the governors accountable to the governed."[2] The same objective underlies constitutional protection of media freedoms, so view FOIA as a tool for citizen journalists. It is almost as if Congress in 1965 imagined the present day when the press has largely become a tool of entrenched political interests.

This public's right to inspect public records guaranteed by FOIA "defines a structural necessity in a real democracy."[3] The act is designed to "pierce the veil of administrative secrecy and to open agency action to the light of scrutiny."[4] It is a transparency-forcing law, consistent with "the basic policy that disclosure, not secrecy, is the dominant objective of the Act."[5]

The law allows the citizenry to learn "what their government is up to."[6] This includes individuals, corporations, unions, pressure groups, the media, etc. Through FOIA, Congress "sought to open agency action to the light of public scrutiny."[7] By so doing, Congress guaranteed access to information that may be publicly disclosed without unwarranted harm. Therefore, in FOIA cases, the burden of proof is on the agency, and all doubts must be resolved in favor of disclosure.[8]

The FOIA is technically part of the Administrative Procedure Act (APA). Section 3 of the APA as enacted in 1946 gave agencies broad discretion concerning the publication of governmental records, followed in 1950 by the Federal Records Act to set forth what was to be kept and disposed and how. Like most laws giving agencies discretion, the APA discretion was abused. So two decades after the APA was enacted, Congress amended the relevant provision to implement "a general philosophy of full agency disclosure."[9]

Like the Presidential Records Act, which followed in 1978,[10] all such laws acknowledge the public necessity of scrutinizing the machinations of a rapidly expanding state—in size, cost, and scope—which is profoundly greater today than at the time of FOIA's enactment. Government continues to move further away from the governed, with power concentrating in Washington at possibly an unprecedented pace. Rightly or wrongly, government is at the same time increasingly viewed as unresponsive, and even out of control. This perception is a dangerous one, as there is great moral hazard in the public losing confidence in the laws, the lawmakers, and those who are charged with executing these authorities. Widespread use and proper execution of FOIA is therefore as important as ever, if not more so.

Who Can FOIA?

At the federal level, anyone can FOIA, for any reason. You need not be a U.S. citizen. "'The Freedom of Information Act may be invoked by any member of the public'—without a showing of need—to compel disclosure of confidential Government documents."[11] Indeed, "the identity of the requesting party has no bearing on the merits of his or her FOIA request. . . . Congress 'clearly intended' FOIA 'to give any member of the public as much right to disclosure as one with a special interest [in a particular document].'"[12] A handful of state statutes limit access to citizens of those states and media outlets with a presence in the state. But this disparate treatment is of dubious constitutionality and is falling away with each challenge.[13]

The Supreme Court has ruled that, generally, the propriety of disclosure hinges not on the requesting party's particular purpose or identity but upon the nature of the requested document and its relationship to FOIA's central purpose of exposing official information to public scrutiny, shedding light on an agency's performance of statutory duties.[14]

While the left seems to believe this law was written by them for them, a requester's motives do not matter. "Fishing expeditions" and "witch hunts"—either chasing a real witch or merely disparaged as such in talking points demonizing your inquiry—are perfectly fine and you need not explain your interest in accessing the records. There are exceptions, requiring a balancing test, weighing another interest against the FOIA-related purpose to be served by the request. These exceptions involve, for example, personal information held by the government, and, when considering your request, having search fees waived.

Under FOIA, there are three distinct categories of requesting parties, but this does not impact access, only costs assessed. They are commercial user; news media, educational, or noncommercial scientific institutions with a scholarly or scientific research purpose; and "other" (personal use, public interest groups, and nonprofit organizations). Although the tax code respects public interest and other nonprofits as educational groups, FOIA does not.

FOIA Is Biased Toward Release

President Obama instructed that FOIA "be administered with a clear presumption: In the face of doubt, openness prevails" and that "a presumption of disclosure should be applied to all decisions involving FOIA."[15] Despite the hype surrounding it, with occasional exceptions concerning national security this merely reflects what federal agencies have always professed their positions on FOIA to be.

FOIA's golden rule is that "[a]n agency seeking to withhold information under an exemption to FOIA has the burden of proving that the information falls under the claimed exemption."[16] That is because the act carries "a strong presumption in favor of disclosure."[17] Certain conditions, as noted above and discussed later, can change that burden, placing it on the requesting party. But the general rule, applicable to most requests, is that it is not you but the agency that must make its case. The agency's reason for withholding documents, or information within released documents, must fall within one of Congress's nine enumerated exemptions. If not, the record is yours.

Too often in practice this is qualified with *if you're willing to fight for it.* More on that momentarily.

Just as no demonstration by the requester is generally required, there is no general requirement to demonstrate the public's interest in disclosure. Still, it is wise in anticipating an appeal to articulate a public interest, and specifically a FOIA-related interest, and whether there are no other means to obtain the requested information.

The aforementioned balancing tests occur when weighing privacy interests versus a FOIA-related purpose because not every record falling under one of FOIA's nine specific exemptions must or even can properly be withheld. Some that may be withheld are subject to discretionary release, and many records that on their face might technically fall under an exemption in fact have no reasonable argument for being withheld. Increasingly, I find appeals result in a reversal of redactions, in full (all redactions overruled), showing that appealing, particularly redactions, should be near-automatic: FOIA officers regularly leave to the higher-ups and the appeal stage the closer look that would lead to discretionary release. This is because the bureaucracy sees no upside for them in erring on the side of disclosure—though the law demands that—but a downside if they do release records only to be later told that this violated some interest (privacy, secrecy, etc.). FOIA officers and appeals counsel affirm this to me.

The above is particularly true of the broadly invoked (b)(5) "predecisional" exemption, discussed below, which is uniquely abused by the Obama administration, despite having been singled out for less-frequent invocation and increased discretionary releases in their numerous homages to just how transparent they would be.

Statutory language and numerous judicial pronouncements of the bias toward disclosure notwithstanding, in practice FOIA officers generally err on the side of withholding. Which means you must go into every request expecting to appeal, in one fashion or forum or another, and regularly do so. This is one of numerous factors militating for getting one's search terms and parameters (relevant time period, offices or employees covered) properly tightened before sending the request.

What Is Covered by FOIA?

The federal act covers the federal executive branch, meaning the White House and agencies, with exceptions for advisory offices of the president. Congress and the federal courts are not covered. State or local government agencies are covered by their state FOIAs, which also generally extend to state universities, again with certain exceptions. Private individuals and companies are never covered, although, as with congressional offices, correspondence to and from them and covered offices is subject to release by the covered office. For example, Michael Mann and the University of Virginia insist that "his" email is sacrosanct. So while they obstruct the school's cache, Landmark Legal, CEI, and ATI have been obtaining tranches of those emails from federal government offices and other universities.

Agency Records

Before information can fall under this federal jurisdiction it must be considered an "agency record."[18] FOIA poorly defined what constitutes an "agency record,"[19] leaving that in practice to the courts. Indeed, the Supreme Court said that Congress really "did not provide any definition of the term."[20] Regardless, we know it is expansive.

"The definition of a record under the Freedom of Information Act (FOIA) is broader than the definition under the Federal Records Act,"[21] with the latter requiring the document to somehow reflect the operations of government at some substantive level while FOIA covers phone logs, annotations, and the most seemingly inconsequential piece of paper or electronic record in an agency's possession. At bottom "the question is whether the employee's creation of the documents can be attributed to the agency for the purposes of FOIA."[22] The United States Code offers a little assistance, defining "records," for purposes of maintenance (and destruction), as "includ[ing] all books, papers, maps, photographs, machine readable materials, or other documentary materials, regardless of physical form or characteristics, made or received by an agency of the United States Government under Federal law or in connection with the transaction of public business and preserved or appropriate for preservation by that agency or its legitimate successor as evidence of the organization, functions, policies, decisions, procedures, operations, or other activities of the Government or because of the informational value of data in them."[23]

In short, presume that whatever information you seek is contained in a record, and request records containing the information.

Documents "generated within the agenc[y]" and "prepared on government time, at government expense and with government materials" are generally agency records, which does not mean the agency will possess the record when you ask for it. Agencies choose to retain only those they determine are "appropriate for preservation . . . as evidence of the organization, functions, policies, decisions, procedures, operations, or other activities of the Government or because of the informational value of the data in them." These documents must be created or obtained by the agency and under its control at the time the FOIA request is made.[24] In practice and by precedent, this means up through the date the search for responsive records is initiated.

The D.C. Circuit has established a four-part test for determining whether an agency is "in control" of documents. These are 1) the intent of the document's creator to retain or relinquish control over the records (that is, if a third party created the document, and the agency possesses it or a copy); 2) the ability of the agency to use and dispose of the record as it sees fit; 3) the extent to which agency personnel have read or relied upon the document (the more this is the case, the greater the likelihood it is an "agency record" in its control); and 4) the degree to which the document was integrated into the agency's record system or files.[25]

So, control can include an agency not possessing the record but having the ability under some agreement, such as a contract, to access a record, or simply that records were created on the agency's behalf. Other considerations in determining a record's status include the content of the records, as well as the process of how the records were generated (did the information "come into the agency's possession in the legitimate conduct of its official duties"?).[26]

It is a basic principle of FOIA that no agency can be forced by the law to create any record to comply with a request, only to provide existing records. An agency is also not required by law to answer questions posed as FOIA requests.[27]

What Is Exempt from FOIA?

Presume records held by the government are yours unless they fall into one of FOIA's nine specific exemptions, which define classes of records that can but do not necessarily exclude records from FOIA's reach. These are found in 5 U.S.C. § 552(b)1–9:

(b)1.   Classified national defense and foreign relations information

(b)2.   Internal agency rules and practices

(b)3.   Information prohibited from disclosure by other federal law

(b)4.   Trade secrets, confidential commercial or financial information

(b)5.   Inter-agency or intra-agency memorandums or letters that would not be available by law to a party other than an agency in litigation with the agency

(b)6.   Information involving matters of personal privacy

(b)7.   Certain information compiled for law enforcement purposes

(b)8.   Information relating to the supervision of financial institutions

(b)9.   Geological information on wells

"These exemptions are explicitly made exclusive, and must be narrowly construed."[28] That is, these are the exemptions, there are no more, and agencies should not seek to read them as excuses to withhold records—as was done with the APA, prompting FOIA's passage in the first place. Regardless, that is still how these are often implemented: a series of reasons to deny requesters access.

Even though FOIA's exemptions are to be interpreted narrowly, with a bias toward releasing records, the U.S. Supreme Court and many lower courts regularly agree with the government's request to read them broadly. Congress has even felt compelled on occasion to amend FOIA in order to narrow exemptions after the courts read them overly broadly or at least running counter to the intended bias toward disclosure.

Categories 1, 3, 4, and 6 are mandatory exemptions, in that information falling under these categories may not be released. However, "Documents protected by . . . Exemptions 2, 5, 7, 8, and 9, can all be subjects of discretionary release"—that is, they give the agency the ability to withhold, but do not require it—so, "Agency FOIA professionals must use their judgment in making such determinations for each document, but they should be guided by the 'fundamental commitment to open government.'"[29]

Although the agency has limited circumstances when it must withhold records, the processing officer, increasingly the political aides who learn of troubling requests, and as we have seen the employee who is expected to have the records and also to volunteer them in response to the request, will read these exceptions broadly and as ways to avoid producing records. This is despite what is called among agency FOIA lawyers "the Obama Standard," the (ignored, unenforceable) order to release records under the discretionary exemptions barring a compelling case of foreseeable harm.[30]

As discussed in detail below, even the most consciously objective searches remain exposed to inherent subjectivity.

The "Pre-decisional" Dodge

Exemptions 5 (interagency memorandums) and 6 (personal privacy) are the most commonly invoked. Exemption 6, like 7, requires the balancing test described below of public interest versus privacy rights. This exemption is less commonly invoked against the FOIA requester interested in policy or politics, although it is nonetheless used to shield embarrassing but not properly exempted information. It was the exemption wrongly tried as a refuge to not release records evincing the close relationship between Cathy Zoi and Solyndra's public affairs firm.

Exemption 5, formally "(b)(5)," 5 U.S.C. § 552(b)(5), offers what Justice Scalia has called "opaque" language,[31] behind which agencies almost ritually hide when seeking to withhold policy-related records. It was identified by Attorney General Holder as the most ripe for reform (that is, subject to abuse).[32] As the left-leaning groups Citizens for Responsibility and Ethics in Washington and OpenTheGovernment.org specifically noted about that supposed transformation to greater transparency, the administration is abusing it, and to a greater degree than its predecessor.[33]

You will surely encounter the oft-abused (b)(5) exemption, which protects attorney-work product, privileged attorney-client discussions (which does not exempt all Department of Justice communications, even if they are now the most secretive agency), presidential communications ("executive privilege"), and, by far the most commonly invoked refuge of the political scoundrel, internal "pre-decisional" communications. A discussion focusing even just on the latter move could go far into the weeds of the various arguments an agency might make in any given situation, so here are some key (b)(5) principles to consider when you inevitably confront this.

The courts have construed this provision to "exempt those documents, and only those documents, that are normally privileged in the civil discovery context."[34] Exemption (b)(5) is a way of viewing FOIA as discovery, outside of litigation. Which is to say, "the public is entitled to all such memoranda or letters that a private party could discover in litigation with the agency."[35] However, "[T]he discovery rules can only be applied under Exemption 5 by way of rough analogies. For example, we do not know whether the Government is to be treated as though it were a prosecutor, a civil plaintiff, or a defendant. Nor does the Act, by its terms, permit inquiry into particularized needs of the individual seeking the information, although such an inquiry would ordinarily be made of a private litigant."[36]

Regardless of the deficiencies of the "discovery" analogy, "the legislative history of Exemption 5 demonstrates that Congress intended to incorporate generally the recognized rule that 'confidential intra-agency advisory opinions . . . are privileged from inspection.'"[37]

The bottom line is that the reluctant or secretive bureaucrat or political appointee—permitted to conduct their own searches for records possibly responsive to a FOIA request—feels a (b)(5) exemption is almost always worth a try when there's information they'd prefer not come out. As such it is nearly always worth a try to appeal a (b)(5) withholding, arguing from the available context that the record is likely not "pre-decisional."

This privilege "clearly has finite limits," extending only to "whether production of the contested document would be 'injurious to the consultative functions of government that the privilege of nondisclosure protects.'"[38] Congress "expressly intended 'to delimit the exception [5] as narrowly as consistent with efficient Government operation.'"[39]

As DOJ writes, "Specifically, three policy purposes consistently have been held to constitute the bases for this privilege: (1) to encourage open, frank discussions on matters of policy between subordinates and superiors; (2) to protect against premature disclosure of proposed policies before they are actually adopted; and (3) to protect against public confusion that might result from disclosure of reasons and rationales that were not in fact ultimately the grounds for an agency's action. . . . In concept, the privilege protects not merely documents, but also the integrity of the deliberative process itself where the exposure of that process would result in harm."[40]

Agencies like to withhold records in full (as opposed to redacting exempt portions and providing the rest), simply notifying you that a document was not provided on the grounds that it represents a deliberative, pre-decisional document. Always appeal that. It is implausible that these aims require that entire documents must be withheld as promiscuously as they are. This is true even if just for the fact that the agency may only redact those portions that meet (b)(5)'s standard, which does not include, for example, "identifying" information—to, from, date, and, usually, subject—unless that would somehow make obvious the information that is rightly withheld.

The deliberative process privilege "applies only to 'deliberative' documents and it ordinarily is inapplicable to purely factual matters, or to factual portions of otherwise deliberative memoranda, which ordinarily must be segregated out and released."[41] "[A]n entire document is not exempt merely because an isolated portion need not be disclosed. Thus the agency may not sweep a document under a general allegation of exemption, even if that general allegation is correct with regard to part of the information. It is quite possible that part of a document should be kept secret while part should be disclosed."[42]

"Virtually all of the courts that have thus far applied Exemption 5 have recognized that it requires different treatment for materials reflecting deliberative or policymaking processes, on the one hand, and purely factual, investigative matters, on the other."[43]

The obvious other test is, is it deliberative? That is, are the records truly "antecedent to the adoption of an agency policy"?[44] Even if so, not all deliberative elements are shielded; arguably, it's only those important elements whose disclosure would chill "honest and frank" internal communications.[45] Further, to get away with this the agency must also identify a decision-making process that prompted the creation of the withheld documents. (However, as discussed below, this is only once you litigate, although the diligent agency counsel will make the case in his memo responding to an appeal. They aren't, however, all diligent.)

As with all withholdings, ultimately the agency is required, when denying information, to at bare minimum permit a reasoned judgment as to the validity of the withholding but also to reasonably identify the record. Unfortunately, if they do not professionally manage the appeal and fail to provide such information, you have to sue somewhat blind until the required Vaughn index, discussed below, is provided.

That is done as a matter of course when suit is filed, and as part of the response to your appeal you are supposed to have been provided a description of what is withheld and why. Reality does not always rise to legal expectations and standards, so in the event you receive no such thing you're in court anyway, having filed at some disadvantage and with little practical chance for sanctioning the derelict agency. At this stage, the bureaucracy is only likely to fulsomely meet its obligations if its legal department recognizes it is in their benefit to properly handle appeals as if they are headed to court. Appeals are discussed in more detail later.

Public Interest Versus Privacy

FOIA does not provide an absolute right to disclosure. Instead, the strong interest in disclosure and the need for an informed citizenry are balanced with the necessity of protecting sensitive information, and the "legitimate governmental and private interests [that] could be harmed by release of certain types of information."[46]

When certain personal information is sought, for example involving personnel, medical, or financial information, privacy implications demand you articulate a FOIA-related purpose to allow this balancing test. That is because the individual who works for or benefits from government expenditures, or otherwise whose personal information the government holds, has a right to privacy, which can be overcome by a public interest. But the former is assumed and, when the privacy is deemed substantial (as opposed to de minimis), the public interest must be demonstrated. At that point, a balancing test determines whether "public interest in disclosure outweighs individual privacy concerns."[47]

The information must be the sort that "sheds light on an agency's performance of its statutory duties."[48] Shedding light instead on an individual is not such a FOIA-related purpose. "[I]nformation about private citizens . . . that reveals little or nothing about an agency's own conduct" does not serve a relevant public interest under FOIA.[49]

Therefore, make sure you state how what you seek sheds light on an agency's statutory duties, how this knowledge is in the public's interest, and how the public benefits from release. Otherwise, the request will be deemed a "clearly unwarranted violation of personal privacy," and denied.

It is possible that, on occasion, your sole interest is to satisfy "'the core purpose of the FOIA,' which is 'contribut[ing] significantly to the public understanding of the operations or activities of the government.'"[50] If that purpose is to determine whether the government has held its employees or others who benefit from taxpayer dollars to comply with various laws, that is, to correctly do their job (which demands compliance with laws, not merely fulfilling a unique statutory purpose), this should be, but is not always, enough to pry information loose.[51]

You'll have to make the case that this illumination will result, and that the possible misconduct is not unsupported, or is mere allegation or suspicion. Demonstrate that the information requested fulfills a FOIA-related public interest in disclosure. Make that case, and the balancing test occurs.

Private Emails on Public Resources

Then of course there is the issue of "personal" emails sent and received using a government email account, provided for official business. Ethics rules require that government equipment be used, with only incidental exception, for official purposes.[52] Regardless, "agency record" is interpreted under federal law narrowly enough to protect genuinely personal emails against disclosure, even if they're held on a government account.

The D.C. Circuit has held that "employing agency resources, standing alone, is not sufficient to render a document an 'agency record.'"[53] As such, an agency official's truly personal correspondence is not subject to FOIA in part because of a "lack of reliance on the correspondence to carry out the business of the agency."[54]

Recall the correspondence between Zoi and Solyndra's public affairs reps, arguably "personal" given the chummy banter about, for example, spending weekend meals together at Zoi's home. However, these are people who had business before the agency, with whom Zoi regularly corresponded about such official public business. That left the presumption, which I successfully argued on two separate appeals, that despite all of that, this indeed was work-related. Which, frankly, places the emails in such troubling light, not exclusively but particularly because of the catastrophic boondoggle that the "green energy" ventures proved to be. We see how these wealth transfers came about, 80 percent of which "went to companies either run by or primarily owned by Obama financial backers—individuals who were bundlers, members of Obama's National Finance Committee, or large donors to the Democratic Party."[55]

If the email exchanges were truly personal, they would not have been revealed, as they would not have been revealing of anything about the government. But they were, because they are.

At the state level, "While 26 states view the use of private emails for government business as public records, the rest have no clear rules or prevailing case law—a source for continuing turmoil in state courts. . . . [G]overnors in Florida and South Carolina have fought to block disclosure of state communications on their private email accounts. In 2011, news organizations pursued a lawsuit to see the emails of former North Carolina Gov. Mike Easley, a Democrat, who used a private email account for state business. The Colorado Supreme Court ruled [in 2011] that Democratic Gov. Bill Ritter was not required to disclose his private cellphone records even though the calls were mostly for state business."[56] State courts that order release of "personal" emails sent or received using government computers typically premise their opinions on the broad language specific to the state FOI law at issue—such as where a public record "*includes, but is not limited to,* any writing containing information relating to the conduct or administration of the public's business"[57] (emphasis added). Nonetheless the decision to order their release still turns on the messages' "relation to legitimate public interest [making] them a public record."[58]

So the key to an "agency record" is its content, not the equipment or account it sits on.

Private correspondence on government computers is an entirely different kettle of fish from that expanding volume of official business sitting on private email accounts or computers, reaffirming the principle: it is the nature of the information that governs, not whether the information sits on Gmail or a government computer.

And the government is awakening to the fact that its employees routinely use Gmail and other private email accounts to conduct official business, however much that is discouraged. This is not always done to escape, or, more specifically subvert, record-keeping and disclosure laws. But sometimes it is.

For what it's worth, a very senior legal officer and University of Virginia administrator informed us, after a typically unpleasant meeting during which they attempted to lecture us for our impertinence, that our suit had caused 90 percent of the faculty to move their email activity to Gmail. If this is done for what is actually personal correspondence, that simply brings them in line with the intended use of a taxpayer-provided email account; if done for work-related correspondence, ultimately this will surely be found to be a futile attempt to dodge required disclosure.

Still, we are told it is not possible to integrate the Gmail and other accounts into the government systems for even those employees who would admit to doing this (who, anyway, aren't generally the employees we need to worry about). As such, and given policies requiring record retention and preservation as well as the tensions this is creating with FRA, PRA, and FOIA compliance, it seems that something close to an outright prohibition on the practice of using private accounts for public business is inevitable, much like the incidental-exception rule about using government resources for private activities.

12.

How-To: Filing Your Own FOIAs

To ensure that the public understands how to request records under the federal FOIA, each agency must publish "where, from whom, and the methods whereby the public may obtain information, make submittals or requests, or obtain decisions."[1] These are published on each agency's website, which is the place to start your process for any request. Each of these posts the agency's own twist on implementing the broader law and general rules.

Thanks to the 1996 amendments to the law, each agency posts frequently requested records as part of a required "reading room"[2] that may answer or help you hone your question. These are records that have been sought (and released) thrice within some ill-defined period of time, indicating a level of public interest in the matter. Agencies do not seek to create more work for themselves nor, generally, do they take initiative to save taxpayers inconvenience down the road (even if, arguably, erring on the side of publication in the reading room should save them response time down the road). As such, look to, but do not hold any irrational exuberance about, the agency's FOIA "reading room."

The agency websites also offer site maps allowing you to narrow your search to the offices you want to directly target in the request, assuming they have their own FOIA officer (some do, some do not), or which one(s) you want to suggest the request be farmed out to.

You want to perfect your request to the best of your ability because the act is judicially enforceable, a resolution will be driven in great part by the quality of the request, and you should proceed from that first request through all subsequent communications with the agency as if you are going to court. Document everything, maintain all emails or other correspondence, and confirm telephone conversations and their content in writing.

The agency's FOIA Web page will inform you whether they accept requests by electronic mail. If you attach your request and use Mac, do so in Word and Pages formats, and state that it is attached in both formats. You may alternately paste the request in the body of the email or in addition to attaching the document. Some agencies only accept electronic requests if by completing a form you complete on their site. So you will have inconveniences placed in your path by these agencies, and by those that do not allow electronic requests at all, which universe includes major agencies, like the Department of Justice.

What to Include

Include all components necessary for a request to be one the agency can respond to without coming back to you first for information or clarification. If it seems that your request would be sent to several offices, break it up and direct one to each office. Some apolitical FOIA officers and many more partisans thrive on reasons to delay. Don't feed them. Try to avoid any opportunity for delay because, particularly if your request is for a there that is there, you can expect people on the receiving end will look for ways to legitimately slow down the process.

Basic components of any request include:

- "Request under the Freedom of Information Act"

- Proper recipient and address

- Your name, address, and in what capacity you write if relevant to establishing your fee category

- The public's interest in the requested records and how you plan and are able to disseminate the information to a broad cross section of the public, and separately a FOIA-related interest as appropriate

Properly specific and narrow search parameters, detailing as precisely as you can, without being overly narrow, what you seek, including:

- The type of documents (include the proper universe of "records," as well; common items to request include emails, including attachments, visitor and phone logs, messages, calendars, meeting notes and minutes, and memoranda)

- That, if the agency possesses the records in electronic format, you request delivery that way (saves copying expenses)

- Correspondence sent to or from, or held by, what offices

- If possible, authors, either senders or recipients, and email addresses if you have them (avoid improperly limiting your request this way, however); also note that you seek responsive emails from any account on which the employee has conducted public business and that the employee and the agency must produce such records no matter the email account on which it is held

- In the event that some portions of the requested records are properly exempt from disclosure, ask the agency to disclose any reasonably segregable, non-exempt portions of the requested records. Cite to 5 U.S.C. § 552(b).

- Include the starting date of the period covered by your request— starting when, "through the date you perform the required search." It is well established in regulation and the courts that, unless stated otherwise, the period the FOIA request runs through the date the search is conducted, not the date the agency logs the request as received.[3]

It makes sense when narrowing that first request to not only strive to avoid providing opportunities for delay, but to specifically design the request to produce answers to select things you know you don't know. Heed the words of one government website: "Make sure you are as specific as possible in describing the information you seek. If you are seeking specific records from a case file or otherwise, include, whenever possible, the date, title or name, author, or subject matter of the record you are requesting. Referencing specific case or report numbers is also helpful in reducing response time. . . . To avoid confusion, we recommend that you describe as clearly as possible the record or information you seek, without putting it into a question format."[4]

When you receive records, then you can read that first production with an eye for revelations of the unknowns that had not occurred to you.

Fees and Fee Waivers

In your request, ask to have fees waived, and the reasons you qualify for what category. State up front that if the fee waiver is denied you agree to pay whatever amount you are comfortable with (usually fifty dollars is sufficient, but this is to taste). This avoids delay.

Three types of fees may be charged: 1) document duplication costs (actual copying costs, only); 2) search time; and 3) costs of reviewing for exemptions (for commercial requesters only). You will most likely be classified as "other" and be required to pay only the actual cost of copying records and search time. FOIA provides that the first two hours of search time are free and typically this leaves most requests from the "other" category as incurring no cost.

Your fees must be waived or reduced when the following test is met: disclosure is in the public interest; it is likely to "contribute significantly to public understanding of the operations or activities of the government"; and it is not primarily in the requester's commercial interest.

Each agency constructs its own test with its own buzzwords, but this is the basic framework for obtaining waiver or reduction of fees.

Therefore, state your case as to how you satisfy each of these, and check the agency's website as you wish for any angles they might fetishize. Also make note of how you satisfy other key considerations, including the relationship of the requested information to public understanding of the operations or activities of government, and your ability to convey that information to other interested members of the public. (Do you have a newsletter or a website? If so, what sort of readership? Do you blog, publish op-eds, provide media commentary? And so on.) This language transfers from request to request, with minor fact-specific modification. So you can work off a template request of your own.

In the event your request for a fee waiver is denied and, objectively, you qualify, you have the option of promptly sending another FOIA request seeking copies of all requests for fee waivers that were granted by that agency or office in the past, say, twelve months (just seek copies of the successful requests, to see what they were and from whom, and how they compare with you and your request). My experience is that this signal that you are prepared to draw negative attention to suspected disparate treatment—exposure of which seems to be of more concern to them than exposure of delays, which nearly all requests experience and the courts have now blessed as acceptable and even to be expected—gets their attention. On one occasion I received a phone call within minutes of emailing such a follow-up, with the caller saying simply, "Don't do this. You'll have your fees waived."

Then again, if you really catch the bureaucracy doing something, they see little to lose in stonewalling. When I discovered and then sought more information on those secret EPA email accounts in mid-2012, the bureaucracy went into the defensive crouch, declaring that I no longer warranted the fee waivers they had agreed to around a dozen times already just that year, without exception and often involving fairly mundane information. Now, they claimed, releasing details of these accounts' origin and use would teach the public nothing significant about the operations of government. Really. This cartoonishly ham-fisted effort at erecting a fee barrier begged an appeal, still pending as of this writing.

How Agencies Handle FOIA Requests

What happens after you send your FOIA request? Even if every bureaucracy and political machine did everything properly—which they do not—the process for agencies handling FOIA requests would differ in practice by agency, and due to the request's specifics. But the process generally moves along the following lines. Ideally, in twenty working days or less the agency mails the records you seek. This occurs quite often for simple, targeted requests, which if simple and targeted enough are not even set on another pile but dealt with immediately. More commonly, the agency receives the request, logs it in to create a record of receipt, and evaluates it for classification and to which office(s) it will be sent. The classifications include "simple," meaning it requires little search or review, and "normal," meaning a modicum of search and review. Many requests are deemed "complex," which has a multitrack system depending on just how complex, due to its search parameters including search terms and time period and how many offices or other agencies must be consulted to respond. The agency typically only informs you of the classification if your request is normal or complex.

For those requests, the agency drafts a written initial response acknowledging receipt, reiterating (or, sometimes to be careful, tweaking) your search terms, notifying you of the classification, to which offices the request has been sent, and your fee category (commercial, educational/media, or most likely "other"). They will often inform you in the same correspondence of an initial determination on your fee waiver request, but they may seek more information before granting or denying that request.

This acknowledgment will inform you that they receive many requests and, like others, yours has been placed in line and will be processed in its turn. Generally, this means on a first-come, first-served basis, although agencies also process requests in separate queues depending on their complexity (simple, normal, and the least complex requests are handled in the order they come to the agency).

Sometimes, as with the Department of Justice, they make a habit of telling you that the twenty days do not begin until the office to which they have farmed out the request receives it. This process then repeats, with another acknowledgment coming from that office, starting the clock.

They should, but oddly do not always, provide you your tracking number, for use in corresponding on the status and otherwise. Use it in all correspondence with the agency.

The bottom line is that they provide you a tracking number and a FOIA officer's contact information for a reason.

Of course, sometimes they do not even acknowledge your request at all. After twenty business days, you may sue, with certain caveats noted below, but may also follow up through the same means (email, snail mail, or fax; agencies requiring you to complete an electronic form make this more difficult) with a copy of the first request, restating it and noting that the date continues to be the date they first received the initial copy. This is one of several reasons to use electronic mail or fax where allowed. The twenty business days that agencies are granted to respond begins on the day the request is actually received by the FOIA office conducting the search for requested records. The statute allows agencies another ten days if they seek it (permissible reasons include collecting records from other offices, consultation with other agencies, or the volume of the responsive records requested). When an extension is needed, you will be notified. But if you are "offered the opportunity" to modify or limit the request, and you can do so meaningfully without materially diluting your request—by correcting a drafting error, ambiguous use of language, or narrowing the request without setting back your purpose—you should agree.

It is good practice to try to work with the agency until you have reasonable grounds to believe your request is being stonewalled. Despite fairly sophisticated tracking software and protocols, it is also possible for a request to get mislaid even now, so follow up if you have received no acknowledgment after a calendar month. It is possible, if you are on to something, that you are being slow-walked. Like everything, discussions should be in writing, or confirmed in writing contemporaneously, setting forth your understanding of what was said.

Stay on top of them, in a friendly way, knowing that they are indeed quite burdened with requests. It is possible to maintain a transactional relationship with the FOIA officers, who are career employees not necessarily predisposed to obstruct you, despite the instinct to withhold when they can and should release, leaving that up to appeals officers. That's the system; it's (usually) not personal. However, as we have seen at various departments, sometimes the partisans catch those requests that should worry them, and they slow-walk and even derail those entirely. There also is only so much a FOIA officer can do to compel a reluctant bureaucrat or appointee to be more responsive.

Opportunities for mischief arise at various points during the process. These include the decision where to send (or not send) the request for a search, the fee waiver determination, and then the issue of the employees who are tasked with the initial search regularly being the ones whose records are sought. If your request is sufficiently of concern to them, either for political reasons or general embarrassment, they may choose not to consider certain records to be responsive or seek to wear you down with protracted and tedious, time-consuming battles involving runarounds, with records when provided being provided late, grudgingly, and in an incomplete and haphazard manner.

With that said, keep in mind that if your request is complex and of a sensitive nature the agency will require a significant amount of time to search and review the responsive records. But when drafting also be aware that it can take years to get a response to a FOIA request (as it can to obtain judicial review at the federal level; states operate differently, often providing that FOIA cases are to be given expedited consideration by the courts, meaning scheduling takes precedence over most of the rest of a court's calendar). Call or write the FOIA office to follow up on requests that have been pending for an unreasonable period of time, and keep a record of all communications.

For complex requests, document production takes the following course: A first production of records to which no party in the internal deliberations objected for possible withholding or redaction. Then, at some later point, a second production, reflecting successful deliberations over some portion of those objected-to/questioned records, now released in full after consultation and agreement that, ultimately, no information will be withheld. This second step can be skipped or repeated, depending on the complexity of the request and the volume of responsive records. After reviewing the first or second (or third) partial production, you may have found further threads to pull. Do not feel a need to wait for final production before pursuing this more targeted follow-up.

Finally, at some point—and this can take months or up to several years depending on the complexity or political sensitivity of your request, and the pressure if any from partisans to derail it or, from the other direction, move it forward—you receive the final production. This may include further documents released in full after further deliberation over possible withholdings or redactions, all documents with redactions, and an acknowledgment, or even a bare-bones description, of the information that's being withheld and under what exception. This is where the real work begins.

What They Owe You

Covered agencies must fully and completely respond to requests for information. This includes for "agency records," with a "reasonable search" meaning reasonably calculated to produce all responsive records (which does not mean they owe you a search that does produce all such records). This process does not advertise subjectivity but in practice cannot escape it. Any unreasonable subjectivity, that is which results in an insufficient search or production, will be resolved on appeal.

Questions to consider while reviewing the productions—other than, what other alleys does this ask me to run down?—are principally, does the search appear to have been adequate? and do the claimed withholdings pass muster on their face?

What Is a "Reasonable FOIA Search" in the Age of Obama?

The term search means to "review, manually or by automated means, agency records for the purpose of locating those records which are responsive to a request."[5] In determining whether or not a search is reasonable, courts are mindful of the purpose of FOIA to bring about the broadest possible disclosure.[6] The requirement, "reasonably calculated to uncover all relevant documents,"[7] raises a practical problem: employees are asked to produce their own records responsive to the request, despite the obvious incentive (proven by experience) to withhold damaging or embarrassing emails or other records. It seems that any search conducted in this way is therefore unreasonable on its face.

This is nonetheless the typical practice unless the employee has left the agency or until a search rises to a certain level, for example, administrative appeal. Then the agency's office of general counsel often becomes involved. These offices approach each case as a matter of course as if preparing for litigation. They perform two steps, the absence of which exposes any potentially revealing FOIA request to corruption: an information officer pulls records from a central resource, and the employee is asked to attest under penalty of perjury how they conducted their search, why they did and did not choose to search where they chose to search or not search, and to answer any questions the lawyer might have when he discovers possible gaps (for example, have you used any personal computer or email account to conduct related business?).

Even though all employees implicitly attest that they are aware of and complied with all laws and policies, the biggest gap is that most FOIA requests never get to this level. When one does, a gap remains if the lawyer does not suspect, does not ask, or otherwise does not learn of facts such as that the employee performs official business on private assets like Gmail or personal computers. The burden is on the employee to raise this, but those who did these things did so despite being expected, like all federal employees, to perform official business on official resources—this is why the resources are provided.

We now know that employees are generally not prohibited from using such private resources but are obligated to retain and preserve the records, and provide them when responsive to a FOIA request. But we have also seen that when given this opportunity to conduct searches for their own records responsive to FOIA requests, sometimes they will search only emails, or avoid certain files, or exclude search terms or fields of records regardless of the language of the request and for their own reasons. That is not per se reasonable under the law and therefore not per se permissible, and it does occur. Unless or until it is caught. Catching it requires a successful appeal. That requires either possessing information that the search and/or production was deficient, or a thorough appeal officer who identifies and fills gaps by going back to employees, as many times as it takes.

Even though each employee should expressly attest to their actions at this stage under penalty of perjury, the most thorough appeal cannot overcome an employee determined to maintain secrecy. That exposes the inadequacy of the safety net to protect against this: an operating assumption that employees, who are all expected to be aware of and comply with record-retention policies, will honestly and fully execute their obligations. That is necessary under any scenario, given our system, though how much room they have to abuse the condition is not.

Alternatively, we can take comfort in the fact that an unsupervised search allowing for abuses is not reasonable and so does not satisfy FOIA's requirements.[8] But you still must demonstrate that the search was or was likely deficient.

An agency must search "those files which officials expec[t will] contain the information requested."[9] So remind the agency, if it appears necessary, that courts inquire into both the form of the search and whether the correct record repositories were searched. "[T]he agency cannot limit its search to only one record system if there are others that are likely to turn up the information requested."[10] Similarly, an agency cannot create a filing system that makes it likely that discrete classes of data will be overlooked.[11]

The reasonableness of a search is determined ad hoc but there are rules, including that it cannot be cursory,[12] and there can be no evidence of bad faith, as demonstrated by, for example, an extraordinary delay ("much longer than the average period of time" as compared to the average delay for that agency or department in recent preceding years).[13] All of this also raises the issue, increasing in importance with federal employees so actively using practices to defeat transparency laws, that agencies cannot tailor their document retention or destruction practices to avoid FOIA's requirements.[14] This also means that an employee cannot conduct their search to the exclusion of email accounts created for them that the public does not know about, and cannot search to the exclusion of private email or personal computers on which they have performed relevant work. But they still do.

Until the appeal stage you are largely at the agency's mercy on its claims of reasonableness, unless you already possess some agency record not produced or identified by the search, or that indicates the existence of other records. The important D.C. Circuit, which handles the bulk of FOIA litigation, has not hesitated to hold searches inadequate where documents in the record make reference to other responsive documents that have not been produced.[15] If you present an agency with evidence that it overlooked responsive documents it must act upon it.[16] And "a law-abiding agency" must "admit and correct error" in its searches "when error is revealed."[17]

Naturally, "there are some limits on what an agency must do to satisfy its FOIA obligations."[18] So, while it is not acceptable to simply reject requests or avoid looking in obvious corners, agencies cannot be forced, for example, to go back into decades of archives. FOIA does not obligate an agency to scour the earth for every last responsive document, but an agency must undertake search efforts reasonably designed to find all responsive records.

The key to prying loose those records revealed in the Big Wind cover-up was a pincer movement: filing requests for the same records with both offices I believed to be involved in the effort ultimately exposed. The field office (NREL), not apparently accustomed to stonewalling and less enamored of the possible attention that would accompany exposure of or being sued over same, put DOE headquarters in a difficult position by coughing up the records ahead of the more politicized (but, I acknowledge, also more heavily burdened) D.C. office's timeline.

And even assuming an honest and diligent search by interested parties, or simply a disinterested search, it is an inescapable truth that FOIA searches remain inherently subjective.

Two versions of the same FOIA request can produce very different responses, whether both confront the same exemptions used to withhold information—or none at all. These exemptions can be applied differently, with neither interpretation necessarily facially unlawful, but simply subjective (although, particularly with Obama's emphasis on the long-standing rule to release unless prohibited, both likely are improper). The same subjectivity can result in two different sets of responsive records claiming no withholdings, as well. By its words the "Obama Standard" made this practice extinct; in deed it is alive and well.

One requesting party might receive a document missing some information provided to the other requesting party, while having other information provided that was redacted for the other party.[19] This is only rectified on appeal. Recall the bureaucratic belief that they have no incentive to err on the side of transparency but great incentive to let you make your case on appeal. So appeal invocation of exemptions, particularly redactions, as a routine matter.

Production under one of my FOIA pursuits was delayed just before the records were to be released, according to the lawyer handling the appeal for the government, because he found inconsistencies in redaction patterns among the various documents, and inconsistent application of exemptions, which had to be harmonized. This took additional months. (Once this was corrected the response was delayed months further when it was discovered materials had not been copied properly, with many pages skipped and blank pages provided instead; a government lawyer spent his time at the photocopier making sure it was done right.)

In a different case, this subjectivity (if I'm in a charitable mood) was egregiously demonstrated by completely different responses given a politically sensitive request by two offices within the same controversial department in the Obama administration. One FOIA officer corresponded, took calls, and was what the term "public servant" denotes; the other provided no status reports when requested and otherwise was completely unresponsive to my several overtures. One went online to locate particular information to better refine the search terms and produced responsive records; the other claimed "no records," even though the first office's production included copies of records that by their nature (congressional correspondence) would be principally held by the second office ("congressional relations").

Sometimes, of course, subjective responses are not so accidental, such as UVa's disparate treatment of Greenpeace and a conservative lawmaker making substantively identical requests. Also, the NOAA example exposed by the previously cited inspector general report reflected just two ways of refusing to properly search, which were to exclude a universe of records from the search and to not farm out the request to parties who would have responsive records, both on a false pretense purely of the (conflicted) employee's invention. It took several years and four requesters before they were caught and immediately abandoned the game (I'm proud to have caught and called them on it).[20] It was another year after this IG report that I learned from NOAA that the employee exposed in the inquiry had also routinely used her private email and personal computer to conduct the very same official business. This did not leave me confident that the records over which she alone had control at all times were all produced.

Is the Document Production Reasonable?

Arguably, any production relying on conflicted employees to produce their own records is inherently unreasonable. Only the searching party knows what he did and did not do. Similarly, only an agency knows what it is withholding. Under FOIA all the agency provides the requesting party is the number of records withheld and a claimed exemption. As such, it is inherently difficult to tell whether an agency's document production is sufficient or deficient. It was this inability of the requesting party to know these facts that was the premise for the landmark

FOIA opinion in the D.C. Circuit Court of Appeals, *Vaughn v. Rosen*. That court recognized that this "lack of knowledge by the party seeing [*sic*] disclosure seriously distorts the traditional adversary nature of our legal system's form of dispute resolution [under which] the facts relevant to a dispute are more or less equally available to adverse parties."[21]

The requester cannot easily determine the validity of the agency's claimed exemptions because, barring a break like that in the British Gmail case, the requesting party typically does not know that certain responsive records exist. (In that case, not even the agency knew the records existed, but only because they didn't think to ask the employee and the employee did not volunteer the information.)

The *Vaughn* court called for implementing the law so as to "(1) assure that a party's right to information is not submerged beneath governmental obfuscation and mischaracterization, and (2) permit the court system effectively and efficiently to evaluate the factual nature of disputed information."[22] This means that agencies must prepare an itemized index, correlating each withholding with a specific FOIA exemption and a justification for that exemption with specificity and particularity enough "for a proper determination of whether they are exempt from disclosure."[23] That means identifying each document withheld, the statutory exemption claimed for each, and how disclosure would damage the interests protected by the claimed exemption. Not "boilerplate explanations" for withholdings.[24] The requester (and the court) must be able to determine if privilege was claimed properly.[25]

This means specificity, separation, and indexing, "detail[ing] which portions of the document are disclosable and which are allegedly exempt . . . itemizing and indexing [to] correlate statements made in the Government's refusal justification with the actual portions of the document."[26]

One of the persistent deficiencies remaining after *Vaughn* is that this requirement only kicks in once you sue, which somewhat incongruously leaves you to administratively appeal, for example, blanket withholdings or redactions of entire documents, without even a reasonably described basis for the withholding. As such, your argument that their basis is insufficient is still often speculative, and is largely premised in context. The same is true when you are denied on appeal, unless a conscientious administration lawyer handled it, which is usually only the case when a request has obtained sufficient legal attention ensuring they prepare their response with an eye toward defending it in court. All agency regulations do provide that they supply (on appeal) adequate justification why a record or redacted information is being withheld. The intention, not uniformly respected and with no meaningful remedy where it is ignored, is to leave little question what is being withheld and why. Not a *Vaughn* index, but close.

What to Do When the Records Don't Come: Appeal, Sue, Neither, or Both?

If the agency's response is either seemingly insufficient or nonexistent production, despite a reasonable time given the request's complexity or lack thereof, you confront the issue of getting around this obstacle. Unlike judicial review of other agency action, requiring you to overcome the difficult burden of demonstrating that the agency's behavior was arbitrary or capricious, FOIA expressly places the burden "on the agency to sustain its action."[27] The 2007 FOIA amendments created an Office of Government Information Services (OGIS), located in the National Archives and Records Administration, to offer mediation services to resolve disputes between FOIA requesters and agencies, as a nonexclusive alternative to litigation.[28] Each agency also provides instructions on its website for this option, as well as for appealing, and many provide directions for these options in their initial determination letter.

When an agency has responded to you in some fashion, including even an acknowledgment letter containing nothing substantive, administrative appeals are generally required under FOIA before suing because of the general rule that you must exhaust available administrative remedies before availing yourself of the courts. FOIA contains a major limitation on this rule, that a FOIA requester "shall be deemed to have exhausted his administrative remedies" whenever an agency fails to comply with a time limit of the act, at which time he can seek immediate judicial review.[29] This seems straightforward, but thanks to a 1991 case it becomes nuanced. Exhaustion will be presumed where there is a "certainty of an adverse decision."[30] Previously, exhaustion was deemed to occur after the statutory deadline for responding had passed, which was ten days and now is twenty. This was true even if the agency responded after the deadline but before suit was filed. No longer.

"Now, in *Oglesby*,[31] the D.C. Circuit has interpreted this 'constructive' exhaustion provision to merely provide FOIA requesters with an 'option to go to court immediately' if they so choose. . . . [I]f a FOIA requester . . . does not exercise his right to go to court directly after the agency breaches its response deadline, then he may lose the benefit of 'constructive' exhaustion if the agency provides him with a proper response (including notification of his administrative appeal right) before he actually files his FOIA lawsuit."[32] That is, "an administrative appeal is mandatory if the agency cures its failure to respond within the statutory time period by responding to the FOIA request before suit is filed."[33]

This is important because a court will bounce your complaint and you will have wasted your time if you were required to appeal before suing. A basic rule to follow is if you do not get a response after twenty working days you have received an adverse determination and may sue without any further requirement of administrative exhaustion by appealing. However, a requester only retains this right to sue, without first appealing, "until such time as the agency provides him with a proper FOIA response."[34] So if you receive a response that is late, but nonetheless before you sue, then you must appeal first. Similarly, with any unsatisfying actual response, pursue the internal appeal according to the instructions set forth in the agency's letter.

Other permutations exist. For example, if the agency gives you a "no records" response, that is now also an adverse determination and if the agency fails to notify you of your right to an administrative appeal, you are not obligated to pursue that course and can proceed straight to court; if they do notify you of your right to appeal, that is essentially a note that you must appeal, and so you should do so but within a fixed time that most agencies specify in their FOIA regulations (usually thirty to sixty days). Their response to you will reference this and point you to the regulations.

Appealing merely extends the process by another month, as you are similarly entitled to sue over an agency not concluding your appeal after the twenty-working-day statutory deadline for adjudicating administrative appeals.[35] Also, administrative appeals are very often effective and much more timely than the courts for challenging deficient searches, fee waiver denials, and the improper full or partial withholdings of responsive documents.

Keep in mind on that count that, although FOI requests are typically given expedited treatment under local court rules, I have a case nearly three years old, with one motion fully briefed sitting before the judge with no action for nearly two of those years. One Washington litigator with whom I have worked on FOIA cases, and who is similarly aware of these delays, bluntly wrote to me, "It is a black hole. FOIA is broken." So try to work within the administrative system as much as it allows.

As with the original request, agencies vary in their requirements of the specifics, so revisit their website for details, beginning with the often different address for appeals, and what enclosures are required (usually all correspondence beginning with the original request). There may be specific format requirements, for example how to set forth your grounds for appeal. You must clearly label it "Appeal under the Freedom of Information Act." State your expectation of a response within twenty business days. And as with the original request, provide no opportunity for delay or denial by not paying attention to these requirements.[36]

The appellate process is typically handled by career attorneys. They will often (but not always) obtain affidavits from the staff who were tasked with searching and producing their own records, and where they see gaps will have them filled. I have found great cooperation among appellate staff, particularly on matters that have drawn the attention of management and are thereby handled diligently; they have identified deficiencies in searches, in responses, and in overly aggressive withholding that I did not possess the information to identify. If your appeal challenges the sufficiency of the search, you also can expect an adequacy-of-search discussion in their response to you, which can resemble a legal memorandum (these are often prepared in anticipation of litigation).

Appealing dramatically increases your chances of having an information officer pull records, as opposed to merely staff whose records are at issue and therefore with an interest in hiding embarrassing records. It does not guarantee that personal email accounts or computers will be searched, so you should provide reasons to believe this step is reasonably necessary. You can raise the odds of the employee at least being called to attest whether he did use private accounts or computers by noting in your original request that they must provide responsive records from any such assets used when performing work-related activity.

Your best hope lies, for various reasons, in the administrative appeal process. FOIA officers routinely leave releasing discretionary information to appeals officers and otherwise err on the side of withholding; the courts can take years and years for even a simple matter despite FOIA cases being granted expedited treatment. Plan to appeal, and prepare for appeal when drafting the first request. Work with the appeals officer without hounding him. Going to court gives them a black mark but gets the matter out of their hands, while expediting nothing for you.

If your request or appeal is denied, either expressly or by virtue of an unresponsive agency (constructively), you may sue, given conditions already discussed. But be warned that as a general matter twenty days no longer really means twenty days. It means "first-in, first-out," and so long as an agency is proceeding with "due diligence," and so long as there is no exceptional reason to favor a requester over others whose requests came before his, the agency is allowed the time reasonably necessary "to complete its review of the records."[37] Again, the reasonableness of a delay is a function of the request's complexity and the agency's average response time over recent years, which is available in the annual FOIA compliance report they are required under the law to publish.

You are free to make a showing of need for expedited treatment. Media outlets regularly do so and in fact some agencies limit this option of expedited treatment to "requesters primarily engaged in disseminating

information." Success on that count is unlikely, and chances are that
even if it rises to a level of appealing that (see DOJ's page giving guidance on this);[38] you'll end up in court anyway seeking recognition that
you warrant that status. Meaning, it is worth asking for, you are unlikely
to be granted it, and if you are not, that's for all practical purposes the
end of the issue.

Further, even media outlets granted priority treatment under the federal FOIA can face an unresponsive bureaucracy. A writer for *ProPublica*
("Journalism in the Public Interest") received a response in mid-2012 for
a request he filed in 2008 seeking information on complaints over TSA
body pat-downs.[39] TSA gave the typical excuses—gee our backlog is big;
gosh we receive so darn many requests—before simply apologizing.

It isn't that *ProPublica's* request was insufficiently narrow and targeted, which limits avenues of escape for the bureaucracy but also sets
up the appeal for success (while positioning the agency as the obvious
obstruction in the event filing suit becomes necessary); but making certain yours is narrowly written should be your primary drafting objective.
All of this also tells you that it makes good sense to gauge what is really
behind the agency's delay in responding to you. Before filing suit, it is
advisable to show what a reasonable person you are by taking the initiative to communicate with the agency, including notifying them of your
intention to protect your appellate rights and asking for a report on the
status of your request. Document it all. This often will change nothing,
but the record will leave you in better standing in the court's eyes, and
the agency worse off if it ignores you. Finally, FOIA.gov and the Department of Justice's FOIA Manual can be helpful resources.[40]

When you sue under the federal FOIA, the proper court to file in is
the local federal court, because FOIA disputes present a federal question.
Venue is proper either where you live, where the appropriate regional
office with which you are dealing resides, or in Washington, D.C. It is
prudent to file in the state where you live. The agency makes life hard
enough on you. Don't add to it.

Conclusion:
Annoy the Statists, Ask What They're Up To

The public deserves and increasingly demands transparency from a government they view, with substantial justification, as growing further out of control and increasingly unresponsive to the governed who pay for it.

Transparency was the liberals' idea, indispensable to good government, and now they have turned it on its head. Liberals demand privacy for public employees and disclosure by private citizens who dare oppose the liberal agenda, all in transparency's name but for political purposes of maintaining secrecy or engaging in intimidation, as the case may be.

Don't let them get away with it. Transparency impacts public policy making, leading to greater citizen interest in policies affecting them, greater participation, and holding taxpayer servants to account. And that, it seems, is the problem that our political class and other elites have with their own long-standing principles that now, we are told, pose grave threats if applied as originally intended, and equally among citizens.

They're different, they've got big plans, and we're getting in their way. They love our system except when it inconveniences them. So they are waging an open as well as a clandestine war on the public transparency guaranteed us by law.

Public institutions increasingly and unlawfully refuse to produce requested records illuminating what their bureaucratic and ideological running mates "are up to." This comes through ad hoc ploys and, as a way of responding to the threat posed and to technology, developing systematic tactics to skirt the laws and frustrate your right to know.

Public employees are using private email accounts and private computers in a growing refusal to create or maintain records, abusing the trust and the discretion granted to them. This is a deliberate attempt to hide things meant by law and policy to be public.

Political appointees and activists serving in career positions have their justifications, or rationalizations, advanced for them by media and other enablers. These distill down to their decision that either they don't want anyone to know about what they're up to, or it's none of your business despite the conditions and the promises made when accepting public employment or otherwise the taxpayer's money.

The new campaign to obstruct taxpayer access is robustly waged at agencies throughout the federal government, and all the way down to state universities. The people who just won't let us be insist that when it comes to learning what it is they're up to, we leave them alone. Except for that part about our paying their way in life.

But our leaving them alone is not going to happen unless and until they succeed in making that "criminal," as they absurdly claim we are by seeking information.

On issues of pressing concern to you, ask, are public servants being faithful to the public? Are they putting special interests before the public interest and subverting their statutory responsibilities to provide us with open, fair, and transparent deliberations? Often the answers to these questions are available through a FOIA request. Sometimes the revelation is that which the requester sought; frequently you merely stumble upon one inconvenient truth while searching for another.

You need to use this tool. Act on evidence, hunch, or routine as you see fit. When you learn through friends, read or overhear somewhere of government excess—from Vegas bacchanals to casting calls for clowns and magicians, or any boondoggle or other disrespect to the taxpayer—ask questions. Get answers. Hold government accountable. Through exposure, force reversals of decisions to misuse your money and the state's authority. Learn the truth about apparent abuses of taxpayer wealth or governmental power at national, state, local, and campus levels.

Narrowly, specifically tailor your request, and reasonably describe what you are looking for so a court cannot say it was your fault that the agency took so long or responded too narrowly. Expect that any crack or wiggle room will be exploited, even manufactured, so try not to leave any. If they rebuff you in whole or in part, appeal.

"Going fishing," unsure what you will find, is perfectly acceptable. And FOIA cares not about your motivation, only that you properly follow the law's requirements in seeking the documents and that the agency similarly follow the law when searching for and providing, or withholding, them.

In any event, be persistent. Make them treat you with respect, or wrench what is due to you from them. Respect will come, even if forced. As will the disinfectant of sunshine.

These transparency laws, providing taxpayers the ability to extract records from a too often resistant bureaucracy against which it can seem one has no recourse, are indispensable for concerned taxpayers to illuminate what might be the most out-of-control federal government in history. Your doing so is "a structural necessity in a real democracy."[1]

Join the fun. Taxpayers learning what their government is up to has become too great a cross for our current political and academic classes to bear. That tells us we should demand to know more.

Do not believe the necessary work is being done, the important questions being asked. "Real journalism" has gone on hiatus. Liberals have so perverted "transparency" that even when they obtain information important to the public's understanding of government, including when it involves scandal, they sit on it if it's the wrong kind of transparency. This is now proved among supposed congressional watchdogs, "real journalists," and others in the tank for their leftist brethren.

When a senior EPA official was captured on video explaining his reprehensible "philosophy" of enforcement that each and every American should be ashamed of—he compared it to the Romans' random method of illustrating the benefits of cooperation by "crucifying" the first five townspeople they came upon, to send a message—the damning video encapsulating Obama's EPA was taken down within hours on the basis of a completely spurious claim of copyright violation.[2] It seems a liberal activist was proud of what he had witnessed and filmed, but when the wrong kind of people took notice, well, this became the sort of information that the public should not see.[3]

The activist even called his work "Citizen Media for We The People." But for the right kind of people. It was meant to encourage liberals that, don't worry, their kind in the administration are up to no good. It wasn't intended to let the public in on the outrage. They might demand such abuses stop, and possibly some accountability. That's certainly transparency and it shows what sunshine can do, but apparently it was the wrong kind of transparency. As HotAir blogger Ed Morrissey wrote, "it seems doubly ironic that a so-called 'citizen media activist' would suddenly fight against openness and transparency. Isn't that the whole point of citizen-media activism? Their YouTube page brags that they bring viewers 'videos that you will not see in the Corporate Media.' Well, congratulations—you found one that scooped the "Corporate Media"! And . . . now [liberal 'citizen media activist' David] McFatridge wants it hidden?"[4] The video was not a public record but it did reveal the ugly truth that was passing as public service. It also simply illustrated the liberals' selective and perverted view of transparency.

Clearly "good government" is in the eye of the beholder. Liberals want their many taxpayer-funded outrages hidden. We need them exposed, and the laws give us that right. It is up to all of us to fill the gap left by the traditional public watchdogs, which are also traditionally liberal. They have fallen down on the job and arguably have stood down, giving a pass to this Orwellian inversion of transparency. We cannot rely upon them.

There also are just not enough bodies in the think tanks and activist groups to pick up where the media has decided to leave off until political circumstances lead them to stir again. In short, we need you to weigh in and demand more, to insist that the public receive the government is it owed under our laws.

The solution is therefore to equip and mobilize you, the citizen journalist and the citizen activist, the private inspectors general, to successfully overcome the new reality of transparency. It is now incumbent upon you, when an idea strikes, to not presume someone's got it covered. If you've got a concern, there is a law to help you learn what you need to learn, or to discover more threads to pull, more bread crumbs to follow. Pull them and follow them. You may be surprised what you find, or it may confirm your suspicion. Most important, however, is that it may make a difference.

NOTES

1. When Freedom of Information Requests Are "Criminal," Only Criminals Will Request Information

1. *NLRB v. Robbins Tire & Rubber Co.*, 437 U.S. 214, 242 (1978).
2. Louis D. Brandeis, "Other People's Money—And How Bankers Use It," 1914, first serialized in essay form in *Harper's Weekly* in 1913. This quote comes from Chapter 5, "What Publicity Can Do," available at http://www .law.louisville.edu/library/collections/brandeis/node/196.
3. Woodrow Wilson, "Committee or Cabinet Government?," *Overland Monthly,* January 1884, no. 1, p. 26, vol. 3, Second Series. Samuel Carson, San Francisco.
4. These admissions are now legion. See, e.g., Anthony "Van" Jones, "When the oil spill had happened in the spring of 2010, there was another moment to say, 'Hold on a second, let's relook at energy policy in America. Should we be subsidizing companies who are risking our health immediately and in the long-term?' We didn't do it. You've never seen the environmental movement more quiet during an oil spill. I guarantee you, if John McCain had been President, with that oil spill, or George Bush had been President with that oil spill, I'd have been out there with a sign protesting. I didn't, because, of who the President was." Afterwords with Van Jones, C-SPAN, April 20, 2012, http://www.c-spanvideo.org/program/304302–1, at 19:14 mark.
5. See, e.g., Order on Motions for Summary Judgment, *Sea Turtle Conservancy et al. v. Locke,* just one of many cases involving EPA and emergency rulemaking authority, under the Endangered Species Act but which authority also exists under the Clean Air and National Environmental Policy Acts applicable in this case I described. N.D. FL, 09-CV-259-SPM-GRJ, available at http://earthjustice.org/sites/default/files/seaturtlesopin ionjuly72011.pdf. EPA regularly uses emergency authority in the name of protecting of a handful of sea turtles; such measures can last as long as needed: for example, until the proposed rule went into place.
6. Michael Fumento, "Polluted Science," *Reason,* August–September 1997, p. 32.
7. See, e.g., James Cerstenzang, "Clean-Air Plan Fuels Backstage U.S. Fight," *Los Angeles Times*, April 20, 1997, p. Al.

8. Declan McCullagh, "Obama Admin: Cap and Trade Could Cost Families $1,761 A Year," CBSNews.com, September 15, 2009, http://www.cbs news.com/8301–504383_162–5314040–504383.html; Declan McCullagh, "Treasury Docs: Enviro Taxes Could Reach $400 Billion A Year," CBSNews .com, September 18, 2009, http://www.cbsnews.com/8301–504383_162 –5322108–504383.html.

9. "Solyndra scandal timeline," *Washington Post,* viewed May 10, 2012, http:// www.washingtonpost.com/wp-srv/special/politics/solyndra-scandal-time line/.

10. This email read, "Subject: Dinner Sunday? In my new kitchen? Mike— Robin's away (again . . .) so I'm making my own social plans for the weekend. If you're around Sunday, wanna join a casual dinner at chez Roy-Zoi (sans Roy)? Missy and a couple of other fun political animals will be there. Lemme know!—cz." (This presumably references Zoi's husband, Robin Roy, who at the time worked for a "green jobs" company and soon migrated over to a green pressure group.)

11. The Anti-Deficiency Act, 31 USC § 1342—Limitation on voluntary services, prohibits the acceptance of voluntary or personal services unless authorized by law.

12. Peter Schweizer, "Obama Campaign Backers and Bundlers Rewarded With Green Grants and Loans," *Daily Beast,* November 12, 2011, http:// www.thedailybeast.com/newsweek/2011/11/13/how-obama-s-alternative -energy-programs-became-green-graft.html.

13. *Presidential Memorandum for Heads of Executive Departments and Agencies,* 75 F.R. § 4683, 4683 (Jan. 21, 2009).

14. Christopher C. Horner, "Newt vs. Eco-Book Co-Author: Released E-mail Begs Questions About Mysteriously Dropped 'Climate' Chapter," BigGovernment.com, January 6, 2012, http://www.breitbart.com/ Big-Government/2012/01/06/Newt-vs-Eco-Book-Co-Author—Released -Email-begs-questions-about-mysteriously-dropped-climate-chapter. Gingrich made this claim on December 29, 2011. A December 7, 2011, email from his coauthor, Terry Maple, to chapter author Katharine Hayhoe of Texas Tech University read:

> From: "Terry L. Maple"
> Date: 7 December 2011 16:00:03 CST
> To: "Hayhoe, Katharine"
> Subject: Book
>
> I just talked to the reporter that talked to you about Newt. I'm sorry that it has been so long since we communicated but I've been swamped with revisions based on things like the Japanese nuclear accident, issues with ethanol (both chapters in

the book) and Newt's availability since he is now so immersed in the campaign. [O]ur editor has been leaning on me to get these revisions together. I don't contemplate any big changes to your submission, I just need to get the transitional material together for Newt to review. I'm hoping to get everything resolved by March 1 so the book can get into some orderly production but don't hold me to that schedule. Of course, you probably have some updated material and you are welcome to make changes. The title has changed a little; it is now "Environmental Entrepreneurs" and the emphasis is on the author's personal story. When I have the revised chapter sequences I'll send you an outline so you can see how it all fits together but I need for Vince (our editor) and for Newt to approve all of it before I can distribute it to the chaper [*sic*] authors. JHP [i.e., Johns Hopkins University Press] doesn't have the book lined up for production yet so there is a way to go before we get to any pre-production publicity. As I told REP, if he becomes president we will see what a green conservative can do. It will be very interesting to see how this different approach work to to [*sic*] advance a new kind of environmental agenda. FYI my retirement as CEO of the palm Beach Zoo gives me a lot more time to work on this project. Thanks again for your patience.

Terry L. Maple, Ph.D.

15. See, e.g., Rachel Levinson-Waldman, "Academic Freedom and the Public's Right to Know: How to Counter the Chilling Effect of FOIA Requests on Scholarship," September 2011, American Constitutional Society, http://www.acslaw.org/sites/default/files/Levinson_-_ACS_FOIA_First_Amdmt_Issue_Brief.pdf.

2. A Life of FOI "Crime"

1. Edward Felker and Stephen Dinan, "Democrats urged to play down 'global warming,'" *Washington Times,* June 19, 2009; available at http://www.washingtontimes.com/news/2009/jun/19/party-memo-urges-democrats-to-fix-pitch-on-climate/.
2. For a compendium of related items, including Enron documents, see the website of former Enron economist Rob Bradley at http://www.masterresource.org/category/enronken-lay/.
3. See, e.g., "The Rector and Visitors of the University of Virginia's Petition to Set Aside Civil Investigative Demands Issued to the University of Virginia,"

May 27, 2010, p. 1, available at http://voices.washingtonpost.com/virginia politics/UVA%20filing.pdf.

4. Christopher Booker, "Climate change: this is the worst scientific scandal of our generation," *Telegraph* (UK), November 28, 2009, http://www.tele graph.co.uk/comment/columnists/christopherbooker/6679082/Climate -change-this-is-the-worst-scientific-scandal-of-our-generation.html.

5. Despite the unsubstantiated talking point that these mostly public records were "hacked" or "stolen," clearly to discourage interest in their content as prurient, fellow global warming supporter Dr. Richard Muller of Berkeley notes, "Then the data came out. They weren't hacked like a lot of people say, most people who know this business believe they were leaked, by one of the members of the team who was, who was really upset with them." Lecture, Dr. Richard Muller, "Climate Change and Energy: Important Recent Developments," available at http://www.youtube.com/watch?v=VbR0EPWgkEI, last viewed May 24, 2012. In July 2012, the Norfolk Constabulary closed their investigation, concluding that the emails were obtained from outside the University of East Anglia computer system, but that their ideas on who actually did obtain the records could only be a "hypothesis," and that, "To be clear, we did not get any indication as to who was responsible."

6. See, e.g., emails from Michael Mann: Email # 0810, May 30, 2008, speaking of academic scientist Dr. Judith Curry of Georgia Tech, who had angered him by substantively engaging those who had exposed Mann's work, "I gave up on Judith Curry a while ago. I don't know what she think's [*sic*] she's doing, but *its* [*sic*] not helping the cause." Email #3115, August 3, 2004, "By the way, when is Tom C going to formally publish his roughly 1500 year reconstruction??? It would help the cause to be able to refer to that reconstruction as confirming Mann and Jones, etc." And email #3940, May 26, 2005, "They will (see below) allow us to provide some discussion of the synthetic example, referring to the J. Cimate paper (which should be finally accepted upon submission of the revised final draft), so that should help the cause a bit." All spelling is as in the originals.

7. See "Brief in Opposition to Petition to Set Aside Civil Investigative Demands," July 13, 2010, available at http://voices.washingtonpost.com/ virginiapolitics/AG%20Mann%20file%20July%2013.pdf.

8. *USA Today* writer and global warming enthusiast Dan Vergano pursued the records of George Mason University professor Edward Wegman, who produced research critical of the global warming "Hockey Stick." Vergano, apparently working with Michael Mann's coauthor, Raymond Bradley, ignored that Bradley "apparently committed academic misconduct in his zeal to smear Wegman." See Anthony Watts, "The Washington Post produces a bigoted editorial against the public's right to know," WattsUp WithThat.com, May 30, 2011, http://wattsupwiththat.com/2011/05/30/

the-washington-post-produces-a-bigoted-editorial-against-the-public-right
-to-know/.

9. George F. Will, "James Q. Wilson, honored prophet," *Washington Post,*
March 2, 2012, http://www.washingtonpost.com/opinions/james-q-wilson
-americas-prophet/2012/03/02/gIQAtEWGnR_story.html.

10. Peggy Noonan, "We're More Than Political Animals," *Wall Street Journal,*
March 2, 2012, http://online.wsj.com/article/declarations.html?mod=WSJ
_topnav_opinion.

11. George F. Will, "James Q. Wilson, honored prophet," *Washington Post,*
March 2, 2012.

12. Video available at, e.g., http://drinkingwateradvisor.wordpress.com/2011
/11/05/lisa-jackson-usepa-administrator-speaks-at-berkeley-law-school/,
November 5, 2011, last viewed February 20, 2012; ellipses reflect a rhetorical pause, not omission.

13. Thomas Friedman, "Down with Everything," *New York Times,* April 21,
2012, http://www.nytimes.com/2012/04/22/opinion/sunday/friedman
-down-with-everything.html.

14. See, e.g., Tish Durkin, "Why Washington needs backroom deals," *Week,*
March 5, 2012, http://theweek.com/bullpen/column/225164/why-wash
ington-needs-backroom-deals.

15. See, e.g., Miles Mogulescu, "NY Times Reporter Confirms Obama
Made Deal to Kill Public Option," *Huffington Post,* March 16, 2010,
http://www.huffingtonpost.com/miles-mogulescu/ny-times-reporter
-confirm_b_500999.html.

16. Thomas R. Friedman interview, *Meet the Press,* NBC, May 23, 2010.

17. See, e.g., Norm Leahy, "The Washington Post's FOIA double standard,"
Washington Examiner, May 31, 2011, http://washingtonexaminer.com
/local/local-opinion-zone/2011/05/washington-posts-foia-double-standard
/145787. Leahy also notes "it is interesting to see this newspaper, the very
one that, back in the day, risked much to publish the Pentagon Papers in an
effort to get the truth out there, should appear so upset when a former state
employee's emails are required to be made public under a long-standing
Virginia law promoting openness." See also "Silence from pressure groups
deafening; media joins hypocrisy," Press Release, American Tradition Institute, May 31, 2011, http://www.atinstitute.org/virginia-university-releases
-correspondence-of-professor-involved-in-hockey-stick-controversy/.

3. Transparency for Me, but Not for Thee

1. Landing page "Freedom of Information: About/History," Society of Professional Journalists, http://www.spj.org/foiabout.asp, reprinting an October
1996 piece, "FOIA: It's always there" in *Quill* by Paul McMasters, First

Amendment ombudsman at the Freedom Forum, a former national president of SPJ, and for four years SPJ's national FOI chair.

2. *U.S. Department of Justice v. Reporters Committee for Freedom of the Press,* 489 U.S. 749, 773 (1989).

3. *Environmental Protection Agency v. Mink,* 410 U.S. 73, 79 (1973).

4. Presidential Records Act (PRA) of 1978, 44 U.S.C. 2201–2207. See, e.g., http://www.archives.gov/presidential-libraries/laws/1978-act.html.

5. Steven Braun, "Mitt Romney Used Private Email Accounts to Conduct State Business While Massachusetts Governor," *Huffington Post,* March 9, 2012, http://www.huffingtonpost.com/2012/03/09/mitt-romney-emails_n_1335712.html.

6. Federal Records Act of 1950 (FRA), 44 U.S.C. 3301 et seq.

7. http://www.spj.org/foiabout.asp.

8. Ibid.

9. Associated Press, "AP and Freedom of Information," http://www.ap.org/foi/journalists.html.

10. This quote, the audio recording of which is played daily as a "bump" on my friend and radio host Joe Thomas's syndicated *Afternoon Constitutional* radio show, available at http://quentinwatson.wordpress.com/2004/02/24/dan-rather-a-trustworthy-voice, is attributed to Rather as spoken to a fellow CBS News employee during coverage of the 1996 elections. See, e.g., RatherBiased.com, http://www.ratherbiased.com/journalism.htm.

11. See, e.g., "Greenpeace lawsuit accuses chemical companies of spying on it," *New Orleans Times-Picayune,* April 28, 2011, http://www.nola.com/politics/index.ssf/2011/04/greenpeace_lawsuit_accuses_che.html.

12. "Mann stays in the hot seat: UVA fights requests for climate scientist's work," *Cville Weekly,* Will Goldsmith, January 18–24, 2011, http://www.c-ville.com/index.php?cat=141404064432695&ShowArticle_ID=12681701113900458.

13. "Harassing climate-change researchers," editorial, *Washington Post,* May 2011.

14. Ed O'Keefe, "New Obama Orders on Transparency, FOIA Requests," *Washington Post,* January 21, 2009.

15. "Change Has Come to WhiteHouse.gov," Macon Phillips, White House Blog, January 20, 2009, available at http://www.whitehouse.gov/blog/change_has_come_to_whitehouse-gov/

16. See, e.g., discussion of the Democrat National Committee ad, "What ELSE is Mitt Romney hiding?," at Ed Morrissey, "Do Democrats really want a fight over transparency?," HotAir.com, April 17, 2012, http://hotair.com/archives/2012/04/17/do-democrats-really-want-a-fight-over-transparency/.

17. "Mr. Romney's Secret Life: The public has a right to know what is on his tax returns and who is raising money for him," *Washington Post,* April

23, 2012, http://www.washingtonpost.com/opinions/mitt-romneys-secrets /2012/04/23/gIQAhvsdaT_story.html?wprss=rss_opinions.

18. Ibid.

19. See, e.g., Steve Pearlstein, "There's the Beef," *Washington Post,* February 22, 2008, http://www.washingtonpost.com/wp-dyn/content/article/2008/02 /21/AR2008022102826.html.

20. Victor Davis Hansen, "10 Things That We Learned from the Trayvon Martin Tragedy," *National Review,* The Corner blog, March 29, 2012, http:// www.nationalreview.com/corner/294779/10-things-we-ve-learned-trayvon -martin-tragedy-victor-davis-hanson.

21. Tim Ross, "Public 'should be charged to see government papers,'" *Telegraph* (UK), February 14, 2012, http://www.telegraph.co.uk/news/politics /9080715/Public-should-be-charged-to-see-government-papers.html.

22. "A Journey," quoted by Martin Rosenbaum, "Why Tony Blair thinks he was an idiot," BBC News, September 1, 2010, http://www.bbc.co .uk/blogs/opensecrets/2010/09/why_tony_blair_thinks_he_was_a.html, viewed February 16, 2012.

23. Nikki Fox, "Concerns over Climategate inquiry," BBC News, December 21, 2011, http://www.bbc.co.uk/news/uk-england-norfolk-16294420, viewed February 20, 2012.

24. "Justice Committee, Post-legislative scrutiny of the Freedom of Information Act 2000. Written evidence received," Exemplar FOI 07, http://www.publi cations.parliament.uk/pa/cm201012/cmselect/cmjust/writev/foi/foi.pdf.

25. Ibid.

26. Ibid.

27. "Larry Keller's visit with Special Agents from the EPA," Asheville (NC) Tea Party, May 10, 2012, http://ashevilleteaparty.org/?p=3690.

28. See, e.g., Ewan MacAskill, "Release of Sarah Palin emails angers US conservatives," *Guardian* (UK), June 11, 2011, http://www.guardian.co.uk/ world/2011/jun/11/sarah-palin-emails-conservative-reaction; see also Ewan MacAskill and Ed Pilkington, "Sarah Palin emails show life in Alaska, from tanning bed to Troopergate," *Guardian,* June 10, 2011, http://www.guard ian.co.uk/world/2011/jun/10/sarah-palin-emails-tanning-troopergate.

29. Media Matters, "2012: A Three-Year Campaign," viewed March 21, 2012, http://www.scribd.com/doc/81500388/25/Corporate-Transparency, pp. 82–84.

30. "The Corporate Disclosure Assault," editorial, *Wall Street Journal,* March 19, 2012, http://online.wsj.com/article/SB100014240527023046928045 77281532246401146.html.

31. See, e.g., Kim Strassel, "The President Has a List," *Wall Street Journal,* April 26, 2012, http://online.wsj.com/article/SB100014240527023047233045 77368280604524916.html.

32. "The President's Hit List," editorial, *Wall Street Journal,* May 12, 2012.
33. "Intimidation by Proxy," editorial, *Wall Street Journal,* May 9, 2012, http:// online.wsj.com/article/SB1000142405270230474660457738188291879 7726.html?mod=WSJ_Opinion_AboveLEFTTop.
34. In February 2012, a scientist/activist impersonated a nonprofit's board member, in apparent violation of the applicable (California and Illinois) laws, in order to obtain documents, from which he "more likely than not" forged another from the contents of these documents, according to a forensic analysis performed pro bono for meteorologist and blogger Anthony Watts of WattsUpWithThat.com ("The world's most viewed site on global warming and climate change", two-time, 2011, 2012, Bloggies Science Blog of the Year). See discussion of this, *infra.* Gleick falsely attributed the faked document to the group, and promoted a campaign against them on the basis of the purloined and forged records. In response, those at the highest levels of the journalistic and scientific establishments rushed to man the ramparts in defense of these actions.
35. The campaign to rationalize and even excuse Gleick's theft of private records, and worse, by some of the same people who condemned using legal means was premised on him and his movement seeking to combat others with whom they disagree. This was acceptable because the perpetrator "was defending a cause that he passionately views as righteous." John Horgan, "Should Global-Warming Activists Lie to Defend Their Cause?," *Scientific American,* February 24, 2012, http://blogs.scientificamerican.com/ cross-check/2012/02/24/should-global-warming-activists-lie-to-defend -their-cause/. In the Australian website for academic discourse we learned that it was okay because he merely "lied to a conservative think tank to access climate change documents." Stephan Lewandoski, "The morality of unmasking Heartland," The Conversation, February 22, 2012, http:// theconversation.edu.au/the-morality-of-unmasking-heartland-5494. It was okay because his "intentions" were right, "justified by the wider good." The "wider good" is defined as suppressing any opposition to the global warming establishment. "What Heartland is doing is harmful, because it gets in the way of public consensus and action," Garvey writes. So, "If Gleick frustrates the efforts of Heartland, isn't his lie justified by the good that it does?" James Garvey, "Peter Gleick lied, but was it justified by the wider good?," *Guardian* (UK), February 27, 2012, http://www.guardian .co.uk/environment/2012/feb/27/peter-gleick-heartland-institute-lie. The *Guardian* wrote a review of the "ethics debate among climate scientists," reporting that most lined up on the side of fraud. After quoting one of the few warmists who denounced Gleick, climate activist turned journalist Andrew Revkin, the article concludes "there were relatively few in the campaign or scientific community who shared that view." Suzanne

Goldenberg, "Gleick apology over Heartland leak stirs ethics debate among climate scientists," *Guardian* (UK), February 21, 2012, http://www.guard ian.co.uk/environment/2012/feb/21/gleick-apology-heartland-leak-ethics -debate?INTCMP=ILCNETTXT3487.

36. See, e.g., Brian Merchant, "Identity of 'DenialGate' Whistleblower Revealed. Is He a Hero or a Huckster?" TreeHugger.com, February 21, 2012, http://www.treehugger.com/corporate-responsibility/identity-denialgate -whistleblower-revealed-he-hero-or-huckster.html.

37. George Monbiot, "Anything to declare, Mr Booker? We need transparency about Heartland," *Guardian* (UK), February 24, 2012, http://www.guard ian.co.uk/environment/georgemonbiot/2012/feb/24/christopher-booker -heartland-climate. See also Don Mikulecky, "Michael Mann is a Modern Hero and we need to acknowledge that!," DailyKos, March 9, 2012, http:// www.dailykos.com/story/2012/03/09/1072828/-Michael-Mann-is-a-Mod ern-Hero-and-we-need-to-acknowledge-that-.

38. Those were from the Climategate affair, ritually claimed without evidence to have been "stolen" but, again, they were public records subject to FOI laws but unlawfully withheld and even destroyed. See *Los Angeles Times* writer Michael Hiltzik equating the "Climategate" scientists victimizing the public by illegally avoiding FOI requests and getting off on a FOIA statute of limitations technicality to Heartland being victimized by an act of criminal wire fraud. Michael Hiltzik, "Subterfuge vs. propaganda in global warming debate," *Los Angeles Times,* February 29, 2012, http://www .latimes.com/business/la-fi-hiltzik-20120229,0,1163347.column.

39. See, e.g., "Peter Gleick, a MacArthur 'genius' grant recipient for his work on global freshwater challenges and president of the Pacific Institute, admitted earlier this month to borrowing a page directly from the denialists' playbook. Posing as someone else. . . ." Editorial, "Michael Mann's counterstrike in the climate wars," *Los Angeles Times,* February 28, 2012, http:// opinion.latimes.com/opinionla/2012/02/mann-climate.html. The *Times* cited no examples of the "denialists" running this play because none exist. So they plainly were analogizing to something the "denialists" do, drawing the ire of outlets like the *Times*. The most likely activity of which is seeking information from the likes of Gleick, through lawful means. See also Stephen Stromberg, "Hurting the climate cause," *Washington Post,* A15, February 22, 2102, stating "Peter Gleick violated a principal rule of the global-warming debate: Climate scientists must be better than their opponents. . . . It's very tempting for scientists and their allies to employ to [*sic*] tactics of their over-aggressive critics. . . . Manipulation and perfidy work much better for the deniers. Whatever the misdeeds of those who attack climate research, however brain-dead the opposition to climate scientists appears to be, advocates degrade themselves when they allow their

frustrations to get the better of their ethical responsibilities." Stromberg cited no equivalent act of the "deniers," as none in fact exist. The obvious intention was that this was the equivalent of obtaining records of alarmists depending on taxpayer funding by lawful means, which Stromberg's paper has editorialized against as strongly as any other. In an update to his piece, after being upbraided, Stromberg referenced Virginia attorney general Ken Cuccinelli's effort using lawful means to obtain records in response to prima facie evidence of fraud.

40. Peter Foster, "'Fakegate' latest climate clash," *Financial Post* (Canada), March 6, 2012, http://opinion.financialpost.com/2012/03/06/peter-foster -fakegate-latest-climate-clash/.

41. Aliza Mirza, "Climate change skeptics call on Oxford to cancel lecture," *Oxford Student,* April 18, 2012, http://oxfordstudent.com/2012/04/18/ climate-change-sceptics-call-on-oxford-to-cancel-lecture/.

42. See, e.g., lecture by Berkeley physics professor Robert Muller, available at http://www.youtube.com/watch?v=8BQpciw8suk, last viewed March 4, 2012.

43. This truncated comparison benefited greatly from the concise summary of the affair by the scientist Dr. Walter Starck, "Heartland vs. Climategate," *Quadrant Online,* February 28, 2012, http://www.quadrant.org.au/blogs/ doomed-planet/2012/02/heartland-vs-climategate.

44. See FN 34, *supra,* and "The Heartland Institute Investigative Report," PRO-TEK, International, Inc., April 20, 2012, http://heartland.org/sites/default /files/protek_heartland_report_-_april_20_2012.pdf. This assessment was produced by expert in computational and forensic linguistics Patrick Juola, PhD, of Juola & Associates, "Stylometric Report—Heartland Institute Memo," March 13, 2012, "Having examined these documents and their results, I therefore consider it more likely than not that Gleick is in fact the author/compiler of the document entitled 'Confidential Memo: 2012 Heartland Climate Strategy,' and further that the document does not represent a genuine strategy memo from the Heartland Institute," available at http://wattsupwiththat.files.wordpress.com/2012/03/memoreport.pdf, at p. 4 (Gleick's employer reinstated him after claiming their own investigation, but they would not make the analysis or product of the inquiry public; see, e.g., Northwestern University professor of law Jim Lindgren's assessment of this move and the Pacific Institute's statement, "Peter Gleick's Possible Involvement in Drafting Fake Heartland Document: Either Not Investigated or the Relevant Results Not Released," at The Volokh Conspiracy blog, run by UCLA law professor Eugene Volock, June 10, 2012, http://www.volokh .com/2012/06/10/peter-gleicks-possible-involvement-in-drafting-fake-heart land-document-either-not-investigated-or-the-relevant-results-not-released/).

45. See, e.g., Matt Patterson, "The Heartland Institute Under Attack: Global Warming Fever Drives Scientists to Desperation," Capital Research Center,

May 2012, https://capitalresearch-zippykid.netdna-ssl.com/wp-content/up
loads/2012/04/GW0512.indd_2.pdf.

46. Remarks made in a radio interview with Univision. See, e.g., Ashley South-
all, "Obama Vows to Push Immigration Changes," *New York Times,* October 25, 2010, http://thecaucus.blogs.nytimes.com/2010/10/25/in-appeal
-to-hispanics-obama-promises-to-push-immigration-reform/.

47. Charles Krauthammer, "Divider in Chief," *Washington Post,* May 3, 2012,
http://www.washingtonpost.com/opinions/divider-in-chief/2012/05/03
/gIQAMPR0zT_story.html.

48. *U.S. Department of Justice v. Reporters Committee for Freedom of the Press,*
489 U.S. 749, 773 (1989).

49. *EPA v. Mink,* 410 U.S. 73, 92 (1973).

50. *National Archives & Records Admin. v. Favish,* 541 U.S. 157,172 (2004);
Reporters Committee for Freedom of the Press, 489 U.S. at 771 (stating that
the requester's identity has "no bearing on the merits of his . . . FOIA request").

51. David Brin, "Politics Redux: Blue New Hampshire, Transparency and the
latest episode of WikiLeaks Mania," January 11, 2012, http://davidbrin
.blogspot.com/2012/01/politics-redux-blue-new-hampshire.html.

52. Andrew C. Revkin, "Private* Climate Conversations on Display," *New York
Times* DotEarth blog, November 20, 2009, http://dotearth.blogs.nytimes
.com/2009/11/20/private-climate-conversations-on-display/.

53. See, e.g., "A Selection From the Cache of Diplomatic Dispatches," *New
York Times,* June 19, 2011, http://www.nytimes.com/interactive/2010/11/28
/world/20101128-cables-viewer.html#.

54. See, e.g., Justin Gillis and Leslie Kaufman, "Leak Offers Glimpse of Campaign Against Climate Science," *New York Times,* February 15, 2012, http://
www.nytimes.com/2012/02/16/science/earth/in-heartland-institute-leak-a
-plan-to-discredit-climate-teaching.html?pagewanted=all; and Andrew C.
Revkin, "The Heartland Files and the Climate Fight," *New York Times*
DotEarth blog, February 15, 2012, http://dotearth.blogs.nytimes.com
/2012/02/15/documents-appear-to-reveal-broad-effort-to-amplify-climate
-uncertainty/.

55. The article that formerly carried this remains up in altered form at Darren Samuelsohn, "Heartland burned by 'DenialGate,'" *Politico,* February
15, 2012, http://dyn.politico.com/printstory.cfm?uuid=5826D160-4705
-4D72-A0BB-44C8C2EDA7DC. In its original form, it stated in pertinent part, "The Chicago-based Heartland Institute has so far declined to
comment on the authenticity of the materials, but Revkin told POLITICO
on Wednesday that he's been able to confirm that the documents are legitimate. The DeSmogBlog's editors said they had received the documents
from an anonymous tipster who dubbed himself a 'Heartland insider.'" See

Tom Nelson, "Heartland: 'Revkin told POLITICO on Wednesday that he's been able to confirm that the documents are legitimate,'" February 15, 2012, http://tomnelson.blogspot.com/2012/02/heartland-told-politico-on-wednesday.html.

56. See, e.g., Stephen Kinzer, "Illinois Senate Campaign Thrown Into Prurient Turmoil," *New York Times,* June 23, 2004, http://www.nytimes.com/2004/06/23/us/illinois-senate-campaign-thrown-into-prurient-turmoil.html?ref=jackryan.

57. See, e.g., Ann Coulter, "David Axelrod's pattern of sexual misbehavior," November 9, 2011, www.anncoulter.com/columns/2011–11–09.html.

58. See, e.g., Glynnis MacNicol, "Bill Kristol's 'Outrageous' Shoutfest With Juan Williams Over Goldman Sachs," Mediaite, April 25, 2010, http://www.mediaite.com/online/bill-kristols-shouting-match-with-juan-williams-over-the-goldman-sachs-emails/.

59. Richard Brearley, "UEA response to EIR requests—it depends who you are," Bishop-Hill blog, July 21, 2011, http://www.bishop-hill.net/blog/2011/7/21/uea-response-to-eir-requests-it-depends-who-you-are.html.

60. Ibid.

61. http://www.publications.parliament.uk/pa/cm201012/cmselect/cmjust/writev/foi/foi.pdf.

62. Written evidence from Nottingham Trent University FOI 13.

63. Written evidence from University of the Arts, London (Europe's largest provider of education in art, design, fashion, communication, and the performing arts) FOI 77.

64. Written evidence from Association of Chief Police Officers FOI 12.

65. "Fit and Unfit to Publish," editorial, *Wall Street Journal,* May 3, 2012, http://online.wsj.com/article/SB10001424052702304050304577378224005694102.html?mod=googlenews_wsj.

66. Sven Böll, Christian Reiermann, Michael Sauga, and Klaus Wiegrefe, "Operation Self-Deceit: New Documents Shine Light on Euro Birth Defects," *Spiegel International,* May 8, 2012, http://www.spiegel.de/international/europe/euro-struggles-can-be-traced-to-origins-of-common-currency-a-831842.html.

67. "Helmut Kohl ignored signs that Italy was unfit to join eurozone," *Times* (UK), May 10, 2012, www.thetimes.co.uk/tto/news/world//europe/article3409714.ece.

4. Rhetoric and Reality: Obama's War on Transparency

1. Josh Gerstein, "President Obama's muddy transparency record," *Politico,* February 5, 2012, http://www.politico.com/news/stories/0312/73606.html. See, e.g., Macon Phillips, "Change Has Come to WhiteHouse.gov,"

White House Blog, Jan. 20, 2009, available at http://www.whitehouse.gov/blog/change_has_come_to_whitehouse-gov/.

2. Obama's Remarks on His Small-Business Plan, Nashua, NH, February 2, 2010, http://www.nytimes.com/2010/02/03/us/politics/03obama.text.html?pagewanted=all.

3. Barack Obama, Remarks at a Town Hall Meeting, Elyria, OH, January 22, 2010.

4. Ben Smith, "Obama administration appeals ruling on White House visitor logs," *Politico*, October 14, 2011.

5. George F. Will, "Obama's disdain for law," *Washington Post*, March 11, 2012, http://www.washingtonpost.com/opinions/obamas-disregard-for-those-pesky-things-called-laws/2012/03/08/gIQAHIA61R_story.html.

6. Josh Gerstein, "President Obama's muddy transparency record," *Politico*, February 5, 2012.

7. Michael Barone, "Fundraising, Chicago Style: The president calls for transparency in all campaigns but his own," *National Review Online*, May 3, 2012, http://www.nationalreview.com/articles/298740/fundraising-chicago-style-michael-barone#.

8. See, e.g., Christopher C. Horner, "Vigilante President, Liberal Fascist," PJMedia.com, April 25, 2012, http://pjmedia.com/tatler/2012/04/25/vigilante-president-liberal-fascist/.

9. Ed Morrissey, "Obama uses WH press corps as threat against Chrysler investors," HotAir.com, May 2, 2009, http://hotair.com/archives/2009/05/02/obama-uses-wh-press-corps-as-threat-against-chrysler-investors/.

10. See, e.g., Andrew Reitman, "No compromise in sight on EU document secrecy," *EU Observer*, May 23, 2012, http://euobserver.com/18/116349.

11. White House, Memorandum for the Heads of Executive Departments and Agencies, January 20, 2009, http://www.whitehouse.gov/the_press_office/FreedomofInformationAct.

12. White House, Memorandum for the Heads of Executive Departments and Agencies, January 20, 2009, http://www.whitehouse.gov/the_press_office/TransparencyandOpenGovernment.

13. Ed O'Keefe, "New Obama Orders on Transparency, FOIA Requests," *Washington Post*, January 21, 2009.

14. Memorandum for Heads of Departments and Agencies, The Freedom of Information Act, President William J. Clinton, October 4, 1993, http://www.justice.gov/oip/93_clntmem.htm.

15. See http://www.fas.org/sgp/clinton/reno.html.

16. See, e.g., George Lardner, Jr. and Susan Schmidt, "Livingstone resigns, denying Ill Intent," *Washington Post*, June 27, 1996.

17. "All of you voted for me," *Politico*, May 9, 2009, http://www.politico.com/blogs/dinnerdish/0509/All_of_you_voted_for_me.html.

18. Attorney General Eric Holder, Memorandum for the Heads of Executive Departments and Agencies, "The Freedom of Information Act," March 19, 2009.

19. OIP Guidance, "President Obama's FOIA Memorandum and Attorney General Holder's FOIA Guidelines, Creating a 'New Era of Open Government,'" http://www.justice.gov/oip/foiapost/2009foiapost8.htm.

20. Ibid.

21. Ibid.

22. Ibid.

23. Attorney General Eric Holder, Memorandum for the Heads of Executive Departments and Agencies, "The Freedom of Information Act."

24. Ibid.

25. OIP Guidance, President Obama's FOIA Memorandum and Attorney General Holder's FOIA Guidelines, "Creating a 'New Era of Open Government.'"

26. David Freddoso, "In Obamaland, transparency is opaque," *Washington Examiner,* March 22, 2012, http://washingtonexaminer.com/opinion/editorials/2012/03/obamaland-transparency-opaque/397156?utm_source=Washington%20Examiner%20Opinion%20Digest%20-%2003/23/2012&utm_medium=email&utm_campaign=Washington%20Examiner:%20Opinion%20Digest%3E.

27. Jonathan Strong, "House Panel Subpoenas Drilling Moratorium Documents," *Roll Call,* April 3, 2012, http://www.rollcall.com/news/house_panel_subpoenas_drilling_moratorium_documents-213607–1.html.

28. Bruce Alpert, "Gulf oil spill moratorium inquiries rebuffed, investigator says," *New Orleans Times-Picayune,* May 08, 2012.

29. See, e.g., the discussion at "The politics of waivers," ObamaCareWatcher, Americans for Limited Government, January 24, 2012, http://obamacarewatcher.org/articles/334; see also Sarah Torre, "Adding Insult to Injury: Obama Admin Refuses to Protect Religious Liberty," Heritage Foundation, January 25, 2012, http://blog.heritage.org/2012/01½5/adding-insult-to-injury-obama-admin-refuses-to-protect-religious-liberty/.

30. See, e.g., Byron York, "Obama: 'I'd like to work my way around Congress,'" *Washington Examiner,* September 15, 2011, http://campaign2012.washingtonexaminer.com/blogs/beltway-confidential/obama-id-work-my-way-around-congress.

31. See, e.g., Alicia Cohn, "Democratic governors discuss bypassing Congress with Obama," *Hill,* February 24, 2012, http://thehill.com/blogs/blog-briefing-room/news/212517-democratic-governors-discuss-bypassing-congress-with-obama.

32. Ari Berman, "Jim Messina, Obama's Enforcer," *Nation,* April 8, 2011, http://www.thenation.com/article/159577/obamas-enforcer.

33. "Emails Reveal How the White House Bought Big Pharma," editorial, *Wall Street Journal*, June 11, 2012, http://online.wsj.com/article/SB100 01424052702303901504577458741425317930.html?mod=googlenews _wsj. See more coverage at the House Energy and Commerce Committee's website at http://energycommerce.house.gov/news/PRArticle .aspx?NewsID=9592.

34. See "E-mails and documents produced through investigation into closed-door health care negotiations, June 8, 2012 Memorandum," http://republicans.en ergycommerce.house.gov/Media/file/PDFs/060812citeddocformemoIII.pdf.

35. See Memorandum to Energy and Commerce Committee Republican Members, from Majority Staff, "Investigation Update: Closed-Door Obamacare Negotiations," http://republicans.energycommerce.house.gov/ Media/file/PDFs/20120531ObamacareDeals.pdf.

36. Ibid.

37. See, e.g., "At a somber post-election press conference, President Barack Obama, ever the pragmatic, conceded that one of his major policy goals, implementing a comprehensive cap-and-trade system, was dead. 'Cap-and-trade was just one way of skinning the cat; it was not the only way,' Obama said." "The Week in Green Energy: The Many Ways to Skin a Cat," *IB Times* (UK), November 8, 2010, http://www.ibtimes.co.uk/ar ticles/20101108/week-green-energy-many-ways-skincat.htm.

38. Citizens for Responsibility and Ethics in Washington, OpenTheGovern ment.org, "Measuring Transparency Under the FOIA: The Real Story Behind The Numbers," December 2011, http://crew.3cdn.net/5911487fbaaa 8cb0f8_9xm6bgari.pdf.

39. Ibid., at p. 3.

40. Ibid., at pp. 41–43.

41. Ibid., at p. 3.

42. Eric Lichtblau, "Report Faults U.S.'s Efforts at Transparency," *New York Times,* March 14, 2010, http://www.nytimes.com/2010/03/15/us/ politics/15open.html.

43. It's easy to forget such gems, but a reporter did, in fact, ask Obama, in a hard-hitting effort to ensure four years of favorable treatment, what had "enchanted you the most from serving in this office?" See, e.g., Brian Montopoli, "Obama's 'Enchanted' Answer," CBS News, April 29, 2009, http:// www.cbsnews.com/8301–503544_162–4979269–503544.html.

44. John Nolte, "LA Times vets Ann Romney's horses," BigJournalism.com, May 22, 2012, http://www.breitbart.com/Big-Journalism/2012/05/22/LA -Times-Vets-Ann-Romney-Horses.

45. Abby Phillip, "Shh! Obama gets anti-secrecy award," *Politico,* March 30, 2011, http://www.politico.com/politico44/perm/0311/not_a_secret_any more_a00ccd98–0d9e-4822–8936–168f3a51b959.html.

46. Byron Tau, "Obama's transparency stumbles," *Politico,* March 5, 2012, http://www.politico.com/politico44/2012/03/obamas-transparency-stum bles-116400.html.

47. Josh Gerstein, "President Obama's muddy transparency record," *Politico,* February 5, 2012.

48. Ibid.

49. Abby Phillip, "Shh! Obama gets anti-secrecy award," *Politico,* March 30, 2011, http://www.politico.com/politico44/perm/0311/not_a_secret_any more_a00ccd98–0d9e-4822–8936–168f3a51b959.html.

50. David Carr, "Blurred Line Between Espionage and Truth," *New York Times,* February 26, 2012, http://www.nytimes.com/2012/02/27/business/ media/white-house-uses-espionage-act-to-pursue-leak-cases-media-equa tion.html?_r=2.

51. Scott Horton, "Prosecution of NSA Whistleblower Collapses," *Harper's,* June 10, 2011, http://www.harpers.org/archive/2011/06/hbc-90008114.

52. David Carr, "Blurred Line Between Espionage and Truth," *New York Times,* February 26, 2012

53. See Paul Bedard, "Obama's bin Laden leaks angered military," *Washington Examiner,* May 17, 2012, http://washingtonexaminer.com/politics/wash ington-secrets/2012/05/obamas-bin-laden-leaks-angered-military/622606.

54. See, e.g., Josh Gerstein, "Pentagon, CIA, White House opened up to Hollywood on bin Laden raid," *Politico,* May 23, 2012, http://www.politico .com/blogs/under-the-radar/2012/05/pentagon-cia-white-house-opened -up-to-hollywood-on-124293.html.

55. Ewan MacAskill, "Underwear bomb plot: British and US intelligence rattled over leaks," Guardian (UK), May 11, 2012, http://www.guardian .co.uk/world/2012/may/11/underwear-bomb-plot-mi6-cia-leaks.

56. Ibid.

57. See, e.g., Andrew Malcolm, "Don't tell anyone, but that al Qaeda mole op had zero to do with the Obama administration," *Investor's Business Daily,* May 15, 2012.

58. See, e.g., Josh Gerstein, "Dianne Feinstein vents ire over 'avalanche of leaks,'" *Politico,* June 6, 2012, http://www.politico.com/blogs/under-the-radar /2012/06/dianne-feinstein-vents-ire-over-avalanche-of-leaks-125513.html.

59. Al Kamen "Where the sunlight doesn't shine," In the Loop, *Washington Post,* February 15, 2012 http://www.washingtonpost.com/politics/2012/02 /14/gIQA9W6SER_story.html.

60. Ibid.

61. Peter Van Buren, "Obama's Unprecedented War on Whistleblowers," Salon.com, February 9, 2012.

62. Edward Wasserman excerpting his 2012 lecture to the Logan Symposium on Investigative Journalism, quoting Steven Aftergood of the Federation of

American Scientists' government secrecy project, in "Media silent when administration targets sources," *Miami Herald*, May 7, 2012, http://www.miamiherald.com/2012/05/07/2783978/media-silent-when-administration.html.

63. Ibid.

64. Rob Kall, "Rough Times for Whistleblowers," OpEdNews.com, September 19, 2011, http://www.opednews.com/articles/Rough-Times-for-Whistleblo-by-Rob-Kall-110919–244.html.

65. Jesselyn Radack, "BREAKING: Another Whistleblower Indicted under Espionage Act," DailyKos.com, January 23, 2012, http://www.dailykos.com/story/2012/01⁄23/1057624/-BREAKING-Another-Whistleblower-Indicted-under-Espionage-Act.

66. Peter Van Buren, "Obama's Unprecedented War on Whistleblowers," Salon.com, February 9, 2012, http://www.salon.com/2012/02/09/obamas_unprecedented_war_on_whistleblowers/.

67. "US Attack on Transparency Continues: CIA Whistleblower Indicted," April 6, 2012, http://www.commondreams.org/headline/2012/04/06–3.

68. Testimony in Q-and-A by Lisa O. Monaco before the Senate Committee on Intelligence, for her nomination to be head of the Justice Department's National Security Division (NSD), May 17, 2011, http://www.fas.org/irp/congress/2011_hr/monaco.pdf.

69. Peter Suderman, "Obama Administration Security Official: We Don't Need to Subpoena Reporters Anymore Because We already Know Who They're Talking To," *Reason*, May 7, 2012, http://reason.com/blog/2012/05/07/obama-administration-security-official-w.

70. Edward Wasserman "Media silent when administration targets sources," *Miami Herald*, May 7, 2012.

71. See, e.g., Josh Gerstein, "President Obama's muddy transparency record," *Politico*, February 5, 2012, at http://www.politico.com/news/stories/0312/73606_Page4.html.

72. Peter Suderman, "Obama Administration Security Official: We Don't Need to Subpoena Reporters Anymore Because We already Know Who They're Talking To," *Reason*, May 7, 2012.

73. Ibid.

74. See, e.g., James Sandler, "The war on whistle-blowers," Salon.com, November 1, 2007, http://www.salon.com/2007/11/01/whistleblowers/singleton/.

75. See, e.g., "WH sought to weaken law on whistleblowing," National Whistleblowers Center, August 7, 2009, http://www.whistleblowers.org/index.php?option=com_content&task=view&id=917&Itemid=71.

76. Steven Aftergood, "Why Are There So Many Leak Prosecutions?," Secrecy News, Federation of American Scientists, April 23, 2012, http://www.fas.org/blog/secrecy/2012/04/why_so_many.html, viewed on May 8, 2012.

77. Eric Lichtblau, "Report Faults U.S.'s Efforts at Transparency," *New York Times,* March 14, 2010, http://www.nytimes.com/2010/03/15/us/politics /15open.html.

78. Ibid. "Obama initially seemed intent on fulfilling his 'new era of transparency' vow. In April 2009, over the objections of CIA officials, he ordered the declassification of Bush-era Justice Department opinions authorizing the use of aggressive interrogation tactics against terrorism suspects. The memos detailed techniques ranging from slapping to waterboarding, along with the legal analysis that concluded the actions were not torture under U.S. law. However, that bout of transparency quickly faded."

79. See, e.g., the formerly top secret but still heavily redacted Thomas R. Johnson, "American Cryptology during the Cold War, 1945–1989. Book III, Retrenchment and Reform, 1972–1980," Center for Cryptologic History, National Security Agency, 1998, http://www.nsa.gov/public_info/_files/ cryptologic_histories/cold_war_iii.pdf.

80. See, e.g., U.S. Environmental Protection Agency, "FOIA ANNUAL REPORT FOR 10/0½2009 THROUGH 09/30/2010," p. 9, http://www .epa.gov/foia/docs/2010report.pdf; "FOIA ANNUAL REPORT FOR 10/0½2008 THROUGH 09/30/2009," p. 9, http://www.epa.gov/foia/ docs/2009report.pdf.

81. Proposed Rule, 28 CFR Part 16, page 15239, March 21, 2011 ("Section 16.6 Responses to Requests, (f)(2)). "When a component applies an exclusion to exclude records from the requirements of the FOIA pursuant to 5 U.S.C. 552(c), the component utilizing the exclusion will respond to the request as if the excluded records did not exist. This response should not differ in wording from any other response given by the component." http:// www.gpo.gov/fdsys/pkg/FR-2011-03-21/html/2011-6473.htm.

82. Al Kamen "Where the sunlight doesn't shine," Federal Page, *Washington Post,* February 15, 2012.

83. Josh Gerstein, "President Obama's muddy transparency record," *Politico,* February 5, 2012.

84. Ibid.

85. Beth Simone Noveck, "What's in a Name? Open Gov and Good Gov," http://www.huffingtonpost.com/beth-simone-noveck/whats-in-a-name -open-gov-_b_845735.html.

86. Josh Gerstein, "President Obama's muddy transparency record," *Politico,* February 5, 2012.

87. Ibid.

88. "More 'junkyard dogs' needed to fight government waste, fraud," editorial, *Washington Examiner,* February 27, 2012, http://washingtonexaminer .com/opinion/editorials/2012/02/more-'junkyard-dogs'-needed-fight-gov ernment-waste-fraud/318721?utm_source=Washington%20Examiner%20

Opinion%20Digest%20-%2002/28/2012&utm_medium=email&utm
_campaign=Washington%20Examiner:%20Opinion%20Digest.

89. Ibid.

5. Obama's Tactics: The Most Transparent Administration Ever's Tricks and Tradecraft to Escape Transparency

1. Eric Lichtblau, "Across From White House, Coffee With Lobbyists," *New York Times,* June 24, 2010, http://www.nytimes.com/2010/06/25/us/politics/25caribou.html?_r=1&scp=4&sq=caribou&st=cse.

2. Chris Frates, "White House meets lobbyists off campus," February 24, 2011, *Politico,* http://www.politico.com/news/stories/0211/50081.html.

3. Ibid.

4. Eric Lichtblau, "Across From White House, Coffee With Lobbyists," *New York Times,* June 24, 2010.

5. Chris Frates, "White House meets lobbyists off campus," http://www.politico.com/news/stories/0211/50081_Page3.html.

6. See, e.g., Ed Morrissey, "Lobbyists 'a steady stream' at White House despite Obama pledge," HotAir.com, May 21, 2012, http://hotair.com/archives/2012/05/21/lobbyists-a-steady-stream-at-white-house-despite-obama-pledge/

7. Timothy P. Carney, "Obama Transparency Fail: Offsite meetings for the purpose of circumventing the Presidential Records Act," *Washington Examiner,* February 24, 2011, http://washingtonexaminer.com/politics/beltway-confidential/2011/02/obama-transparency-fail-offsite-meetings-purpose-circumventing.

8. Ibid.

9. Eric Lichtblau, "Across From White House, Coffee With Lobbyists," *New York Times,* June 24, 2010, http://www.nytimes.com/2010/06/25/us/politics/25caribou.html?pagewanted=all.

10. Nick Bauman, "Starbucksgate: Obama's Lobbyist/Email Scandal," *Mother Jones,* June 28, 2010, http://motherjones.com/mojo/2010/06/starbucksgate-crew-calls-investigation-white-house.

11. See also Memo from OSTP Director John Holdren to all OSTP staff, titled "Subject: Reminder: Compliance with the Federal Records Act and the President's Ethics Pledge," May 10, 2010, http://assets.fiercemarkets.com/public/sites/govit/ostp-employees.pdf.

12. See, e.g., Charlie Spiering, "Rosen's firm deeply involved in 'War on Women,'" *Washington Examiner,* April 12, 2012, http://campaign2012.washingtonexaminer.com/blogs/beltway-confidential/rosens-firm-deeply-involved-war-women/477191.

13. Josh Gerstein, "President Obama's muddy transparency record," *Politico,*

February 5, 2012, at http://www.politico.com/news/stories/0312/73606 _Page3.html.

14. Ibid.

15. "A New Era of Openness? How and Why Political Staff at DHS Interfered with the FOIA Process," Staff Report, Prepared for Chairman Darrell Issa, U.S. House of Representatives Committee on Oversight and Government Reform, 112th Congress, March 30, 2011, House Committee on Oversight and Government Reform, http://oversight.house.gov/images/stories/ Reports/DHS_REPORT_FINAL_FINAL_4_01_11.pdf, viewed February 6, 2012.

16. See, e.g., House Energy and Commerce Committee Background Memo, November 1, 2011, to Members, Subcommittee on Oversight and Investigation, from Subcommittee Staff, http://Republicans.EnergyCommerce .house.gov/Media/file/Markups/Oversight/112th/110311/Memo.pdf.

17. See, e.g., "White House Solyndra Stonewall Reveals Broken Promises of Transparency," Press Release, House Energy and Commerce Committee, Majority, February 3, 2012, http://energycommerce.house.gov/news/ PRArticle.aspx?NewsID=9268.

18. Andrew Restuccia, "White House delivers Solyndra documents, rebuffs full GOP subpoena," *Hill,* November 11, 2011, http://thehill.com/blogs/ e2-wire/e2-wire/193169-white-house-provides-solyndra-documents-rebuffs -subpoena-request.

19. Press release, "Investigation Update: Committee Continues Inquiry Into the Development of Obamacare," House Committee on Energy and Commerce, Majority, April 17, 2012, http://energycommerce.house.gov/News/ PRArticle.aspx?NewsID=9461.

20. Ibid.

21. See October 14, 2011, letter from White House Counsel Kathryn Ruemmler to House Energy and Commerce Committee Chairman Fred Upton, Subcommittee on Oversight and Investigation Chairman Cliff Stearns, http://Republicans.EnergyCommerce.house.gov/Media/file/ Letters/112th/101411whresponse.pdf.

22. See, e.g., "Ken Cuccinelli's climate-change witch hunt," editorial, *Washington Post,* March 12, 2012, http://www.washingtonpost.com/opinions/ken -cuccinellis-climate-change-witch-hunt/2012/03/08/gIQApmdu5R_story .html.

23. Mark Hemingway, "Is a lawsuit finally forcing transparency at the Department of Labor?," *Washington Examiner,* November 2009, http:// washingtonexaminer.com/politics/beltway-confidential/2009/11/lawsuit -finally-forcing-transparency-department-labor/8582.

24. When my notices to NASA of my intention to sue them obtained front-page coverage (see Stephen Dinan, "Researcher: NASA hiding climate data,"

Washington Times, December 3, 2009, http://www.washingtontimes.com/news/2009/dec/03/researcher-says-nasa-hiding-climate-data/?page=all) and treatment as an item on Fox News Special Report's popular "Grapevine" segment, NASA began falling all over itself to assert a concentrated effort to respond to something that they insisted, despite my repeated notices to them of their delinquency, had just fallen through the cracks.

25. Josh Gerstein, "President Obama's muddy transparency record," *Politico,* February 5, 2012, http://www.politico.com/news/stories/0312/73606_Page 2.html.

26. Colin Sullivan, "Vow of silence key to White House-Calif. fuel economy talks," *New York Times,* May 20, 2009, http://www.nytimes.com/gwire/2009/05/20/20greenwire-vow-of-silence-key-to-white-house-calif-fuel-e-12208.html.

27. Ibid.

28. See, e.g., Mike Spitzer, "AP: EPA Head Browner Asked for Computer Files to Be Deleted," Associated Press, June 30, 2001, available at http://www.mail-archive.com/ctrl@listserv.aol.com/msg70823.html; Associated Press, "EPA held in contempt over documents," *Deseret News,* July 25, 2003, http://www.deseretnews.com/article/998899/; Michelle Malkin, "Down on Browner," *National Review Online,* December 12, 2008, http://article.nationalreview.com/380776/down-on-browner/michelle-malkin. See also Horner, "Power Grab," pp. 63–70.

29. See, e.g., "On FOIA, Obama wants a license to lie," editorial, *Washington Examiner,* October 30, 2011, http://washingtonexaminer.com/opinion/2011/10/foia-obama-wants-license-lie/119851, addressing a proposed regulatory change to falsely claim that records requested under FOIA do not exist.

30. In addition to what Christian Adams revealed about the Department of Justice and what the House Committee on Oversight and Government Reform exposed at the Department of Homeland Security, see also "Union Watchdog Files Second Disclosure Request to Investigate Obama Labor Department Stonewalling," Press Release, National Right to Work Foundation, December 2, 2009, http://www.nrtw.org/en/press/2009/12/union-watchdog-files-second-disclosure-request-12022009.

31. J. Christian Adams, "Bombshell: Justice Department Only Selectively Complies with Freedom of Information Act," February 10, 2011, PJMedia, http://pjmedia.com/blog/bombshell-justice-department-only-selectively-complies-with-freedom-of-information-act-pjm-exclusive/, viewed February 6, 2012.

32. Ibid.

33. J. Christian Adams, *Injustice: Exposing the Racial Agenda of the Obama Justice Department* (Washington, DC: Regnery, 2011), pp. 92–93.

56 NOTES

34. Ibid., chap. 3, at p. 261 fn.
35. Ibid., at p. 94.
36. Ibid., chap. 3, at p. 261 fn.
37. Adams, "Bombshell."
38. Staff Report, House Committee on Oversight and Government Reform, "A New Era of Openness? How and Why Political staff at DHS Interfered with the FOIA Process," March 30, 2011, p. 15, http://oversight.house .gov/images/stories/Reports/DHS_REPORT_FINAL_FINAL_4_01_11 .pdf.
39. See, e.g., Alex Spillius, "Osama bin Laden dead: Robert Gates criticises handling of aftermath," *Telegraph* (UK), May 13, 2011, http://www.tele graph.co.uk/news/worldnews/al-qaeda/8512836/Osama-bin-Laden-dead -Robert-Gates-criticises-handling-of-aftermath.html.
40. See, e.g., Greg Jaffe, "Gates, Mullen appeal for end to disclosures of Osama bin Laden raid details," *Washington Post,* May 18, 2011, http:// www.washingtonpost.com/world/national-security/gates-mullen-appeal -for-end-to-disclosures-of-osama-bin-laden-raid-details/2011/05/18/AF 3jsk6G_story.html; see also, "Gates: SEALs who killed bin Laden con- cerned for their safety," CNN.com, May 12, 2011, http://news.blogs.cnn .com/2011/05/12/gates-seals-who-killed-bin-laden-concerned-for-their -safety/?hpt=C1.
41. Patrick B. Pexton, "Post's reporting on SEAL Team 6 provokes cries of 'treason,'" *Washington Post,* May 20, 2011, http://www.washingtonpost .com/opinions/posts-reporting-on-seal-team-6-provokes-cries-of-treason /2011/05/20/AFq9627G_story.html.
42. "Gates: SEALs who killed bin Laden concerned for their safety," CNN .com, May 12, 2011.
43. Erica Martinson, "CO2 rules: Now you see 'em, now you don't," *Politico,* April 16, 2012 http://www.politico.com/news/stories/0412/75216.html.
44. Juliet Eilperin, "EPA e-mails reveal frustration with White House," *Wash- ington Post,* May 3, 2012, http://www.washingtonpost.com/national/ health-science/epa-e-mails-on-anti-pollution-rules-reveal-agencys-frustra tion-with-white-house/2012/05/03/gIQAYeQDzT_story.html.
45. Recall *Rolling Stone*'s cover story on EPA administrator Lisa Jackson, by Tim Dickinson, "The Eco-Warrior: Lisa Jackson's EPA: President Obama has appointed the most progressive EPA chief in history—and she's moving swiftly to clean up the mess left by Bush," *Rolling Stone,* January 20, 2010, http://www.rollingstone.com/politics/news/the-eco-warrior-20100120, and of course EPA's Region 6 administrator Al Armendariz, who compared his enforcement "philosophy" to random Roman crucifixions to instill order and thereby ensure a docile, compliant population.
46. See, e.g., P. J. Gladnick, "Audio: Obama Tells SF Chronicle He Will

Bankrupt Coal Industry," Newsbusters, November 2, 2008, http://news busters.org/blogs/p-j-gladnick/2008/11/02/hidden-audio-obama-tells-sf -chronicle-he-will-bankrupt-coal-industry.

47. "Obama camp spies endgame in Oregon," Agence France-Presse, May 16, 2008, http://afp.google.com/article/ALeqM5h-wpxs1Re-8vx2Zk5xnYygW 1W67w.

48. "Can't Get No Respect," editorial, *Wall Street Journal,* May 8, 2012.

49. See, e.g., Richard Belzer, "Regulatory cost estimates are often murky or avoided," letter, *Wall Street Journal,* May 17, 2012, http://online.wsj.com/article/SB10001424052702304371504577403960943794618.html.

50. "Obama's Marriage Act," editorial, *Wall Street Journal,* May 10, 2012.

51. It seems the Obama team tried to silence a whistleblowing energy body, the North American Electric Reliability Corporation (NERC), which was calling foul on his war on American energy, "for questioning the 'pace and aggressiveness' of the Environmental Protection Agency's regulatory wave in a 2010 report. NERC's position is that the EPA goal of mothballing many or most coal-fired power plants could endanger the security of the electric-power grid, with possible blackouts and much higher energy costs. In a follow-up report last year it found that 'Environmental regulations are shown to be the number one risk to reliability over the next one to five years.' Apparently that was too honest for Washington. Earlier this month the Federal Energy Regulatory Commission disclosed that it has spent months conducting a highly unusual audit of NERC." "Getting even on Reliability," *Wall Street Journal,* May 20, 2012, http://online.wsj.com/article/SB10001424052702304192704577406273583732622.html.

52. Eric Lichtblau, "Report Faults U.S.'s Efforts at Transparency," *New York Times,* March 14, 2010. As usual, these recognitions of the problem are one-offs, often apologetic, like this piece, and serving as a requisite "Sunshine Week" item, checking a box but seeing no need to look any further.

53. Ibid.

54. Citizens for Responsibility and Ethics in Washington, OpenTheGovernment.org, "Measuring Transparency Under the FOIA: The Real Story Behind The Numbers."

55. "A New Era of Openness? How and Why Political Staff at DHS Interfered with the FOIA Process," Staff Report, March 30, 2011, House Committee on Oversight and Government Reform, p. 1, viewed February 6, 2012.

56. Ibid., at p. 3.

57. Citizens for Responsibility and Ethics in Washington, "Measuring Transparency Under the FOIA."

58. "A New Era of Openness?," p. 3.

59. Ibid., at p. 15, citing Ted Bridis, "Playing politics with public records requests," Associated Press, July 21, 2010.

60. Ibid.
61. Ibid., citing Bridis, "Playing politics with public records requests."
62. Ibid., at p. 80.
63. Ibid., at p. 3.
64. Ibid., at pp. 3–4.
65. Ibid., at p. 5.
66. Ibid.
67. Ibid., at p. 6.
68. Ibid.
69. Ibid.

6. You Never Know What You'll Find: Obama's "Big Wind" Cover-up

1. News Transcript, DOD News Briefing—Secretary Rumsfeld and General Myers, U.S. Department of Defense, February 12, 2002, http://www.de fense.gov/transcripts/transcript.aspx?transcriptid=2636.
2. April 11, 2008, letter from EPA records officer John B. Ellis from to Paul Wester, National Archives and Records Administration. In this letter EPA indicated that it had no knowledge whether she had ever used this secret account set up for the first time on her orders; recall that Browner violated a federal court order and had her computers wiped clean, destroying all records that might have remained. From this admission it seems that EPA's servers also were cleaned in pertinent part.
3. See, e.g., Darren Goode, "GOP: Save Browner documents," *Politico,* February 9, 2011, http://www.politico.com/news/stories/0211/49196.html.
4. See, e.g., Anthony Watts, "Friday Funny Bonus: Kenji gets mail," Watts UpWithThat, March 9, 2012, http://wattsupwiththat.com/2012/03/09/friday-funny-bonus-kenji-gets-mail/.
5. Calzada et al., "Study of the effects on employment of public aid to renewable energy sources," Universidad Rey Juan Carlos, Madrid, March 2009, http://www.juandemariana.org/pdf/090327-employment-public-aid-re newable.pdf.
6. Henrik Meyer and Hugh Sharman, "Wind Energy: The Case of Denmark," CEPOS, Copenhagen, September 2009, http://www.cepos.dk/fileadmin/user_upload/Arkiv/PDF/Wind_energy_-_the_case_of_Denmark.pdf. The response from windmill advocates in Denmark was similar: such studies threaten Danish industry by reducing the chances that the United States will serve as the hoped-for massive new market to make inefficient energy sources profitable for their foreign manufacturers. For example, on Danish Radio TV News, Thursday, February 25, 2010.
7. Manual Frondel, Nolan Ritter, Christoph M. Schmidt, and Colin Vance, "Economic impacts from the promotion of renewable energy technologies:

The German experience," Rheinisch-Westfälisches Institut für Wirtschafts-forschung (Essen), Energy Policy, vol. 38, no. 8, August 2010, pp. 4048–56, original version, Manual Frondel, Nolan Ritter, Christoph M. Schmidt, and Colin Vance, "Economic impacts from the promotion of re-newable energy technologies: The German experience," Ruhr economic pa-pers, No. 156, 2009, available at http://www.econstor.eu/bitstream/10419 /29912/1/614062047.pdf.

8. Chris Horner, "Wound-up Windmill Welfare Queens," *National Review* Planet Gore Blog, September 23, 2009, http://www.nationalreview.com/ planet-gore/14853/wound-windmill-welfare-queens/chris-horner (links to external sources not included).

9. Daniel Kessler, "Gore's Green Group Loses CEO Cathy Zoi to the Obama Administration," TreeHugger.com, March 28, 2009, http://www.treehug ger.com/files/2009/03/zoi-goes-to-dc.php.

10. See biography of Jason Miner, http://www.gloverparkgroup.com/our-team/ jason-miner/, viewed May 10, 2012.

11. LinkedIn profile of Udai Rohatgi, http://www.linkedin.com/pub/udai-ro hatgi/21/45b/122, viewed May 12, 2012.

12. The relevant emails produced by NREL/DOE are available at http://pjme dia.com/files/2010/03/DoE-and-AWEA-et-al0001.pdf.

13. See Russ Choma, "Overseas firms collecting most green energy money," In-vestigative Reporting Workshop, American University, October 29, 2009, http://investigativereportingworkshop.org/investigations/wind-energy -funds-going-overseas/story/overseas-firms-collecting-most-green-energy -money/, and Russ Choma, "Renewable energy money still going abroad, despite criticism from Congress," February 8, 2010, http://investigative reportingworkshop.org/investigations/wind-energy-funds-going-overseas/ story/renewable-energy-money-still-going-abroad/.

14. Institute for Energy Research, "The Department of Special Interests," May 25, 2010, http://www.instituteforenergyresearch.org/2010/05/25/the-de partment-of-special-interests/.

15. Email from Doug Arent to David Kline, June 29, 2009, at 6:19 p.m., Su-zanne Tegen to Arent, Kline at 9:39 a.m.

16. Email from David Kline, NREL, to Doug Arent of NREL, June 29, 2009.

17. See Shannon Bream, "Spanish Study Sparks Skepticism About Green Jobs," Fox News, April 14, 2009, http://www.foxnews.com/politics/2009/04/14/ spanish-study-sparks-skepticism-green-jobs/.

18. Spain adopted the Royal Decree of April 30, 2009, saying in part that the scheme "is deeply harming the system and puts at risk not only the finan-cial situation of the electric sector companies but also sustainability of the system itself. This dis-adjustment turns out to be unsustainable and has grave consequences since it deteriorates the security and financial capacity

of the investments necessary for providing electricity at the levels of quality and security that the Spanish society demands." See Testimony Before the House Select Committee on Energy and Energy Independence and Global Warming, Gabriel Calzada Alvarez, PhD, September 24, 2009, http:// globalwarming.house.gov/files/HRG/092409Solar/calzada.pdf. An internal PowerPoint file was also leaked, affirming the findings. See also Pajamas Media, "Leaked Doc Proves Spain's 'Green' Policies—the Basis for Obama's— an Economic Disaster," May 18, 2010, http://pjmedia.com/blog/spains -green-policies-an-economic-disaster/. See also, e.g., Cristina Blas, "Espana admite que la economia verde vendio a Obama es una ruina" (Spain admits the green economy sold to Obama is a disaster), *La Gaceta,* reprinted in Pajamas Media, May 21, 2010, http://pjmedia.com/blog/leaked-spanish-re port-obamas-model-green-economy-a-disaster-pjm-exclusive/2/.

19. "The Department of Special Interests," Institute for Energy Research, May 25, 2010, http://www.instituteforenergyresearch.org/2010/05/25/the-de partment-of-special-interests.

20. Email from Suzanne Tegen to David Kline and Eric Lantz, titled "Spanish jobs report response—questions about its release," June 29, 2009.

21. "Energy drives our world and our economy. It's also the leading contributor to Global Warming and climate change," Clipper Windpower, About Us, http://www.clipperwind.com/aboutus.html, viewed March 7, 2012.

22. See the opinion in *Stuart Dimmock v. Secretary of State for Education and Skills,* UK High Court (2007), available at http://www.elaw.org/ node/2284.

23. Email from Robert Hawsey to David Kline, August 12, 2009.

24. National Renewable Energy Laboratory, "NREL Response to the Report Study of the Effects on Employment of Public Aid to Renewable Energy Sources from King Juan Carlos University (Spain)," White Paper NREL/ TP-6A2–46261 ("Prepared under Task No. SAO9.2011"), Eric Lantz and Suzanne Tegen, August 2009, http://www.nrel.gov/docs/fy09osti/46261.pdf.

25. "The Big Wind-Power Cover-Up," editorial, *Investor's Business Daily,* March 12, 2010.

7. Artless Dodgers: Liberal Scheming to Dodge Disclosure, from the UN to the Obama White House

1. Email from Phil Jones to Warwick Hughes, February 21, 2005.

2. For an online tutorial slide show, see, e.g., Dr. M .D. Kandiah, "The UK Freedom of Information Act—A Practical Guide for Academic Research- ers," Cambridge, England, February 16, 2011, available at http://www .slideshare.net/Incremental2/cambridge-fo-imichaelkandiahpresentation.

3. See also the Environmental Information Regulations (2004), a statute

providing a right of access to environmental information that is held by British public authorities. In addition to recorded data, it "includes information about decisions, policies or activities that could affect these aspects of the environment." U.K. National Archives, "Accessing Environmental Information," http://webarchive.nationalarchives.gov.uk/+/www.direct.gov.uk/en/Environmentandgreenerliving/Greenerlivingaquickguide/DG_068192. EIR came into effect at the same time as U.K. FOIA, January 1, 2005.

4. Email from Phil Jones to Michael Mann, February 2, 2005.

5. Email from Phil Jones to Raymond Bradley at University of Massachusetts and Malcolm Hughes at University of Arizona, February 21, 2005.

6. Email from Phil Jones to Ray Bradley, Michael Mann and Malcolm Hughes, all academics at public universities in the United States, November 16, 1999.

7. See account of the proceeding by participant Don Keillor, with Andrew Montford, at "A major FOI victory," Bishop-Hill blog, January 23, 2012, http://bishophill.squarespace.com/blog/2012/⅟23/a-major-foi-victory.html.

8. Email from Phil Jones to authors of the "Hockey Stick," Raymond Bradley, Michael Mann, and Michael Hughes, November 16, 1999, available at, e.g., Steve McIntyre, "Mike's Nature Trick," ClimateAudit.org, November 20, 2009, http://climateaudit.org/2009/1⅟20/mike%e2%80%99s-nature-trick/.

9. From behind the assumed safety of NCAR claiming his records were already shielded from disclosure, Wigley seems to have been less enamored of this behavior. See, e.g., Climategate email 1254756944, dated October 5, 2009, styled "Message from Tom Wigley," forwarded from Jones to Keith Briffa, http://di2.nu/foia/1254756944.txt.

10. In one email Jones acknowledged that "as national measures to reduce emissions begin to affect people's lives, we are all going to get more" requests for their information underlying the agenda, noting that "[o]ne way to cover yourself and all those working in AR5 would be to delete all emails at the end of the process. Hard to do, as not everybody will remember to do it." Email from Phil Jones to Thomas Stocker and Pauline Midgley, May 13, 2009.

11. See, e.g., a summary of the various evidence with embedded links at Andrew Montford, "Acton and Parliamentary Privilege," Bishop Hill blog, May 10, 2012, http://www.bishop-hill.net/blog/2012/5/10/acton-and-parliamentary-privilege.html.

12. IPCC governing principles state its role is "to assess on a comprehensive, open, and transparent basis the scientific, technical, and socio-economic information relevant to understanding the scientific basis." http://www.ipcc.ch/organization/organization_history.shtml, IPCC, History, viewed March 13, 2012.

13. Richard Tol, Key Economic Services and Sectors, "IPCC, CoI, FOI,"

December 13, 2011, http://ipccar5wg2ch10.blogspot.com/2011/12/ipcc
-coi-foi.html.

14. See, e.g., Steve McIntyre, "Another IPCC Demand for Secrecy," Climate
Audit, January 26, 2012, http://climateaudit.org/2012/0½6/another-ipcc
-demand-for-secrecy/.

15. For a detailed discussion of the history of this matter, see Steve McIntyre,
"Climategate: A Battlefield Perspective: Annotated Notes for Presentation
to Heartland Conference," Chicago, May 16, 2010, http://www.climate
audit.info/pdf/mcintyre-heartland_2010.pdf, pp. 13–15.

16. Ibid.

17. Ibid.

18. Email from Phil Jones to NOAA's Thomas Peterson, July 29, 2009, Climategate email 1248902393.txt.

19. For an overview of what IPCC did, see, e.g., "Were skeptic scientists kept
out of the IPCC," SkepticalScience.com, http://www.skepticalscience.com/
print.php?r=316, viewed February 21, 2012.

20. Even this rather interested (as in, not unbiased) group pulled too many
punches given that those deficiencies were scandals of the sort that put private sector entities in bankruptcy and lead governments to fall. Regardless,
they all were on the same page when it came to shielding their work from
undue scrutiny from those who paid for it and who were on tap to pay for
the agenda the work sought to justify.

21. http://www.ipcc.ch/meetings/session32/inf04_p32_review_ipcc_proc
_proced_notes_informal_task_group.pdf, Busan, October 11–14, 2010,
document viewed and captured on October 12, 2011. Specifically: "E.
Security and confidentiality. E1. The issues of security and confidentiality
in the work of preparing the next IPCC Assessment Report require urgent
attention in order to meet the challenges of modern methods of working
and communication and given the experiences during and since AR4.
While IPCC is an institution that is open and transparent, the process of
producing the reports (e.g., approval meetings, the deliberations by LAs
within their Chapters, during LA meetings, and in related electronic communications) are pre-decisional processes which are not open to the public.
In order to facilitate exchange, closed electronic discussion fora could be
established when needed. The WG TSUs are already actively considering
these issues." This meeting led to the "REVIEW OF THE IPCC PRO-
CESSES AND PROCEDURES Background and Introduction (Submitted
by the IPCC Secretariat on behalf of the Task Group Co-chairs)," May
10–13, Abu Dhabi, http://www.ipcc.ch/meetings/session33/doc09_p33
_review_ipcc_processes_procedures.pdf.

22. https://www.ipcc-wg1.unibe.ch/guidancepaper/WG1_GuidanceNote_Con
fidentiality.pdf, document viewed and captured on October 12, 2011. This

illustrates a practice now running throughout all IPCC Working Groups. See, e.g., re: WGII at http://ipcc-wg2.gov/organization/procedures/WG2 _Confidentiality_FINAL.pdf, and WGIII at http://www.ipcc-wg3.de/ login_form.

23. This is related in thorough detail by McIntyre at "Stocker's Earmarks," ClimateAudit.org, January 12, 2012, http://climateaudit.org/2012/01/12/ stockers-earmarks/.

24. "Progress Report: Working Group II contribution to the Fifth Assessment Report," submitted by the Co-Chairs of the IPCC Working Group II, Thirty-Third Session of the IPCC, Abu Dhabi, United Arab Emirates, 10–13 May 2011, IPCC-XXXIII/Doc. 3 (I.IV.2011), Agenda Item: 10.1, p. 3 (http://opcc.ch/meetings/session33/doc03_p33_progress_report_wg2 .pdf, as provided in a November 7, 2011, letter to OSTP director John Holdren to Chairmen James Sensenbrenner and Paul Broun, oversight prompted by my FOIA request to OSTP seeking all records discussing or downloading records from such servers.

25. Ibid.

26. See David Holland, "Stocker in Action," Bishop Hill blog, May 14, 2012, http://www.bishop-hill.net/blog/2012/5/14/stocker-in-action.html.

27. Ibid., at David Holland comment linking to IPCC documents reflecting their response.

28. Email from Phil Jones to NASA's Gavin Schmidt, August 20, 2008; MOHC stands for Met Office Hadley Centre, and CRU/UEA the Climatic Research Unit and University of East Anglia.

29. Richard Tol, Key Economic Services and Sectors, "IPCC, CoI, FOI."

30. Further affirming this intent and that it is well-known, note the following comment made at a widely attended (more than one hundred) public forum hosted on October 5, 2011, by NOAA in Boulder, Colorado, for William H. Brune of Pennsylvania State University. Although in keeping with this new IPCC line, Brune requested no electronic recording of his remarks, contemporaneous notes posted by Dave Bufalo, P.E., reported that "Bruen [sic] stated that the IPCC has directed all of its principal authors and reviewers to NOT use email in communicating among themselves" (emphasis in note-taker's original). Steve McIntyre, "Seminar on Penn State Inquiry," ClimateAudit.org, October 4, 2011, http://climateaudit .org/2011/10/04/seminar-on-penn-state-inquiry/.

31. See, e.g., Andrew Montford, "UN seeks to undermine FOI," Bishop-Hill blog, December 6, 2011, http://www.bishop-hill.net/blog/2011/12/6/un -seeks-to-undermine-foi.html, citing email 1251.txt.

32. See, e.g., re: WGII at http://ipcc-wg2.gov/organization/procedures/WG2 _Confidentiality_FINAL.pdf, and WGIII at http://www.ipcc-wg3.de/login _form.

33. This was acknowledged in a January 30, 2012, letter from OSTP director John Holdren to Chairmen James Sensenbrenner and Paul Broun,
responding to oversight prompted by my October 17, 2011, FOIA request
to OSTP seeking all records discussing or downloading records from such
servers.

34. http://www.ipcc.ch/meetings/session32/inf04_p32_review_ipcc_proc
_proced_notes_informal_task_ group.pdf, Busan, October 11–14, 2010,
document viewed and captured on October 12, 2011, para. E2. In a nod
to reality, the IPCC instructed participants, "You are encouraged to consult
with the legal advisors of your institution as to whether this is compatible
with prior and local regulations."

35. https://www.ipcc-wg1.unibe.ch/guidancepaper/WG1_GuidanceNote_Con
fidentiality.pdf.

36. Concerns about the economic harms they would be responsible for led
the UN Framework Convention on Climate Change to seek such im-
munities beginning at its December 2005 meeting in Montreal. See
also George Russell, "Mammoth new green climate fund wants United
Nations–style diplomatic immunity, even though it's not part of the UN,"
Fox News, March 22, 2012, http://www.foxnews.com/world/2012/03/22/
mammoth-new-green-climate-fund-wants-un-style-diplomatic-immunity
-even-though/#ixzz1q3dndk8F.

37. http://www.ipcc.ch/organization/organization.shtml.

38. Department of Commerce Inspector General, "Examination of issues
related to internet posting of emails from Climatic Research Unit," alternately styled "Response to Sen. James Inhofe's Request to OIG to Examine Issues Related to Internet Posting of Email Exchanges Taken from
the Climatic Research Unit of the University of East Anglia, UK," herein
"OIG Report," February 18, 2011, pp. 15–16, available from http://www
.oig.doc.gov/Pages/Response-to-Sen.-James-Inhofe's-Request-to-OIG-to
-Examine-Issues-Related-to-Internet-Posting-of-Email-Exchanges-Taken
-from-.aspx. See also November 17, 2011, letter from OSTP director John
Holdren to Chairmen Sensenbrenner and Broun stating in pertinent part,
"If a U.S. government employee accesses a document through the Portal, a
copy of the document is downloaded onto the employee's Federal government computer . . . all documents downloaded from or uploaded to the
Portal remain on the employee's Federal government computer, where they
are subject to applicable Federal laws, including the Freedom of Information Act."

39. For the curious, Steve McIntyre has doggedly chronicled these abuses. See
index of McIntyre posts at http://climateaudit.org/category/foia/. See also
science writer Andrew Montford's collection at his Bishop-Hill blog, http://
www.bishop-hill.net/blog/category/foi. For the perspective of Australians'

involvement, see also Geoffrey H. Sherrington, "THAT famous email explained and the first Volunteer Global Warming Skeptic," JoannNova.com, http://joannenova.com.au/2012/01/that-famous-email-explained-and-the-first-volunteer-global-warming-skeptic/, last viewed February 20, 2012.

40. Email from Phil Jones to Dave Palmer and Tim Osborn, July 16, 2009, emphasis added.

41. Email from Phil Jones to Neville Nicholls, July 6, 2005.

42. Email from Phil Jones to Dave Palmer, Jonathan Colam-French, Michael McGarvie, and Annie Ogden, July 28, 2009.

43. Email from Phil Jones to John Kennedy, Philip Brohan, Simon Tett, and Linda Livingston, May 13, 2009. He repeated these sentiments in a July 28, 2009, email to 1577.

44. Email from Phil Jones to undetermined parties, found in a response to Jones from Michael McGarvie, January 30, 2007.

45. Maxim Lott, "Climategate Bombshell: Did U.S. Gov't Help Hide Climate Data?," FoxNews.com, December 16, 2011, http://www.foxnews.com/scitech/2011/12/16/complicit-in-climategate-doe-under-fire/.

46. This is the FRA's definition of records, 44 USC § 3301. See also 36 C.F.R. § 1236.20, "What are appropriate recordkeeping systems for electronic records?"

47. See, e.g., DOE Administrative Records Schedule 20: Electronic Records, September 2010, Revision 2, # 14, "Electronic Mail Records: (GRS 20, item 14)," http://energy.gov/sites/prod/files/cioprod/documents/ADM_20%282%29.pdf.

48. Sari Horwitz and Ellen Nakashima, "Data on citizens to be kept longer," *Washington Post,* March 23, 2012, http://www.washingtonpost.com/world/national-security/new-counterterrorism-guidelines-would-permit-data-on-us-citizens-to-be-held-longer/2012/03/21/gIQAFLm7TS_story.html.

49. See Juliet Eilperin, "Long Droughts, Rising Seas Predicted Despite Future CO2 Curbs," *Washington Post,* January 27, 2009, http://www.washington post.com/wp-dyn/content/article/2009/01/26/AR2009012602037.html.

50. The unhappy history of Santer's involvement with the IPCC was detailed by a past president of the National Academy of Sciences, Dr. Frederick Seitz, "A Major Deception on Global Warming," *Wall Street Journal,* June 12, 1996.

51. OIG Report, pp. 13–14.

52. Ibid., at p. 14.

53. Ibid.

54. McIntyre explains his decision thus: "At the time, I observed the absurdity of NOAA's reply (later even calling it 'mendacious'), but, since IPCC had relented, the issue appeared to be mostly moot and I didn't bother trying to overturn NOAA's refusal." Steve McIntyre, "Solomon's

'Divergence' Problem," Climate Audit, February 24, 2011, http://climate
audit.org/2011/02/24/solomons-divergence-problem/.

55. Ibid., at p. 15.
56. Ibid.
57. Ibid., at p. 16.
58. March 9, 2012, letter from NOAA's Director of Legislative and Intergov-
    ernmental Affairs John Gray to Chairman of the House Science Subcom-
    mittee on Investigations and Oversight, Paul Broun (R-GA).
59. April 26, 2012 letter from House Chairmen James Sensenbrenner and Paul
    Broun to NOAA Administrator Jane Lubchenco.

8. Technological Trickery, Exposed: The Scandalous Epidemic of Hiding Public Service on Personal Email Accounts

1. 5 C.F.R. 2635.704 Use of Government Property, and 5 C.F.R. 2635.705
   Use of Official Time.
2. Jessica Guynn, "Watchdog Group Requests White House Official's E-mail
   After Google Buzz Mishap," *Los Angeles Times* Technology Blog, April 1,
   2010, http://www.consumerwatchdog.org/story/watchdog-group-requests
   -white-house-officials-e-mail-after-google-buzz-mishap.
3. Press release, "Consumer Watchdog Files White House FOIA Request
   For Ex-Googler's Email," Consumer Watchdog, April 1, 2010, http://
   www.consumerwatchdog.org/newsrelease/consumer-watchdog-files-white
   -house-foia-request-ex-googlers-email.
4. Steven Braun, "Mitt Romney Used Private Email Accounts to Conduct State
   Business While Massachusetts Governor," *Huffington Post*, March 9, 2012, http://
   www.huffingtonpost.com/2012/03/09/mitt-romney-emails_n_1335712
   .html.
5. Statement, House Committee on Oversight and Government Reform,
   "The Hatch Act: The Challenges of Separating Politics from Policy," June
   21, 2011, http://oversight.house.gov/hearing/the-hatch-act-the-challenges
   -of-separating-politics-from-policy/. This statement was made in the context of a law precluding federal employees from using taxpayer-provided
   resources, including time, phones, computers, etc., to engage in certain unofficial activity, specifically politicking. It seems nearly everyone in Washington has their own anecdotal stories of observing Hatch Act violations,
   federal employees using private email accounts to perform political activity
   on official time.
6. United States Government Accountability Office, "Report to the Ranking
   Member, Committee on Finance, U.S. Senate: NATIONAL ARCHIVES
   AND RECORDS ADMINISTRATION Oversight and Management

Improvements Initiated, but More Action Needed," October 2010, http://www.gao.gov/assets/320/310933.pdf, p. 18.

7. Ibid., at p. 19.
8. Braun, "Mitt Romney Used Private Email Accounts to Conduct State Business While Massachusetts Governor."
9. Guynn, "Watchdog Group Requests White House Official's E-mail After Google Buzz Mishap."
10. Tony Bradley, "Mixing Business and Personal Email: Is It a Good Idea?," About.com Network Security, September 19, 2008, http://netsecurity.about.com/od/newsandeditoria2/a/palinemail.htm.
11. See, e.g., Emily Kopp and Jack Moore, "Agencies have 120 days to start getting e-records in shape," Federal Radio News, November 29, 2011, http://www.federalnewsradio.com/?nid=493&sid=2648774. This reported an Obama "memo that recognizes emails, tweets and other electronic communications play a key role in government decisions . . . directing agencies to improve their archiving of digital records." This only addresses emails on government computers, however. Memorandum is available at http://www.whitehouse.gov/the-press-office/2011/11/28/presidential-memorandum-managing-government-records.
12. "Interim Report: Investigation of Possible Presidential Records Act Violations," prepared for Chairman Henry A. Waxman, United States House of Representatives Committee on Oversight and Government Reform Majority Staff, June 2007, available at http://usspi.org/resources-emailsgone/interim-report.pdf, pp. 4–6.
13. Ibid., see, e.g., Executive Summary, p. ii.
14. 44 U.S.C. 2901, et seq.
15. *Public Citizen v. Carlin*, 184 F.3d 900, 902 (D.C. Cir. 1999), citing to Armstrong v. EOP, 1 F.3d 1274, 1279 (D.C. Cir.1993).
16. GAO, "NATIONAL ARCHIVES AND RECORDS ADMINISTRATION Oversight and Management Improvements Initiated, but More Action Needed," p. i.
17. 44 U.S.C. Sections 3105, 3106, which prohibit the actual, pending or threatened, removal, defacing, alteration or destruction of documents, including documents or records of a Federal Agency and set forth procedures in these events.
18. 36 C.F.R. § 1236.22(a), "What are the additional requirements for managing electronic mail records?," http://www.archives.gov/about/regulations/part-1236.html.
19. Government Accountability Office, "Federal Records: National Archives and Selected Agencies Need to Strengthen E-Mail Management," GAO-08–742, June 2008, http://www.gao.gov/assets/280/276561.pdf, p. 6.

20. Ibid., at p. 7.

21. Ibid., at p. 9.

22. Ibid., at p. 11.

23. Ibid., at p. 37.

24. Government Accountability Office, "Federal Records: Agencies Face Challenges in Managing E-Mail," Statement of Linda Koontz, Director, Information Management Issues, April 23, 2008, http://www.gao.gov/new .items/d08699t.pdf, p. 11.

25. GAO, "Federal Records: National Archives and Selected Agencies Need to Strengthen E-Mail Management," at p. 33.

26. Ibid., at p. 35.

27. Ibid., at p. 37.

28. "Interim Report: Investigation of Possible Presidential Records Act Violations," House of Representatives Committee on Oversight and Government Reform Majority Staff, available at http://usspi.org/resources-emails gone/interim-report.pdf, p. 7, citations omitted.

29. See Memo from OSTP Director John Holdren to all OSTP staff, titled "Subject: Reminder: Compliance with the Federal Records Act and the President's Ethics Pledge."

30. See, e.g., *Citizens for Responsibility and Ethics in Washington v. U.S. Department of Education*, 538 F. Supp.2d 24 (D.D.C. 2008). The court found the plaintiff did not have standing and, in this case, had scant evidence that the practice affected the records cited by the challenger.

31. *Oglesby v. Department of the Army*, 920 F.2d 57, 68 (D.C. Cir. 1990); see also *Founding Church of Scientology*, 610 F.2d at 838; *Greenberg*, 10 F. Supp. 2d at 30 n.38.

32. *Oglesby*, 920 F.2d at 68.

33. *Friends of Blackwater v. Department of the Interior*, 391 F. Supp. 2d 115, 120–21 (D.D.C. 2005).

34. Christopher Williams, "Civil servants to be forced to publish Gmail emails," *Telegraph* (UK), December 15, 2011, http://www.telegraph.co.uk/ technology/news/8958198/Civil-servants-to-be-forced-to-publish-Gmail -emails.html.

35. Julie Henry, "Michael Gove aides 'destroyed government emails,'" *Telegraph* (UK), March 3, 2012, http://www.telegraph.co.uk/news/politics/9120506/ Michael-Gove-aides-destroyed-government-emails.html.

36. Williams, "Civil servants to be forced to publish Gmail emails," *Telegraph*. See also Andrew Montford, "Education Secretary used private emails," Bishop-Hill blog, September 20, 2011, http://www.bishop-hill.net/blog /2011/9/20/education-secretary-used-private-emails.html, referencing Jeevan Vasager, "Michael Gove faces questions over department's use of private email," *Guardian* (UK), September 19, 2011, http://www.guardian.co.uk/ politics/2011/sep/20/michael-gove-department-private-email.

37. "ICO Statement: Department for Education decision notice," March 2, 2012, http://www.ico.gov.uk/news/latest_news/2012/statement-depart ment-for-education-decision-notice-02032012.aspx.

38. ICO, Decision notice, March 1, 2012, PDF available by link at http:// www.ico.gov.uk/news/latest_news/2012/statement-department-for-educa tion-decision-notice-02032012.aspx, at p. 2.

39. Ibid. at p. 1.

40. Ibid., at p. 3.

41. Ibid.

42. Ibid. at p. 4.

43. Ibid., at p. 6.

44. Williams, "Civil servants to be forced to publish Gmail emails."

45. Ibid.

46. ICO, Decision notice., at p. 5.

47. Ibid., at p. 8.

48. Ibid., citing to Information Commissioner, Guidance, "Information held in private email accounts," December 15, 2011, http://www.ico.gov.uk/ for_organisations/guidance_index/~/media/documents/library/Freedom _of_ Information/Detailed_specialist_guides/official_information_held _in_private_email_accounts.ashx, at p. 1.

49. Ibid., at p. 2.

50. Ibid., at p. 1.

51. Henry, "Michael Gove aides 'destroyed government emails.'"

52. Information Commissioner, Guidance, "Information held in private email accounts," at p. 4.

53. 44 U.S.C. § 3301. We also note 44 U.S.C. § 3101: "Records management by agency heads; general duties. The head of each Federal agency shall make and preserve records containing adequate and proper documentation of the organization, functions, policies, decisions, procedures, and essential transactions of the agency and designed to furnish the information neces- sary to protect the legal and financial rights of the Government and of persons directly affected by the agency's activities; § 3105. Safeguards. The head of each Federal agency shall establish safeguards against the removal or loss of records he determines to be necessary and required by regulations of the Archivist. Safeguards shall include making it known to officials and employees of the agency—(1) that records in the custody of the agency are not to be alienated or destroyed except in accordance with sections 3301– 3314 of this title, and (2) the penalties provided by law for the unlawful removal or destruction of records; and § 3106. Unlawful removal, destruc- tion of records."

54. Gavin Clarke, "Beware Freedom of Info law 'privacy folktale'—ICO chief," Register (UK), February 7, 2012, http://www.theregister.co.uk/2012/02/07/ foia_review_information_commissioner/.

55. "White House Use of Private E-mail Accounts," Committee on Oversight and Government Reform, http://oversight-archive.waxman.house.gov/investigations.asp?ID=251.

56. Henry, "Michael Gove aides 'destroyed government emails.'"

57. Christopher Williams, "Civil servants to be forced to publish Gmail emails," *Telegraph* (UK), December 15, 2011, http://www.bishop-hill.net/blog/2011/12/15/on-her-majestys-public-service.html. See also Andrew Montford, "Education Secretary used private emails," Bishop-Hill blog, September 20, 2011, http://www.bishop-hill.net/blog/2011/9/20/education-secretary-used-private-emails.html, referencing Jeevan Vasager, "Michael Gove faces questions over department's use of private email," *Guardian* (UK), September 19, 2011, http://www.guardian.co.uk/politics/2011/sep/20/michael-gove-department-private-email.

9. Using Private Computers to Keep Official Business from Prying Eyes

1. GAO, "NATIONAL ARCHIVES AND RECORDS ADMINISTRATION Oversight and Management Improvements Initiated, but More Action Needed," p. 16.

2. See, e.g., Susan Jones, "EPA: 'Ask If You Can Work From Home' to Save Energy," CNSNews.com, April 2, 2012, http://cnsnews.com/news/article/epa-ask-if-you-can-work-home-save-energy.

3. Ibid., at p. i.

4. See, e.g., Christopher C. Horner, *Power Grab: How Obama's Green Policies Will Steal Your Freedom and Bankrupt America* (Washington, DC: Regnery, 2010), pp. 71–79.

5. See, e.g., William Yeatman, "Dr. John P. Holdren 'De-development' Advocate is the Wrong Choice for White House Science Adviser," Competitive Enterprise Institute, Washington DC, January 13, 2009, http://cei.org/cei_files/fm/active/0/William%20Yeatman%20-%20Holdren%20WebMemo.pdf. See also this survey of related items of curious Holdren stances, Marc Morano, "Obama Czar John Holdren wants to 'educate' GOP on global warming—But it is Holdren who 'desperately needs remedial climate science education!,'" ClimateDepot.com, January 30, 2011, http://www.climatedepot.com/a/9596/Obama-Czar-John-Holdren-wants-to-educate-GOP-on-global-warming—But-it-is-Holdren-who-desperately-needs-remedial-climate-science-education.

6. Horner, *Power Grab,* pp. 71–79.

7. John P. Holdren, "Too much energy, too soon, a hazard," *Windsor* (Ontario) *Star,* August 25, 1975, available at http://hauntingthelibrary.wordpress.com/2011/01/31/flashback-1975-holdren-says-real-threat-to-usa

-is-cheap-energy/, or in its original at http://news.google.com/newspapers ?id=IjU_AAAAIBAJ&sjid=jFEMAAAAIBAJ&pg=3972,2528093&dq=john +holdren&hl=en, last viewed February 20, 2012.

8. See, e.g., David Boaz, "Should the Government Ban ATMs and Create 'Spoon-ready' Projects?," Cato Institute, http://www.cato-at-liberty.org/ should-the-government-ban-atms-and-create-spoon-ready-projects/, and Jake Tapper, "O on ATMs," June 15, 2011, ABC News Political Punch, http://abcnews.go.com/blogs/politics/2011/06/o-on-atms/.

9. Letter from John Holdren to Chairmen James Sensenbrenner and Paul Broun, December 16, 2011.

10. Letter from John Holdren to Chairmen James Sensenbrenner and Paul Broun, January 30, 2012.

11. Stanford University is now hosting, e.g., the IPCC WGII Technical Support Unit, "c/o Carnegie Institution for Science," as noted at, e.g., http:// www.ipcc.ch/pdf/press-releases/ipcc-wg2-ar5-authors.pdf.

12. Duffy is cited by IPCC as an AR5 WGII author. See http://www.ipcc .ch/pdf/press-releases/ipcc-wg2-ar5-authors.pdf and http://www.ipcc.ch/ meetings/session32/inf07_p32_ipcc_ar5_authors_review_editors.pdf. However, this is in his capacity as a private-sector, activist-group employee, with Climate Central, Inc. The biography associated with that service notes he "won numerous honors, including the 2007 Nobel Peace Prize"; in this capacity he was also listed as, coincidentally, "a Visiting Scholar at Stanford University and at the Carnegie Institution for Science" (http://nofrakkingconsensus.com/2011/05/06/slivers-of-the-nobel -pie/). It is possible that Duffy may have been added by IPCC as a U.S. government author following his transition into the Obama administration but, if so, that transition is not yet complete as of this writing. Duffy was still listed on the September 30, 2011, index provided by OSTP in its response to me, and as of June 13, 2012 on the link provided in that index, http://ipcc.ch/pdf/ar5/ar5_authors_review_editors_updated.pdf (cited as last being updated on 5/12/2012, even though this update came well after Duffy joined the White House). This indicates otherwise but we must presume Duffy terminated this private affiliation upon his employment with the federal government. Regardless, from this it is reasonable to conclude that OSTP employees who are not IPCC authors, even those listed as private-sector authors, are provided access to IPCC author portals.

13. From Declaration of Larry D. Travis in Support of Defendant's Motion for Summary Judgment dated September 17, 2010, submitted to the United States District Court for the District of Columbia in the matter of *Competitive Enterprise Institute v. National Aeronautics and Space Administration,* D.D.C. CV 10–0883, September 20, 2010, pp. 12–13.

14. From NASA/Defendant's Memorandum of Points and Authorities in Support of Defendant's Motion for Summary Judgment, submitted to the United States District Court for the District of Columbia in the matter of *Competitive Enterprise Institute v. National Aeronautics and Space Administration,* D.D.C. CV 10–0883, September 20, 2010, p. 27.
15. Ibid., at p. 25.
16. Ibid.
17. Ibid., at pp. 28–29.

10. It's Academic: Campus Activists Want Your Money, Not Your Scrutiny

1. Glenn Reynolds, "Confidence in Science by Conservatives Has Declined Since 1974," Instapundit, March 30, 2012, http://pjmedia.com/insta pundit/139873/, citing research published at Scott Jaschik, "Conservative Distrust of Science," *Inside Higher Ed,* March 29, 2012, http://www .insidehighered.com/news/2012/03/29/study-tracks-erosion-conservative -confidence-science.
2. Email from Michael Mann to Phil Jones, August 29, 2007, http://climate gate2011.blogspot.com/2011/11/1680txt.html.
3. Gavin Clarke, "Beware Freedom of Info law 'privacy folktale'—ICO chief," *Register* (UK), February 7, 2012, http://www.theregister.co.uk/2012/02/07/ foia_review_information_commissioner/, viewed February 16, 2012.
4. See, e.g., David Matthews, "UUK fails in bid for amendment to FoI Act," *Times Higher Education* (UK), February 18, 2012, http://www.timeshigher education.co.uk/story.asp?storycode=419058#.T0IX3mKzz6Q.twitter, viewed February 21, 2012.
5. The video may be viewed at Andrew Montford, "Dark Matter: What's science got to hide?," Bishop-Hill blog, December 13, 2011, http://www .bishop-hill.net/blog/2011/12/13/dark-matter-whats-science-got-to-hide .html, viewed February 16, 2012.
6. Ibid.
7. "Climate Change and the Integrity of Science," *Science,* Letters, May 8, 2010, http://www.sciencemag.org/content/328/5979/689.full.pdf.
8. See discussion of Juola and Associates analysis and the Pacific Institute's response, *supra.*
9. Anne Jolis, "The Climate Kamikaze," *Wall Street Journal,* March 15, 2012, http://online.wsj.com/article/SB100014240527023044500045772791639 50476028.html?mod=WSJ_Opinion_LEFTTopOpinion.
10. Gary Stix, "Effective World Government Will Be Needed to Stave Off Climate Catastrophe," *Scientific American,* March 17, 2012, http://blogs.scientificamerican.com/observations/2012/03/17/

effective-world-government-will-still-be-needed-to-stave-off-climate-catas
trophe/.

11. F. Bierman et al., "Navigating the Anthropocene: Improving Earth System Governance," *Science*, March 16, 2012, vol. 335, no. 6074, pp. 1306–1307 , DOI:
10.1126/science.1217255, http://www.sciencemag.org/content/335/6074/1306
.summary.

12. Letter to UVa president Teresa Sullivan, American Association of University Professors, American Geophysical Union, Climate Science Watch,
Union of Concerned Scientists, August 10, 2011, http://www.ucsusa.org/
assets/documents/scientific_integrity/sullivan-letter-8–10–11.pdf.

13. Letter to UVa President Teresa Sullivan, Alliance for Justice, American
Association of University Professors, American Civil Liberties Union of
Virginia, Center for Inquiry, Climate Science Watch, Council of Environmental Deans and Directors, National Coalition Against Censor-
ship, National Council for Science and the Environment, People for the
American Way, Robert O'Neil, Director of the Thomas Jefferson Center
for the Protection of Free Expression, Ornithological Council, Union of
Concerned Scientists, April 14, 2011, http://www.ucsusa.org/assets/docu
ments/scientific_integrity/Letter-to-UVA-President-Teresa-Sullivan-regard
ing-academic-freedom.pdf (emphasis added)

14. *Urofsky v. Gilmore*, 216 F.3d 401, 411–412 (4th Cir. Va. 2000), http://law
.justia.com/cases/federal/appellate-courts/F3/216/401/570332/.

15. Eisenhower's Farewell Address to the Nation, January 17, 1961, available at
http://mcadams.posc.mu.edu/ike.htm.

16. David Schnare, "Faculty email: Point Counterpoint," *Roanoke Times*, April
1, 2012, http://blogs.roanoke.com/roundtable/2012/04/faculty-email-point
-counterpoint/.

17. Ibid., at 411, n.12, citing *Minnesota State Board for Community Colleges v.
Knight*, 465 U.S. 271, 288 (1984).

18. Ibid., at 414.

19. Press release, "AAAS Board: Attacks on Climate Researchers Inhibit
Free Exchange of Scientific Ideas," American Association for the Advancement of Science, June 29, 2011, http://www.aaas.org/news/
releases/2011/0629board_statement.shtml. Full statement available at
http://www.aaas.org/news/releases/2011/media/0629board_statement.pdf.

20. Ibid.

21. See, e.g., Anthony Watts, "East Anglia Climatic Research Unit shown to
be liars by results of latest FOIA ruling and investigation," Watts Up With
That, May 7, 2012, http://wattsupwiththat.com/2012/05/06/east-anglia
-climate-research-unit-shown-to-be-liars-by-results-of-latest-foia-ruling
-and-investigation/.

22. See, e.g., Joanne Nova, "Pathological exaggerators caught on 'death threats':

How 11 rude emails became a media blitz," JoNova: Science, carbon, climate and tax, May 3, 2012, http://joannenova.com.au/2012/05/patho logical-exaggerators-caught-on-death-threats-how-11-rude-emails-became -a-media-blitz/.

23. "Academic freedom," *Nature* 479, 149 (November 10, 2011), DOI: 10.1038 /479149a, http://www.nature.com/nature/journal/v479/n7372/full/479149a .html?WT.ec_id=NATURE-20111110.

24. George Monbiot, "Pretending the climate email leak isn't a crisis won't make it go away," *Guardian* (UK), November 25, 2009, http://www.guard ian.co.uk/environment/georgemonbiot/2009/nov/25/monbiot-climate -leak-crisis-response.

25. Clive Crook, "More on Climategate," *Financial Times,* November 30, 2009, http://blogs.ft.com/crookblog/2009/11/more-on-climategate/#axzz1 pggSfpzp.

26. See the relevant statements and parallels at and linked to in, e.g., Steve McIntyre, "Penn State President fired," ClimateAudit.org, November 10, 2011, http://climateaudit.org/2011/11/10/penn-state-president-fired/.

27. See, e.g., Shawn Lawrence Otto, "Shocking New Oil Propaganda Plan to Fool Americans," *Huffington Post,* May 8, 2012, http://www.huffington post.com/shawn-lawrence-otto/wind-energy-opponents_b_1501533.html.

28. Joe Romm, "Much-vindicated Michael Mann and Hockey Stick get final exoneration from Penn State—time for some major media apologies and retractions," ThinkProgress.com, July 1, 2010, http://thinkprogress.org/ climate/2010/07/0½06340/michael-mann-hockey-stick-exonerated-penn -state/?mobile=nc.

29. RA-10 Inquiry Report: Concerning the Allegations of Research Misconduct Against Dr. Michael E. Mann, Department of Meteorology, College of Earth and Mineral Sciences, Pennsylvania State University February 3, 2010, http://www.research.psu.edu/orp/documents/Findings_Mann_Inquiry.pdf, p. 5.

30. Ibid., p. 3.

31. Ibid., at pp. 5–6.

32. Department of Commerce Inspector General, "Examination of issues related to internet posting of emails from Climatic Research Unit," alter- nately styled "Response to Sen. James Inhofe's Request to OIG to Examine Issues Related to Internet Posting of Email Exchanges Taken from the Cli- matic Research Unit of the University of East Anglia, UK," February 18, 2011, p. 5, available from http://www.oig.doc.gov/Pages/Response-to-Sen. -James-Inhofe's-Request-to-OIG-to-Examine-Issues-Related-to-Internet -Posting-of-Email-Exchanges-Taken-from-.aspx.

33. Steve McIntyre, "New Light on 'Delete Any Emails'," ClimateAudit.org, February 23, 2011, http://climateaudit.org/2011/02/23/new-light-on-delete -any-emails/, last viewed February 17, 2012.

34. See Steve McIntyre, "New Information on the Penn State Inquiry Committee," November 15, 2011, http://climateaudit.org/2011/11/15/new-information-at-penn-state/.

35. Clive Crook, "Climategate and the Big Green Lie," *Atlantic,* July 14, 2010, http://www.theatlantic.com/politics/archive/2010/07/climategate-and-the-big-green-lie/59709/# .

36. Ibid.

37. "Penn State thumbed their noses at Office of Research Integrity procedures for academic misconduct. These procedures state that first-stage inquiries are only charged with determining prima facie evidence and should not attempt to make the findings that are the province of an investigation. Instead of adhering to ORI procedures, Penn State purported to make final findings on key issues (including deletion of emails) without a full investigation. The issue of email deletion should have been passed from the inquiry to an investigation and the investigation committee should have interviewed Wahl, before purporting to dispose of the matter." See Steve McIntyre, "New Light on 'Delete Any Emails.'"

38. RA-1O Final Investigation Report Involving Dr. Michael E. Mann, The Pennsylvania State University, June 4, 2010,, http://live.psu.edu/pdf/Final_Investigation_Report.pdf, p. 13.

39. See McIntyre, "New Information on the Penn State Inquiry Committee."

11. FOIA: What It Is and How It Works

1. The Department of Justice opened its 1985 history of the law's treatment at the hands of the Supreme Court with the unsettling boast that a recent victory "cap[ped] off an extremely successful twelve years of FOIA litigation before the Supreme Court. In the nineteen FOIA cases that the Court has decided, involving a wide array of FOIA issues, the Government's position has prevailed all but once. These decisions have touched on all of the FOIA's major exemptions, as well as some critical procedural issues, and have had an enormous impact on FOIA administration govemmentwide [*sic*]." FOIA Update, vol. 6, no. 2, 1985 FOIA Supreme Court History, http://www.justice.gov/oip/foia_updates/Vol_VI_2/page2.htm.

2. *NLRB v. Robbins Tire & Rubber Co., 437* U.S. 214, 242 (1978).

3. *NARA v. Favish,* 541 U.S. 157, 172 (2004).

4. *Department of the Air Force v. Rose,* 425 U.S. 352 (1976).

5. Ibid.

6. "FOIA is often explained as a means for citizens to know what 'their Government is up to.'" *Favish* at 171 (quoting *U.S. Department of Justice v. Reporters Committee for Freedom of the Press,* 489 U.S. 749, 773 [1989]).

7. *Department of Justice v. Reporters Comm. for Freedom of Press,* 498 U.S. 749, 772 (1989) (internal citations omitted).

8. See, e.g., *Federal Open. Market Committee v. Merrill,* 443 U.S. 340, 352 (1979).

9. *Reporters Committee* at 754.

10. The Presidential Records Act (PRA) of 1978, 44 U.S.C. ß2201–2207. See, e.g., http://www.archives.gov/presidential-libraries/laws/1978-act.html, requiring among other things that a president and vice president properly create and maintain records, and allow for public access to presidential records through FOIA beginning some years after the end of the particular administration, all on the grounds that ownership of these records does not rest with the officeholder, but with the public.

11. *EPA v. Mink,* 410 U.S. 73, 92 (1973).

12. *Reporters Committee,* citing *NLRB v. Sears, Roebuck & Co.,* 421 U. S. 132, 421 U. S. 149 (1975) and referencing *NLRB v. Robbins Tire & Rubber Co.,* 437 U. S. 214, 437 U. S. 221 (1978), *FBI v. Abramson,* 456 U. S. 615 (1982).

13. See, e.g., "List of who can make public record requests by state," "Eight states currently have a law that says that only state residents can request copies of public documents: Alabama, Arkansas, Delaware, Georgia, New Hampshire, New Jersey, Tennessee and Virginia. In 2006, a federal appeals court (the Third Circuit) in the case *Lee v. Minner* rejected the constitutionality of Delaware's law that disallowed non-residents from making public record requests. The Third Circuit's rulings apply to Delaware, New Jersey and Pennsylvania. As a result, the provision in the New Jersey Open Public Records Act that prohibits non-residents from access to records is likely to be considered invalid." *Sunshine Review,* last viewed March 9, 2012, http://sunshinereview.org/index.php/List_of_who_can_make_pub lic_record_requests_by_state.

14. *U.S. Department of Justice v. Reporters Committee for Freedom of the Press* et al., 489 U.S. 749, 771 (1989).

15. Presidential Memorandum for Heads of Executive Departments and Agencies, 75 F.R. § 4683, 4683 (Jan. 21, 2009).

16. *GC Micro Corp. v. Defense Logistics Agency,* 33 F.3d 1109, 1113 (9th Cir. 1994); see also *Lewis v. IRS,* 823 F.2d 375, 378 (9th Cir.1987). See also *EPA v. Mink,* 410 U.S. at 93, citing to 5 U.S.C. 552(a)(3), "The burden is, of course, on the agency resisting disclosure."

17. *Local 598 v. Department of Army Corps of Engineers,* 841 F.2d 1459, 1463 (9th. Cir. 1988).

18. See *Citizens for Responsibility and Ethics in Wash. v. U.S. Department of Homeland Security,* 527 F. Supp. 2d 76, 88 (D.D.C. 2007), at 88 ("Under 5 U.S.C. § 552(a)(4)(B) federal jurisdiction is dependent upon a showing that an agency has (1) improperly; (2) withheld; (3) agency records." (Quoting *Kissinger v. Reporters Committee for Freedom of Press,* 445 U.S. 136, 150 [1980]) (internal quotations omitted).

19. 5 U.S.C. § 552(f). These include "(A) any information that would be an agency record subject to the requirements of this section when maintained by an agency in any format, including an electronic format; and (B) any information described under subparagraph (A) that is maintained for an agency by an entity under Government contract, for the purposes of records management."

20. *Forsham v. Harris,* 445 U.S. 169, 178 (1980).

21. See, e.g., Environmental Protection Agency, "What Is a Federal Record?" http://www.epa.gov/records/tools/toolkits/procedures/part2.htm.

22. *Consumer Fed. of Am.,* 455 F.3d. at 287; *see also Burka v. Department of Health and Human Services,* 87 F.3d 508, 515 (D.C. Cir. 1996). See also *Tax Analysts,* 492 U.S. at 144–45 (holding that, for documents to qualify as "agency records," an agency "must either create or obtain the requested materials" and "must be in control of the requested materials" in the sense that they "have come into the agency's possession in the legitimate conduct of its official duties" [internal quotation marks omitted]).

23. 44 U.S.C. § 3301. Also note 44 U.S.C.§ 3101: "Records management by agency heads; general duties. The head of each Federal agency shall make and preserve records containing adequate and proper documentation of the organization, functions, policies, decisions, procedures, and essential transactions of the agency and designed to furnish the information necessary to protect the legal and financial rights of the Government and of persons directly affected by the agency's activities; § 3105. Safeguards. The head of each Federal agency shall establish safeguards against the removal or loss of records he determines to be necessary and required by regulations of the Archivist. Safeguards shall include making it known to officials and employees of the agency—(1) that records in the custody of the agency are not to be alienated or destroyed except in accordance with sections 3301–3314 of this title, and (2) the penalties provided by law for the unlawful removal or destruction of records; and § 3106. Unlawful removal, destruction of records."

24. *DOJ v. Tax Analysts,* 492 U.S. 136, 144–45 (1989).

25. *Burka v. U.S. Department of Health & Human Services,* 87 F.3d 508, 515 (D.C. Cir. 1996)).

26. *Tax Analysts,* at 145.

27. See, e.g., *DiViaio v. Kelley,* 571 F.2d at 542–43 (10th Cir. 1978).

28. *Milner v. Department of the Navy,* 131 S. Ct. 1259, 1262 (2011) (internal quotations and citations omitted) (citing *FBI v. Abramson,* 456 U.S. 615, 630 [1982]); see also *Public Citizen, Inc. v. Office of Management and Budget,* 598 F.3d 865, 869 (D.C. Cir. 2010).

29. U.S. Department of Justice, FOIA Post, "OIP Guidance: President Obama's FOIA Memorandum and Attorney General Holder's FOIA

Guidelines—Creating a New Era of Open Government," posted April 17, 2009, http://www.justice.gov/oip/foiapost/2009foiapost8.htm.

30. As set forth in Memorandum from Attorney General Eric Holder to Heads of Executive Departments and Agencies, March 19, 2009, available at http://www.justice.gov/ag/foia-memo-march2009.pdf.
31. *DOJ v. Julian,* 486 U.S. 1, 19 n.1 (1988) (Scalia, J., dissenting and commenting on a point not reached by majority).
32. Memorandum from Attorney General Eric Holder to Heads of Executive Departments and Agencies, March 19, 2009, available at http://www.justice.gov/ag/foia-memo-march2009.pdf, p. 3.
33. Citizens for Responsibility and Ethics in Washington, OpenTheGovernment.org, "Measuring Transparency Under the FOIA: The Real Story Behind The Numbers," December 2011, http://crew.3cdn.net/5911487fbaaa8cb0f8_9xm6bgari.pdf.
34. *NLRB v. Sears, Roebuck & Co.,* 421 U.S. 132, 149 (1975); see *FTC v. Grolier Inc.,* 462 U.S. 19, 26 (1983); *Martin v. Office of Special Counsel,* 819 F.2d 1181, 1184 (D.C. Cir. 1987).
35. *Mink,* 410 U.S. at 86.
36. *Mink,* 410 U.S. at 87, quoting *Kaiser Aluminum & Chemical Corp. v. United States,* 157 F. Supp. 939, 946 (1958).
37. Ibid.
38. Ibid., citing S. Rep. No. 813, p. 9. See H.R. Rep. No. 1497, p. 10.
39. Ibid. at 89.
40. U.S. Department of Justice FOIA Guidelines 2009, Exemption 5, p. 366, citations omitted, http://www.justice.gov/oip/foia_guide09/exemption5.pdf.
41. Ibid., at p. 380 (citations omitted).
42. *Vaughn v. Rosen,* 484 F. 2d 820 (DC Cir. 1973), internal citations omitted.
43. *Mink,* 410 U.S. at 89.
44. *Jordan v. DOJ,* 591 F.2d 753, 774 (D.C. Cir. 1978).
45. See *Coastal States Gas Corp. v. Department of Energy,* setting forth document-specific facts for determining the validity of declaring the (b)(5) exemption. 644 F.2d 854, 866 (D.C. Cir. 1980).
46. *United Techs. Corp. v. U.S. Department of Defense,* 601 F.3d 557, 559 (D.C. Cir. 2010); see also *Critical Mass Energy Project v. Nuclear Regulatory Commission,* 975 F.2d 871, 872 (D.C. Cir. 1992).
47. *National Association of Home Builders v. Norton,* 309 F.3d 26 (D.C. Cir. 2006).
48. *Reporters Committee for Freedom of the Press,* 489 U.S. 749 (1989).
49. Ibid.
50. *U.S. Dept. of Defense v. Federal Labor Relations Authority,* 510 U.S. 487 (1994).
51. *Multi AG Media v. Department of Agriculture,* 515 F.3d 1224 (D.C. Cir. 2008).

52. "The Standards of Ethical Conduct for Employees of the Executive Branch" issued by the Office of Government Ethics provide that "[a]n employee has a duty to protect and conserve Government property and shall not use such property, or allow its use, for other than authorized purposes." 5 C.F.R. § 2635.704(a). The regulation makes clear that electronic mail and telephones are both included within the meaning of "Government property" and that "authorized purposes" are purposes "authorized in accordance with law or regulation." See 5 C.F.R. § 2635.704(b). The regulation does not attempt, however, to set forth the purposes that are authorized. See also Office of Government Ethics opinion letter, September 24, 1993, Personal Use of Government E-Mail System, http://www.oge.gov/OGE-Advisories/Legal-Advisories/93x24—Personal-Use-of-Government-E-Mail-System/.

53. *Gallant v. NLRB,* 26 F.3d 168, 172 (D.C. Cir. 1994).

54. Ibid.

55. Schweizer, "Obama Campaign Backers and Bundlers Rewarded With Green Grants and Loans."

56. Steven Braun, "Mitt Romney Used Private Email Accounts to Conduct State Business While Massachusetts Governor," *Huffington Post,* March 9, 2012.

57. See, e.g., *Cowles Publishing Co. v. Kootenai County Board of County Commissioners,* 144 Idaho 259, 159 P.3d 896, 898, 900–901 (2007). The opinion set out the statutory definition of a public record as "includ[ing], but is not limited to, any writing containing information relating to the conduct or administration of the public's business prepared, owned, used or retained by any state agency, independent public body corporate and politic or local agency regardless of physical form or characteristics." The high court held that because of the language, "but is not limited to," under the statutory definition of public record, "other records and writings may qualify even if they do not meet this definition." Combining Idaho's broad statutory definition of public record with facts in the case showing a possible inappropriate relationship, the high court in Cowles held that the emails involved "a public concern" and were therefore public records. Further, Cowles held that "[i]t is not simply the fact that the emails were sent and received while the employees were at work . . . that makes them a public record. Rather, it is their relation to legitimate public interest that makes them a public record."

58. Ibid.

12. How-To: Filing Your Own FOIAs

1. 5 U.S.C. § 552(a)(1).

2. See, e.g., U.S. Department of Justice, "FOIA Counselor Q&A: 'Frequently

Requested" Records'," http://www.justice.gov/oip/foiapost/2003foiapost28. htm. The "frequently requested record" provision of the FOIA, 5 U.S.C. § 552(a)(2)(D) (2000), involves a "rule of three." The 1996 amendments "created an additional category of reading room records by requiring all federal agencies to give 'reading room' treatment to certain records after they are processed for, and released to, a FOIA requester. . . . It provides that such treatment must be given to any FOIA-processed records that, 'because of the nature of their subject matter, the agency determines have become or are likely to become the subject of subsequent requests for substantially the same records.'"

3. Staff Report, House Committee on Oversight and Government Reform, "A New Era of Openness? How and Why Political staff at DHS Interfered with the FOIA Process," March 30, 2011, p. 96, citing to language throughout FOIA regulations, specifically here DHS's implementing regulation 6 C.F.R.s.5.4(a): "In determining which records are responsive to a request, a component ordinarily will include only records in its possession as of the date the component begins its search for them. If any other date is used, the component shall inform the requester of that date." Also citing to *Edmonds Institute v. United States Department of the Interior,* 383 F. Supp.2d 105 (D.D.C. 2005), finding that the agency must include records through the date the search begins, as the "fair and sensible outcome." Ibid. at 111. The Court also reiterated that "[t]he D.C. Circuit has all but endorsed the use of date-of-search as the cut-off date for FOIA requests." Ibid. See also *Public Citizen v. Department of State,* 276 F.3d at 637 (D.C. Cir. 2002), stating that the appropriate cutoff was the date of the search, unless another date was specified.

4. Office of Special Counsel, Freedom of Information Act (FOIA) Handbook, http://www.osc.gov/foia.htm.

5. 5 U.S.C. § 552(a) (3). See also *Iturralde v. Comptroller of the Currency,* 315 F.3d 311, 315 (D.C. Cir. 2003); *Steinberg v. Department of Justice,* 23 F.3d 548, 551 (D.C. Cir. 1994).

6. See *Campbell v. Department of Justice,* 164 F.3d 20, 27 (D.C. Cir. 1999) ("reasonableness" is assessed "consistent with congressional intent tilting the scale in favor of disclosure").

7. See, e.g., *Nation Magazine v. U.S. Customs Serv.,* 71 F.3d 885, 890 (D.C. Cir. 1995).

8. See *Kempker-Cloyd v. Department of Justice,* W.D. Mich. (1999) (holding that the purpose of FOIA is defeated if employees can simply assert that they've searched, unsupervised, claiming, e.g., that records are personal without agency review).

9. *Greenberg v. Department of Treasury,* 10 F. Supp. 2d 3, 30 n.38 (D.D.C. 1998).

10. See, e.g., *Oglesby v. Department of the Army,* 920 F.2d 57, 68 (D.C. Cir. 1990).

11. *Founding Church of Scientology v. NSA,* 610 F.2d 824, 837 (D.C. Cir. 1979).

12. See *Citizens For Responsibility and Ethics in Washington v. U.S. Department of Justice,* 2006 WL 1518964 *4 (D.D.C. June 1, 2006) ("CREW"). "The Court is troubled by the fact that a mere two-hour search that started in August took several months to complete and why the Government waited [for several months] to advise plaintiff of the results of the search."

13. *CREW,* 2006 WL 1518964 at *5.

14. See *Citizens for Responsibility and Ethics in Washington v. Department of Homeland Security,* 527 F. Supp. 2d 76, 94 (D.D.C. 2007). "Although an agency's treatment of documents for preservation purposes may provide some guidance . . . an agency should not be able to alter its disposal regulations to avoid the requirements of FOIA," quoting *Bureau of Nat'l Affairs v. U.S. Department of Justice,* 742 F.2d 1484, 1493 (D.C. Cir. 1984).

15. See *Kean v. NASA,* 480 F. Supp. 2d 150, 158 (D.D.C. 2007) ("[g]iven the fact that NASA recently amended one of these documents . . . it appears likely that there are responsive documents regarding the satellite").

16. *Campbell,* 164 F.3d at 28–29.

17. *Meeropol v. Meese,* 790 F.2d 942, 953 (D.C. Cir. 1986).

18. *Nation Magazine, Wash. Bureau v. U.S. Customs Service,* 71 F.3d 885, 891 (D.C. Cir. 1995) (finding it unreasonable to require agency to search through twenty-three years of unindexed files for records); cf. *Ancient Coin Collectors Guild v. U.S. Department of State,* 641 F.3d 504, 514 (D.C. Cir. 2011).

19. See, e.g., Jennifer Lynch, "The FBI Arbitrarily Covers Up Evidence of Misconduct: Is This the Transparency Obama Promised?," Electronic Frontier Foundation, December 8, 2010, https://www.eff.org/deeplinks/2010/12/fbi-arbitrarily-covers-evidence-misconduct.

20. See generally, Department of Commerce, Office of Inspector General, "Response to Sen. James Inhofe's Request to OIG to Examine Issues Related to Internet Posting of Email Exchanges Taken from the Climatic Research Unit of the University of East Anglia, UK," February 18, 2011, pp. 12–16, available at http://www.oig.doc.gov/Pages/Response-to-Sen.-James-Inhofe's-Request-to-OIG-to-Examine-Issues-Related-to-Internet-Posting-of-Email-Exchanges-Taken-from-.aspx.

21. *Vaughn v. Rosen,* 484 F. 2d 820, 825–26 (DC Cir. 1973) cert. denied, 415 U.S. 977 (1974).

22. Ibid., at 826.

23. *Rein v. U.S. Patent and Trademark Office,* 553 F. 3d 353, 368 (4th Cir. 2009).

24. *Ctr. for Biological Diversity v. OMB,* No. 07–4997, 2008 WL 5129417, at *7 (N.D. Cal. Dec. 4, 2008).
25. *Morley v. CIA,* 508 F.3d 1108, 1127 (D.C. Cir. 2007).
26. *Vaughn* at 827.
27. 5 U.S.C. § 552(a)(4)(B).
28. The National Archives, "The Office of Government Information Services," http://www.archives.gov/ogis/. 16 5 U.S.C. § 552(b).
29. 5 U.S.C. §552(a)(6)(C). See, e.g., *Jenks v. United States Marshals Service,* 514 F. Supp. 1383, 1384–87 (S.D. Ohio 1981); *Information Acquisition Corp. v. Department of Justice,* 444 F. Supp. 458, 462 (D.D.C. 1978).
30. *Tesoro Refining v. FERC,* 552 F.3d 868, 874 (D.C. Cir. 2009) (quoting *Communications Workers v. AT&T,* 40 F.3d 426, 433 (D.C. Cir. 1994)).
31. *Oglesby v. Department of the Army,* 920 F.2d 57 (D.C. Cir. 1990). DOJ says, "The most significant aspect of the Oglesby decision is its entirely new application of the rule of exhaustion of administrative remedies under the FOIA."
32. U.S. Department of Justice, FOIA Update, vol. XII, no. 2 (1991), OIP Guidance, "Procedural Rules Under the D.C. Circuit's *Oglesby* Decision," http://www.justice.gov/oip/foia_updates/Vol_XII_2/page2.htm (internal citations omitted).
33. *Oglesby,* 920 F.2d at 63.
34. U.S. Department of Justice, FOIA Update, vol. XII, no. 2 (1991), OIP Guidance, "Procedural Rules Under the D.C. Circuit's *Oglesby* Decision, http://www.justice.gov/oip/foia_updates/Vol_XII_2/page2.htm, which offers a thorough walk-through of these issues.
35. See 5 U.S.C. § 552(a)(6)(A)(ii).
36. The National Security Archive offers a sample FOIA appeal, at http://www.gwu.edu/~nsarchiv/nsa/foia/guide.html.
37. *Open America v. Watergate Special Prosecution Force,* 547 F.2d 605, 616 (D.C. Cir. 1976).
38. U.S. Department of Justice, OIP Guidance, FOIA Update, When to Expedite FOIA Requests, vol. IV, no. 2, 1983, http://www.justice.gov/oip/foia_updates/Vol_IV_3/page3.htm.
39. Michael Grabell, "TSA Reveals Passenger Complaints . . . Four Years Later," ProPublica, May 4, 2012, http://www.propublica.org/article/tsa-reveals-passenger-complaints-four-years-later.
40. http://www.justice.gov/oip/foia_guide09.htm.

Conclusion: Annoy the Statists, Ask What They're Up To

1. *National Archives and Records Administration v. Favish,* 541 U.S. 157 (2004).

2. Bob King, "Inhofe's office wants answers on vanishing of 'crucify' video," *Politico,* April 27, 2012.

3. See Lachlan Markay, "Video of EPA Official's 'Crucify' Remarks, Removed by Environmental Activist, Reappears Online," Heritage Foundation, April 27, 2012, http://blog.heritage.org/2012/04/27/video-of-epa-officials -crucify-remarks-removed-by-environmental-activist-reappears-online/. The activist was Sierra Club member David McFatridge.

4. Ed Morrissey, "Whodunit: The case of the missing EPA "crucifixion" video," HotAir.com, April 27, 2012, http://hotair.com/archives/2012/04/27/who dunit-the-case-of-the-missing-epa-crucifixion-video/ (emphases in original.

INDEX

United Nations Environmental Pro-
   gramme (UNEP), 118, 120
Urofsky v. Gilmore, 177, 179
USA Today, 30, 72, 238*n*

Vaughn index, 204, 223–24
Vaughn v. Rosen, 223–24
Vergano, Dan, 238*n*
Virginia, 176–77
Virginia, University of (UVa):
   and academics, 15, 174–76, 178–79,
      183–86, 188
   Board of Visitors of, 183
   campaigns of retaliation at, 179
   and Climategate, 14–15, 17, 184
   and comparisons between IPCC,
      112
   delaying tactics of, 73
   and emails, 14–18, 20, 30, 112, 127,
      174–76, 179, 183–84, 198, 207–8,
      238*n*-39*n*
   Environmental Sciences Department
      of, 184
   faculty handbook of, 176
   and fee barriers, 18, 73
   and FOIA, 14, 16–18, 20, 28–30,
      73, 169, 174, 176, 178, 180–81,
      183–86
   hearings and lawsuits on, 13–18, 20–
      21, 28–31, 100, 112, 127, 168–69,
      171, 174–76, 178–86, 188, 207–8,
      222, 238*n*-39*n*
   and Mann, 15–18, 21, 30, 108, 127,
      169, 174, 176, 183–86, 188, 198,
      238*n*-39*n*
   open letters to president of, 174–76
   and scientists, 15–18, 20, 30, 100,
      174–75, 179–85
   and temperature data shielding, 110
   "Use of Electronic Communications
      and Social Media: Certificate of
      Receipt" of, 182
   and what FOIA is and how it works,
      198

Virginia Fraud Against Taxpayers Act,
   15–16
Virginia Freedom of Information Act,
   28, 239*n*
voting rights, 39, 76

Wahl, Eugene:
   IPCC and, 187–89
   NOAA and, 188–89
   and self-policing of academia, 185,
      187–91, 275*n*
Wall Street Journal:
   anti-pollution rules and, 80
   ObamaCare and, 52
   scientists and, 172
War on Fox News, 68
War on Women initiative, 68
Washington & Lee University, 58
Washington Examiner, 62–63
Washington Post, 23, 95
   anti-pollution rules and, 79–80
   criminally acquiring private records
      and, 243*n*
   and Obama's alleged commitment to
      transparency, 28, 58
   politicizing transparency and, 77,
      79
   on Romney, 29
   selective views on transparency of,
      28–31
   and storage of personal information,
      122
   and using transparency for intimida-
      tion, 36
   UVa case and, 28–30, 175
Washington Times, 77, 126
Wasserman, Edward, 58
Watergate Presidential Records Act, 74
Watts, Anthony, 242*n*
Waxman, Henry, 144
   and events in UK, 151
   and private email accounts in
      conducting government business,
      133–34, 139–40, 151–52